D1624754

BEACON TO THE WORLD

BEACON TO THE WORLD

A History of Lincoln Center

JOSEPH W. POLISI

Yale

UNIVERSITY PRESS

New Haven and London

Yale University Press books may be purchased in quantity for
educational, business, or promotional use. For information, please
e-mail sales.press@yale.edu (U.S. office) or sales@yaleup.co.uk
(U.K. office).

Set in Janson type by Newgen North America, Austin, Texas.
Printed in the United States of America.

Library of Congress Control Number: 2021947403
ISBN 978-0-300-24996-5 (hardcover : alk. paper)

A catalogue record for this book is available from the British Library.

This paper meets the requirements of ANSI/NISO Z39.48-1992
(Permanence of Paper).

10 9 8 7 6 5 4 3 2 1

To
Creighton, Adeline, Teague, and Will

Contents

Preface   ix

PROLOGUE   1

1.   The Expansion of an Idea   6

2.   A Mighty Influence for Peace and Understanding   21

3.   No Longer a Dream but a Reality   38

4.   You Have Made Something That Will Last   54

5.   It Was Not a Matter of Friendship but Principle   70

6.   Opening Night and Amateur Night at the Same Time   91

7.   The Cursed Inheritance   109

8.   It's Called Accountability   124

9.   It Will Flourish as Long as a Civilized Society Survives   141

10.   This Is a Dream Come True   160

11.   An Innovative, Risk-Taking, Adventurous, Artistic Entity   173

12.   We're Going to Have to Put Our Dreams on Hold   185

13.   I Would Have Preferred a More Collegial Approach   196

14.   Welcome to the Urbanism of Lilt and Swoon   206

15.   She Had Bet the Ranch   220

16.   We Don't Have a Playbook for This   233
       EPILOGUE   258

Notes   265
Bibliography   293
Acknowledgments   297
Index   301

Preface

AS A YOUNG CHILD growing up in Flushing, Queens, I viewed Manhattan as a distant destination that I would visit occasionally through Sunday family dinners on Mott Street, school field trips to the American Museum of Natural History, and concerts in Carnegie Hall, where my father would perform as principal bassoonist of the New York Philharmonic. My mother, sister, and I would often be seated in a side box, where I would speak to my mom in a proud, loud voice so that audience members in adjacent boxes would be aware that the bassoonist in the orchestra was *my* father.

By the time the orchestra moved to Lincoln Center in 1962, I was a sophomore in high school and a fledgling bassoonist in my own right. I saw the members of the Philharmonic as equivalent to the starting lineup of the New York Yankees, and the orchestra's new home at Lincoln Center was a larger-than-life edifice that represented for me the highest reaches of musical performance. What was even more exciting was my new membership as the fourth bassoonist of the All-City Orchestra, an ensemble that was one of the first youth orchestras to play in Philharmonic Hall in May 1963, with the entire concert broadcast live on local television station WPIX, channel 11.

Lincoln Center has been a part of my life for decades, culminating, in September 1984, with my appointment as president of The Juilliard School, one of the Center's constituents. Lincoln Center has always existed for me as a magical place providing large expanses for the eye to explore, so different from the dense and congested neighborhoods of Manhattan. It is a unique destination, where putting on a tie and jacket, even as a youth, manifested a gesture of respect for what an audience member would experience in one of the Center's halls.

When I realized that the only extant comprehensive history of Lincoln Center ended in the late 1970s, I felt that an expanded and up-to-date chronicle would be of interest not only to arts cognoscenti but also to individuals curious about New York City's cultural and business affairs.

Beacon to the World highlights numerous artistic presentations which occurred over several decades, featuring towering personalities such as George Balanchine, Leonard Bernstein, Rudolf Bing, Lincoln Kirstein, Richard Rodgers, Beverly Sills, and many others. In addition, such distinguished architects as Max Abramovitz, Pietro Belluschi, Lew Davis, Elizabeth Diller, Wallace Harrison, Philip Johnson, and Eero Saarinen will be shown to have played significant roles in shaping not just the campus's physical aesthetic but also the audience's experience of the arts of drama, dance, and music. Supporting these artistic ambitions were the financial and political initiatives developed by John D. Rockefeller 3rd, Robert Moses, and other city and national leaders who were an important part of the birth of Lincoln Center.

My research has brought me to individuals, organizations, and idealistic philosophies which span the diverse landscape we know as New York City. *Beacon to the World* presents those stories through an investigation of the evolution of Lincoln Center from its exploratory discussions in late 1955 to the challenging and unique experiences that fell upon the entire world in 2020.

This history focuses on Lincoln Center, Inc., the "umbrella organization" that oversees the constituent members and its campus buildings. Although I present all the Center's constituents, I ask the reader to excuse me for not including the many details that encompass the full story of each one.

This history tells the story of an idealistic concept that came to fruition and then adapted to changing political, economic, social, and artistic forces. The final product of Lincoln Center is the art that is presented daily in each of the campus's halls, with the hope that these performances enrich our cultural environment and our individual personas.

The philosophical tenets developed for Lincoln Center in its earliest years have had to adapt to changing times. The stories of these adaptations show how the performing arts have flourished, permitting audiences to take solace and intellectual stimulation from great works of art that provide a portal through which to experience our humanity. *Beacon to the World* is dedicated to a better understanding of that experience.

BEACON TO THE WORLD

Prologue

AS THE SUNLIGHT FADED ON New York City's West Side during an early spring evening, hundreds of individuals gathered in small groups or hastily walked to close-by entries, faintly illuminated by the ambient light of the surrounding buildings. It was a time filled with expectation, as performances were about to take place at Lincoln Center for the Performing Arts.

Patrons created a palpable energy on the Center's plaza, as the playful waterspouts of an iconic fountain added a sonic and visual ambience rarely found in New York City. Whether attending an opera at the Met, a concert of the Philharmonic at Geffen Hall, a dance presentation of the New York City Ballet at Koch Hall, a play at the Lincoln Center Theater, a chamber music concert at Alice Tully Hall, a film at the Lincoln Center Film Society, or a contemporary music concert at The Juilliard School, those present that evening understood that they were in a special place. It was a place founded with an idealistic spirit and, like all artistic endeavors, it had experienced challenges in its quest for excellence and financial solvency.

The creation of an arts organization the size of Lincoln Center was based on the fundamental belief in the mid-1950s that Americans would benefit from bringing together a diverse array of performing organizations in one place to create an entity whose whole would be greater than the sum of its parts. Although a naive concept when one considers the highly independent qualities of performing arts practitioners and ensembles, this belief reinforced the view that hope can be stronger than pessimism when attempting to realize change and innovation in American society.

America after World War II represented a unique mixture of supreme military might, global economic dominance, and a type of idealism born out of the defeat of fascism and the belief that the United States represented the best of human values as manifested in its form of government and the diversity and moral strength of its people.

Yet the postwar world between 1955 and 1960 was also an ominous time for American interests. In the span of just those six years, the Warsaw Pact was created, countering the strength of the North Atlantic Treaty Organization; the recently deposed British prime minister, Winston Churchill, spoke of an "Iron Curtain" across Eastern Europe deepening the reality of a Cold War between the United States and the Soviet Union; the Soviets invaded Hungary while Israel, Great Britain, and France attacked Egypt over control of the Suez Canal; *Sputnik* was launched by Russia, initiating the space race; Fidel Castro began his revolution in Cuba, prevailing in 1959; a U-2 spy plane flown by an American pilot was downed over the Soviet Union; and for the first time, American military personnel were attacked and killed by enemy forces in Vietnam.

On the domestic front, the racial divide in America was manifested by the heroic stance of Rosa Parks when she refused to sit in the back of a Montgomery, Alabama, bus, and the stubborn refusal of Arkansas governor Orval Faubus to allow the integration of Little Rock's Central High School. Conversely, the Civil Rights Act was passed in 1960 to secure voting rights for all citizens, followed by the historic Civil and Voting Rights Acts of 1964 and 1965, and a youthful John F. Kennedy was elected president.

This period, although fraught with domestic and international anxiety, brought together a group of visionary and well-positioned New York City civic leaders to develop an idea for the creation of a multi-institution center in support of the performing arts. These leaders embraced a patriotic obligation to highlight the cultural attributes of America and show both friends and foes abroad that the United States could be a cultural as well as a political and economic leader in a new world order.

The history of the birth and growth of this extraordinary institution reflects the political and social values of the time in New York City and the nation. It is a story of determination, economic acumen, political machinations, institutional arrogance, and personality conflicts, but, above all, of the strong belief that the arts are at the center of the fabric of American society and should be supported and experienced by all citizens. This concept was presented by John D. Rockefeller 3rd when he stated, "The arts are not for the privileged few, but for the many. Their place is not on the periphery of daily life, but at its center."[1]

Rockefeller worked resolutely to achieve the goal of having the arts be accessible to everyone, regardless of their social or financial standing, writing, "Let us enrich the lives of people everywhere with the form and the movement, the color and gesture, the rhythm and song of the arts. Let us, by enriching our lives, enrich our America."[2] This idealistic perspective of Lincoln Center viewed its creation as a "beacon to the world," where post–World War II America could now take its rightful place as a global thought leader as well as a financial and military force.[3]

Lincoln Center as we know it today would not have been realized without the exceptional vision and leadership of John D. Rockefeller 3rd, who was chair of the venture throughout its formative years and who brought together, through his personal gravitas and reputation, a remarkable group of civic, business, and political leaders to navigate the highly complex process of developing government authorizations, construction schedules, organizational structure, and, of course, fundraising.

In today's world, Lincoln Center, as envisioned by its founders, might not have been built. An enormous arts complex dedicated to the presentation of canonical and mostly Western-based artistic works in music, dance, and drama would be viewed with considerable suspicion. The overall cost of the project would be beyond the financial resources of any organization, and the flattening of entire neighborhoods to build an arts center would certainly be anathema to the beliefs of most twenty-first-century American political leaders.

A persistent problem with the Center's legacy is manifested in the "original sin" it committed in the 1950s of displacing thousands of families living in the Lincoln Square neighborhood. As with most retrospective historical scenarios, evaluating through a revisionist lens the decisions made at the birth of the Center may be a pointless exercise. It would be futile to apply the political and sociological standards of the third decade of the twenty-first century to a project developed sixty years earlier.

The political environment of the 1950s, characterized by a widespread effort to make America the dominant economic and political player on the world scene, energized Americans to start initiatives which would eradicate the old, making the United States a leader in not only world politics but also culture—a concept that would have been unthinkable in America prior to World War II.

The diaspora caused by the building of Lincoln Center represented the driving belief that nothing was sacred or untouchable in this new America—an America that saw "urban blight" as a manifestation of an earlier, less triumphant era in the country's history. Nevertheless, the moral miasma caused by the eradication of a large and vital Manhattan neighborhood continues to hover over the Center's legacy.

Even the founders' idealistic belief in having various arts organizations situated in one place to generate collective artistic activities that would dwarf individual efforts might be contested. America's current urban landscapes often celebrate the placement of arts organizations throughout a city, working with local resources and communities to define the particular identities of each venue.

In seeking to create a unique community of artists interacting in innovative ways to explore the development of new artistic experiences, the founders underestimated the difficulty of bringing together the various constituents of the Center to work for a common goal. Lincoln Center's campus was conceived by its founders as a catalytic environment where its collective performances and arts education programs would provide a cornucopia of artistic activities found nowhere else. During the Center's more than sixty-year history, individuals and institutions would test such collective objectives, as well as the will of Lincoln Center leadership, which invariably led to controversies never envisioned by Rockefeller or his colleagues.

"Styles change. Ideas move on. Nothing escapes fashions in art and life."[4] Such a view applies to the Lincoln Center saga. Over decades, the history of Lincoln Center contains elements of idealism and realism brought together in support of the performing arts and the artists who populate that universe. As the future unfolds, this complex organization will need to adapt to changing times and mores. *Beacon to the World* is about Lincoln Center's challenges and successes throughout its history, and its resolute quest for excellence in the demanding profession of the performing arts.

CHAPTER ONE

The Expansion of an Idea

THE DENSE URBAN ENVIRONMENT of today's West Side of Manhattan was once home to the Lenni-Lenape, the Native American tribe that first populated what they called "Mannahatta," the "island of many hills," before white settlers forced them to move west.[1] The settlers arrived after Henry Hudson sailed up the "Great River of the Mountains" in 1609, and by 1660 this area of Manhattan had been settled by Dutch farmers drawn by its ample resources: plentiful fertile land, game, and fish.[2] Two hundred years later, Washington Irving described the West Side as a "sweet and rural valley, beautiful with many a bright wild-flower . . . enlivened here and there by a delectable Dutch cottage, sheltered under some sloping hill and almost buried in embowering trees."[3]

Soon after the American Revolution, the area became a type of spa for the well-to-do, whose visitors included George Washington, King Louis Philippe of France, and Charles-Maurice de Talleyrand-Périgord.[4] In 1868 its principal thoroughfare, Bloom-ingdale Road, a main route to Boston, was developed into a high-way, later renamed Broadway.[5] The name "Bloomingdale," taken from the Dutch "Bloemendael" (vale of flowers), was used for a long stretch of Manhattan's West Side until the mid-nineteenth century.[6]

When Central Park was created in the 1850s, squatters—driven by an economic depression and their displacement due to the construction of the park—came to the West Side and set up shanty towns.[7] Later, after the Civil War, brownstone dwellings were built, and a construction boom came to the area along with more paved roads, the installation of underground power lines, the extension of the West Side and Yonkers Patent Elevated Railway to Eighty-First Street in 1879, and the opening of the Broadway subway in 1918.[8]

The New York City Board of Aldermen named the area Lincoln Square in 1906, though land deeds issued from the mid-seventeenth century to the beginning of the twentieth reveal that no landowner in the area went by the name of Lincoln.[9] The precise relationship of Abraham Lincoln to the area is murky, perhaps in deference to New York mayor George B. McClellan, the son of the Civil War general who lost to Lincoln in the presidential election of 1864 and who earlier was a source of great frustration to Lincoln as the less-than-aggressive commanding general of the Union Army.[10] Knowing of Mayor McClellan's potentially negative view of the sixteenth president, the aldermen may have underplayed the naming of the square in honor of Lincoln.

As in other parts of New York, by the late nineteenth century "dumbbell" or "railroad" tenements came to dominate the area, providing overcrowded and unsanitary housing units. This type of building had been outlawed by 1901, and since the tenements were obsolete almost at the time of their construction, the owners had little motivation to renovate. Amid this lower-income housing environment, in 1887 the U.S. Army established an armory complete with Norman-style turrets on Columbus Avenue between Sixty-First and Sixty-Second Streets, similar in design to armories built at the same time on the city's East Side. This West Side armory would stand until the middle of the next century.

For the first half of the twentieth century, the Lincoln Square area, also known as San Juan Hill in honor of Black residents who were veterans of the Spanish-American War, was described as "the toughest neighborhood in town, a spawning ground for violence and crime . . . where grimy rooming houses, oil-soaked garages, and fly-specked bars and luncheonettes [existed together]."[11] However, it was also home to a thriving Black and Puerto Rican community, with many schools, churches, and jazz and social clubs. Jazz legends such as Thelonious Monk and James P. Johnson lived nearby, and

Johnson purportedly composed "The Charleston" for performances in one of the San Juan Hill clubs. By the second half of the twentieth century, Leonard Bernstein had immortalized the area by using it as the setting for his great musical of 1957, *West Side Story* (and the 1961 film version). Contrary to urban mythology, the opening scenes of the movie were not filmed in Lincoln Square but immediately northwest on Sixty-Eighth Street between Amsterdam and West End Avenues, where the Lincoln Towers housing development now stands.

The initial thrust in developing what was to become Lincoln Center for the Performing Arts had less to do with the arts and more with the redevelopment of so-called blighted sections of New York City through "slum clearance." This term had great currency during the early post–World War II years in American cities, where populations were growing as America's economy became the most powerful in the world. The Federal Housing Act of 1949 gave unique authority and funding to American municipalities confronting urban overcrowding and decline. The greatest strategist behind the utilization of this sweeping federal legislation in New York City was Robert Moses. Although never elected to any public office, Moses served in so many prominent positions, from New York City Parks commissioner to chair of both the Triborough Bridge and Tunnel Authority and the New York State Power Authority, that his influence appeared ubiquitous and infinite—and perhaps it was. Included in these myriad posts was chair of the City's Committee on Slum Clearance.

Moses's vision for a future New York City was built on his belief that the automobile would become the primary means of transport in urban centers, superseding public transportation.[12] In building highways, Moses evicted as many as 250,000 people and destroyed countless communities in what a 1954 City Planning Commission report called "an enforced population displacement completely unlike any previous population movement in the City's history."[13] The techniques that Moses used in clearing enormous tracts of urban land might be considered draconian in the twenty-first century, but his methods prevailed during the 1950s. When asked about the personal impact of his public works on those who were forced to move from their homes, he brazenly responded, "There's very little real hardship in the thing. There's a little discomfort, and even that is greatly exaggerated."[14]

In 1958 Lincoln Center's management agents, Braislin, Porter & Wheelock, pledged to "make the Lincoln Square project a model for site practices," although that was not how the hundreds of displaced families saw it.[15] In fact, Moses completely ignored the essential requirement in the federal legislation that the slum clearance would "improve the quality of life for neighborhood residents and focused instead on razing unseemly sectors of the central city— displacing the African Americans, Italians, and Hispanics who had made these neighborhoods their home."[16]

Moses viewed the development of Lincoln Center as a project befitting the ambitions of a great city like New York, one that would make it a world-class center for the arts.[17] He believed that the prestige of a new cultural center would overcome any objections to the project.[18] Some civic leaders like Dean Rusk, president of the Rockefeller Foundation at the time, expressed qualms about condemning private property, but the destruction of a city neighborhood and the resulting diaspora of residents moved ahead with a single-mindedness that left the affected individuals and families in its wake.[19]

Despite the brutal destruction of large swaths of Manhattan's Upper West Side neighborhoods, Lincoln Center boosters worked toward what they considered a benign mission: a multibuilding arts center which would enhance citizens' lives by making the arts accessible to all. Although the need for improved concert halls and opera houses in New York City had been evident since much earlier in the twentieth century, a confluence of three separate issues occurred in the mid-1950s which brought the concept of an arts center into focus.

The first element was the passage of the federal urban renewal program. The all-powerful Moses, who often was referred to as the "real mayor" of New York, much to the chagrin of Mayor Robert Wagner, had in 1955 designated the stretch of Manhattan's West Side that Lincoln Center would come to occupy as a redevelopment area, appropriately named the Lincoln Square Urban Renewal

Project. Although Moses envisioned the traditional mix of commercial and residential buildings for the project, he also saw the potential for the creation of an opera house in the area.

Such a new opera venue was the second element of the project. Moses's longtime friend, the architect Wallace K. Harrison, had worked for years on the concept of a new Metropolitan Opera House to replace the antiquated and logistically challenged venue on Thirty-Ninth Street and Broadway, exploring new locations for the opera at Rockefeller Center and even as part of the overall project to build the United Nations soon after World War II, but to no avail. Charles M. Spofford, chair of the Met's executive committee, was enthusiastic about the idea, and the Met's board voted on April 14, 1955, to formally pursue the building plan. Moses proposed the Lincoln Center site to Harrison, thus completing the second action that moved forward the concept of a new musical arts center.

The third factor involved the New York Philharmonic–Symphony Society's need to leave their home at Carnegie Hall. In 1955, Carnegie Hall was privately owned, and the owners felt that razing the building and selling the land would bring them a handsome profit. The orchestra's lease was to end in 1959. Arthur A. Houghton, Jr., soon to become chair of the orchestra's board, turned to Harrison for advice on where to resettle. Harrison logically brought the Philharmonic into the Lincoln Square discussion.

A statement issued in 1957 by the Exploratory Committee for a Musical Arts Center cited a perceived "evolution" in the social fabric of the nation, pointing to "America's growing audience of opera, music, drama and the dance . . . [and the] emergence of brilliant American talent . . . [and arguing that] the arts are important if not essential to the human mind and spirit."[20] Such a statement reinforced the concept that the America emerging from the chaos of World War II could now look to the human spirit of its citizens as well as to their economic successes, reflecting what one writer called a "Cold War urban renewal vision."[21] A similar sentiment was expressed in the words of C. D. Jackson, one of the original members of the Center's Exploratory Committee, in 1959: "We haven't thought of [cultural achievements] as positive, dynamic, and essential assets in the great and dangerous game that we must play today.

... [Lincoln Center would be a] new, visible, artistically impeccable, majestic, cultural asset [for the United States]."[22]

The idea of performing arts organizations working together in New York City was not entirely new. The New York City Opera and earlier iterations of the New York City Ballet, along with a drama component, had been functioning within one administrative entity at the New York City Center of Music and Drama on West Fifty-Fifth Street since 1943. In 1954, the Metropolitan Opera and the New York Philharmonic created an unusual entity called Music, Inc., a nonprofit fundraising organization.[23] The effort was short-lived and eventually replaced by the Lincoln Square project.

Lincoln Square, unlike earlier collaborative efforts, had strong political and financial backing. Organizational work started in the fall of 1955 with a $50,000 seed grant from John D. Rockefeller, Jr. The successful solicitation letter to Rockefeller noted Lincoln Center's appeal "from the standpoint of mass subway transportation" as well as "the Cadillac trade."[24] A $25,000 grant also came from the New York Foundation, together with contributions from the New York Community Trust and John D. Rockefeller 3rd to offset the $89,500 paid to the firm of Day & Zimmermann, the principal planning consultant for the project.

The project clearly needed a strong civic leader to bring credibility and political clout to the venture, and that person was John D. Rockefeller 3rd (often referred to in correspondence and business meetings as JDR 3rd). Once again Wallace K. Harrison was the go-between, making the connection through his friend Dean Rusk, who felt that Rockefeller would be the perfect person for the task. Rockefeller was born in New York City in 1906 and followed in the footsteps of his father, John D. Rockefeller, Jr., in devoting his life to philanthropic work. He graduated from Princeton University in 1929 with a major in economics and then set out on a world tour during which he became fascinated with the culture of Japan and the subject of foreign affairs in general. He joined the navy during World War II and helped plan postwar Japan policy. He revived the Japan Society and established the Asia Society in the 1950s, and became chair of the Rockefeller Foundation, serving in that position

John D. Rockefeller 3rd at the Lincoln Center construction site
of an almost completed Philharmonic Hall, ca. 1962. (Photo by
Arnold Newman / Arnold Newman Collection via Getty Images)

from 1952 to 1971.[25] His influence in philanthropic circles was second to none.

Rockefeller viewed his work on Lincoln Center as part of his responsibilities as a citizen of New York. Though he was not a frequent attendee at the opera, symphony, or ballet, he recognized the positive role that the arts could play in the lives of New Yorkers.[26] Motivated by a genuine idealism regarding the power of the arts to enhance the quality of life for all citizens, he consistently saw the creation of Lincoln Center as realizing such a lofty goal. Rockefeller and the initial group of members of the Exploratory Committee for a Musical Arts Center—Charles Spofford (Metropolitan Opera board member), Floyd Blair (New York Philharmonic board chair, soon to be succeeded by Arthur Houghton), Wallace Harrison, and Lincoln Kirstein (representing the New York City Ballet)—believed that the city "must achieve a greater measure of cultural eminence if we are to maintain the political leadership we now enjoy."[27] JDR 3rd saw that American business could also "build a healthier, happier and better educated America."[28] Furthermore, he felt that Lincoln Center would, "by enriching our lives, enrich our America."[29] Lincoln Kirstein, who became a powerful force in developing Lincoln Center's mission, noted, regarding education at the Center, that "the emphasis [must be] on quality. The mass education idea is out of the question. The Center could be a kind of West Point for the performing arts, as a visible token of the United States' interest in things of the pure spirit."[30]

Future scholars did not embrace this idealized philosophical position. Cultural historians William B. Scott and Peter M. Rutkoff wrote four decades later that "in the 1950s and 1960s, the working poor in New York were the victims, rather than the beneficiaries, of urban renewal. Working with the Rockefeller family, Robert Moses manipulated federal largesse, using funds earmarked for the improvement of urban housing, to build a center for the performing arts comparable in scope to Rockefeller Center."[31]

The Exploratory Committee for a Musical Arts Center first met on October 25, 1955, at the venerable Century Association on West Forty-Third Street.[32] They agreed at this first meeting that Devereaux Josephs, chair of the board of the New York Life Insurance Company; Robert Blum, vice president of Abraham & Straus and president of the Brooklyn Institute of Arts and Sciences; C. D. Jackson, Metropolitan Opera Board member, formerly publisher of *Fortune* magazine and publisher of *Life* magazine in 1960, as well as a close adviser to President Eisenhower; and Irving S. Olds, partner in the law firm of White and Case, former chair of U.S. Steel, and a director of the Metropolitan Opera, would also be invited to join the committee. The committee represented a classic assemblage of highly placed businessmen who felt a responsibility to give back to society through volunteering for projects that would benefit the community as a whole, with a secondary agenda that included the reinforcement of business relationships that would benefit them and their stockholders.

Every two weeks, the group met for lunch at the Century. Rockefeller was quickly elected chair, and new participants David Keiser, board member of The Juilliard School of Music and the New York Philharmonic, and John Drye, chair of both The Juilliard School of Music and the Juilliard Musical Foundation and a founding partner of the law firm Kelley Drye & Warren, joined the meetings. A. L. Fowler represented the committee's consultant, Day & Zimmermann, and Edgar Young provided precise minutes.

At a Musical Arts Conference on February 17, 1956, the committee invited many luminaries in the fields of music, dance, drama, arts education, and architecture, as well as business leaders, to discuss plans for the Center.[33] The conference brought forward a wide array of issues that were eventually addressed by the Exploratory Committee: the drafting of a philosophical statement for the new venture, the creation of a financial and administrative structure, discussions on possible new participants beyond the Metropolitan Opera and the New York Philharmonic, the role of education at the Center, the creation of advisory groups in determining the quality and direction of various Center activities, the architectural design to be overseen by Wallace K. Harrison, land acquisition and price, traffic and parking facilities, fundraising, and the crucial relationship that the Center's leadership would have with Robert Moses in his role as chair of the city's Committee on Slum Clearance.

In June, the Board of Directors of Lincoln Center for the Performing Arts was officially created. The Exploratory Committee and the board often met on the same day in consecutive sessions, sharing membership between the two entities.

Contrary to some perceptions of the dignified and patrician Rockefeller as simply a figurehead in the realization of this enormous venture, Rockefeller threw himself completely into the vast organizational process, attending meetings; visiting potential donors and lobbying city, state, and federal officials involved in financing the project; and overseeing the demolition process and the relocation of thousands of residents and businesses.

Rockefeller claimed to take the relocation aspect of the venture particularly seriously: "We will undertake this responsibility [of relocation] with full respect for the rights of these families and with maximum consideration for their comfort," although the evidence suggests that he would show considerable indifference to the suffering caused by the creation of the Center.[34] In one example of the many letters sent to Rockefeller from displaced residents of San Juan Hill, Basil Fellrath of 125 West Sixty-Third Street writes:

> I am a 77-year-old having lived here for 18 years in the back parlor of this well-kept house at the low rent of six dollars a week. . . . The important question for me is where will I be able to get another suitable place like this at such low rent? . . . It is next to impossible at my age to get work. . . . God has blessed the great Rockefeller Heritage as an instrument to benefit mankind in many ways, and the peoples [*sic*] are grateful for it. I hope somehow a way can be found for the thousands of poor people in this Center to assist them to find homes with rents they can afford to pay.[35]

The response came not from Rockefeller but from Otto L. Nelson, construction head for Lincoln Center: "I am sorry this is necessary but hope that when you see the completed Lincoln Center for the Performing Arts, you will feel that the inconvenience has been for a good cause. You should feel a sense of satisfaction and participation in that you too have helped in bringing about what we believe will be a great civic improvement that will be enjoyed by many thousands of people over the next hundred years."[36] Such a tone-deaf and unempathetic response showed the inexorable insistence that the Lincoln Center leaders exhibited in pushing forward the project. The displaced residents of Lincoln Square would be relocated to public housing projects in the outer boroughs or left to find housing in abandoned tenements in the South Bronx.[37] For many of those displaced, the sense of community they had enjoyed before would be lost forever.

As early as March 1956, Wallace Harrison presented a preliminary plot plan and recommended the creation of two groups of architects, one to consult with the board on general planning and one to carry out the designs.[38] In the autumn, leading architects, acousticians, and arts professionals from Europe and the United States, including Alvar Aalto, Pietro Belluschi, Richard Bolt, Marcel Breuer, and Philip Johnson were invited to participate in a two-week conference to discuss the Center's architecture.

The original slum clearance plan allowed the new arts center to stretch north from Sixty-Second Street to the point of the triangle that is formed by the convergence of Amsterdam Avenue and Broadway at Seventieth Street. This large tract of land proved unwieldy for both financial and logistical reasons, and the plan was cut back considerably, with the Center projected to be built between Sixty-Second and Sixty-Fifth Streets, bounded on the west by Amsterdam Avenue and on the east by Columbus Avenue. Eventually, the Center acquired property between Sixty-Fifth and Sixty-Sixth Streets to provide space for the construction of the Juilliard building.

The Exploratory Committee set about in earnest to shape the project. Following Harrison's plan, they determined that the Center would not only include an opera house and a concert hall but also provide space for chamber music, ballet, light opera, spoken drama, an educational program, and a performing arts library. Contiguous to the Center on Sixty-Second Street, and part of the overall slum clearance program overseen by Moses, would be a Manhattan campus for Fordham University, as well as a new headquarters for the American Red Cross on Amsterdam Avenue, and a combined arts high school merging the High School of Music & Art and the High School of Performing Arts, eventually named the Fiorello H. La Guardia High School of Music & Art and Performing Arts. The committee considered the idea of including painting and sculpture in the Center but decided against it on the grounds that the visual arts were already well housed in New York.

Early on the Exploratory Committee had to consider the idea of inviting the New York City Center of Music and Drama to join the venture. Kirstein wanted City Ballet to be an integral part of the new complex, with the City Center administrative support system assisting it in its new home, but Moses was opposed and Newbold Morris, City Center's chair, seemed noncommittal.[39] The Lincoln Center board decided that there were enough participants at the moment, and advised City Center that it would not be possible for them to join the project at that time. Morris reacted with disappointment—perhaps, Rockefeller thought, because of financial difficulties he was weathering at City Center, whose solution might be found in its association with Lincoln Center.[40] The committee would readdress this question in short order.

Purchasing the land for the Center turned out to be an extraordinarily complex process. The Metropolitan Opera and the New York Philharmonic initially bid on the purchase of the redevelopment site before the Exploratory Committee was even constituted, offering to buy the land at eight dollars per square foot, a price that corresponded to the land cost at the nearby redevelopment area known as the Coliseum project, located at Broadway and Fifty-Ninth Street.[41] Both the Met and the New York Philharmonic eventually revised their offers, adding more acreage, for a total cost of $1.2 million. There was also an extended process in acquiring the so-called Cadillac Building, also known as the Kennedy Building, at 60–74 Columbus Avenue, owned by Joseph P. Kennedy, father of the future president. Built in 1927 as an automobile sales, service, and distribution center, the building had twelve floors in a loft structure. Unlike most buildings in the clearance area, the Kennedy Building was in respectable shape and housed several federal agency offices based in New York. There was a concern that its demolition would be illegal under the Federal Housing Act. Eventually, the building was purchased by Lincoln Center at a price of $2.5 million and razed along with the other buildings on the site.

By early 1957, it was becoming apparent that the expanded size of the parcel required the Exploratory Committee to reconsider the cost of the land acquisition. Accordingly, the Lincoln Square project lowered its offer to five dollars per square foot and, concurrently, the Met and the Philharmonic withdrew their eight-dollar offer. Moses was not entirely against this change, but the federal government needed to authorize the adjustment. As the request came during a drive to reduce the federal budget, the lower square footage price was rejected.

Rockefeller reluctantly agreed to the $8 price, but on the condition that Lincoln Center would not pay for land in a planned park, the public plaza, or the street.[42] By July 1957 further negotiations brought the price down to $6.75 a square foot. The price paid for

John D. Rockefeller 3rd is shown presenting a check to Mayor Wagner to pay for acquiring the land for Lincoln Center. (Left to right): Mayor Robert F. Wagner, Robert Moses, and John D. Rockefeller 3rd. (Photo by Bob Serating)

the Lincoln Center acreage initially amounted to $3,993,667 and then grew to $4,848,171 with the purchase of the half block between Sixty-Fifth and Sixty-Sixth Streets that would be used by The Juilliard School.[43]

Even before the negotiations for the land were finished, the Exploratory Committee engaged professional assistance in developing their plan. They settled on the engineering and consulting firm of Day & Zimmermann of Philadelphia, with A. L. Fowler as the supervising executive, to develop a study for the committee. In its first drafts of the report, Day & Zimmermann explored with a good deal of imagination, if not realistically, how the new Center's halls could be used. The basic assumptions for all four principal halls (an opera house, a concert hall, a recital hall, and a theater for dance and operetta) included air-conditioned year-round venues with fully equipped, multipurpose stages.[44] This "multipurpose" approach was anathema to how the Met and the Philharmonic envisioned their halls, and the idea was quickly dropped.

In addition to the expected use of the halls by the Metropolitan Opera and the New York Philharmonic, the consultants proposed that the theater—known initially as the Theater for Dance and Operetta and eventually the New York State Theater, with a proposed seating capacity of 2,200—would be primarily designated as the home of the ballet and the venue for touring foreign productions, although there was no explicit strategy for booking those attractions.[45] Planners envisioned many domestic and international orchestras performing in Philharmonic Hall. The summer was seen as a time for the presentation of "folk operas" and musicals, ranging from Aaron Copland's *The Tender Land*, to Richard Rodgers and Oscar Hammerstein's *Oklahoma!*, and even a film festival. Finally, organizers suggested a grandiose summer festival utilizing all four halls on the scale of the Edinburgh and Bayreuth Festivals.[46]

Plans for programming of the Theater for Dance and Operetta eventually moved to mostly ballet, musical theater, and opera, but a strategy for the recital and repertory hall (eventually named Alice Tully Hall) took a particularly eclectic direction as planners considered it as a multi-use space. The proposed thousand-seat auditorium was originally recommended to accommodate drama, light opera, small ensembles, and recitals or debuts.[47] It was planned to be constructed in the basement of Philharmonic Hall, but engineers and architects quickly learned that an underground stream, moving northwest to the Hudson River, crossed directly below where Philharmonic Hall and the Met were to be placed.[48] As a result, the recital space was eventually built across Sixty-Fifth Street as part of the Juilliard building.

During this early stage there was no shortage of suggestions from professionals and the public having to do with the correct seating capacity for each venue at the new Center. Eugene Ormandy, the music director of the Philadelphia Orchestra, let Rockefeller know that the concert hall should have at least three thousand seats.[49] The *Herald Tribune* urged Lincoln Center leaders to think big, arguing "New York . . . hasn't become the greatest city in the country by building things too small."[50]

The impresario Sol Hurok, one of the world's preeminent arts presenters, argued that the new Center should include an exceptionally large hall for visiting theatrical productions, since New York City lacked a home for productions that could attract large audiences. Hurok bemoaned the fact that while earlier in the century New York City had had at least three other opera houses in addition to the Metropolitan Opera House, each having an average capacity of 3,100 seats, all had been transformed to serve other purposes (e.g., as apartment houses, movie theaters, or meeting halls). He recommended that one Lincoln Center hall be built, in addition to the proposed 3,800-seat Metropolitan Opera House, with a capacity of 3,500 to 4,000 seats.[51] Rockefeller viewed Hurok's suggestions as a minor annoyance and asked his lieutenants to respond to the impresario's letters. For acoustical, logistical, and financial reasons Hurok's idea of a mammoth concert hall for the Center was never seriously considered.

For Rockefeller, however, his grand, even audacious idea now needed a formal administrative structure, backed by considerable financial resources and an architectural vision that would bring the Center's disparate units together to provide a unified campus supporting not only the Center's performing arts ensembles but also the members of the public who would frequent the imagined halls, creating a synergy that did not yet exist anywhere else.

CHAPTER TWO

A Mighty Influence for
Peace and Understanding

T O KEEP THE CENTER PROJECT on track during its formative years, John D. Rockefeller 3rd was pushed to utilize all
his diplomatic skills as well as his considerable patience and
gravitas. He chaired numerous exploratory meetings dealing with finances, fundraising, and government affairs in the run-up
to the groundbreaking in 1959.

JDR 3rd asked questions at these gatherings as to whether the
concept of the Center was a valid one: Does a Center have advan-
tages over merely new houses for the Metropolitan Opera and the
Philharmonic? Should the Center include educational facilities?

The most creative meetings he chaired included artists, educators, scholars, and critics debating what the Center should artistically
achieve. Luminaries who participated included composer Aaron Copland, composer and critic Virgil Thomson, choreographer George
Balanchine along with his professional partner Lincoln Kirstein, architect Pietro Belluschi, composer and record producer Goddard Lieberson, producer Roger Stevens, producer, director, and cofounder
of the Actors Studio Elia Kazan, and performing arts critics Irving
Kolodin, Paul Henry Lang, Howard Taubman, and Walter Terry.

One conference included only music and dance critics from
the major New York City periodicals. The critics were asked to

comment on the new complex's basic philosophy and educational mission. The participants agreed that the concept of the Center was sound, and they expressed the hope that future constituents would work together to provide artistic inspiration for all.

Another conference specifically focused on education at the Center. A mix of artists and educators participated, including George Balanchine, composer and Juilliard president William Schuman, Elia Kazan, director of the Neighborhood Playhouse School of the Theater Sanford Meisner, drama critic Walter Kerr of the *New York Herald Tribune*, and *New York Times* music critic Howard Taubman.

What was clear to those discussing education at the Center was that the fundamental emphasis for such an effort had to be on training for a professional career. There were recommendations to invite existing schools to be constituents, and there was also a strong endorsement that the Center's educational program must include dance and drama as well as music. However, Day & Zimmermann stated that there was not a drama school in the United States worthy of inclusion.[1]

By early 1956, The Juilliard School of Music had become the favored candidate to provide music instruction at the Center, although there was hardly unanimous support in this regard. In dance, because of the strong presence of Lincoln Kirstein as a member of the Exploratory Committee, the School of American Ballet was a prime candidate. However, there was also mention of the Opera Ballet School of the Metropolitan Opera and the Catherine Long group as institutions under consideration.[2]

By late 1956 the basic educational principles of the Center were coming into shape, suggesting the development of "a unique form of training."[3] This approach necessitated "a bridge . . . between the best of training . . . with actual professional performance . . . [and that the] atmosphere for such a training center should be highly practical and professional—not academic."[4] It was also recommended that no academic degrees be awarded at the end of the educational process.

These discussions involved a good deal of negativity about Juilliard being the educational entity for the Center, with selected participants in the conference stating, "Why disturb a good going concern for a[n] untried development; no matter how much Juilliard has changed, it would face prejudices and opposition based on attitudes towards the present Juilliard."[5] The report concluded, "The consensus of the group was in support of a new development rather than an invitation to Juilliard or any other music school to move into the center."[6]

Howard Taubman of the *New York Times* expressed his belief that graduates of American conservatories were not ready to become members of professional orchestral or operatic ensembles, and that Juilliard was "too academic and lacked both the personnel and experience needed to put the finishing touches on professional musicians."[7] For his part, Max Rudolf of the Metropolitan Opera showed a "moderate contempt for American conservatories . . . [and] that neither Juilliard nor any other existing American music school is competent to do what needs to be done to bridge the gap between formal classroom training and professional work."[8]

According to Edgar Young's notes of the Kirstein interview with Charles Dollard on July 17, there was a "firm impression that Kirstein was himself uneasy about handing over the direction of musical education in the Center to Juilliard and Schuman. He thinks that Schuman is a fine person and a gifted composer but no great shakes as a musical educator."[9]

In drama, Day & Zimmermann could not come up with a preferred school that would teach both classical and modern dramatic repertory: "Investigation to date, however, has not brought to light any single group that qualifies in drama. The programs of the Actors Studio, the American Academy of Dramatic Arts, the Theatre Wing, the Neighborhood Playhouse and others have been reviewed, but none seems to offer what is desired. . . . As far as can be determined, there is no good school in the country with this emphasis."[10]

By November, the Exploratory Committee drafted a prospectus for the Center's new educational entity and named it "The Institute of Advanced Training in the Performing Arts."[11] The prevailing intention in 1956 was to utilize "a new small flexible institution rather than an old one with fixed ideas and traditions."[12] Nevertheless, in addition to The Juilliard School of Music, the Columbia University School of the Arts was under consideration, as was a proposed arts school within New York University.

In retrospect, it is surprising that a formal invitation from JDR 3rd to The Juilliard School of Music to become one of the constituents of the Center was tendered on December 17, 1956, little more than a month after the November proposal to create an entirely new educational entity.[13] Without doubt, the reason for this turnaround was the intense and successful lobbying by Juilliard president William Schuman to convince JDR 3rd and his colleagues that Juilliard should be part of the Center.

In a succinct five-page report written by Schuman for the Juilliard board on December 7, 1956, and shared with the Exploratory Committee, the Juilliard president outlined how the School would need to change in order to join Lincoln Center. Schuman proposed a transformation of the "old Juilliard" by not just changing location but also dissolving its thousand-student preparatory division, downsizing its degree student enrollment, transforming the structure of its dance division, and creating an entirely new drama program.

Schuman was convinced that as the primary educational arm of Lincoln Center, it would be inevitable that Juilliard would remain one of the most prominent institutions of its type in the world. His persuasive report of early December realized that objective for Juilliard, and on February 7, 1957, The Juilliard School of Music joined Lincoln Center.

In addition to the artistic issues concerned with the proposed activities in the various halls, Rockefeller and his colleagues grappled with how the Center's management should function. All the organizations eventually choosing to join Lincoln Center were quite concerned about maintaining their institutional autonomy in all matters. Rockefeller was in favor of such independence and emphasized that each institution would be responsible for not only its artistic programming but also its financial solvency. In the early years of planning, the Exploratory Committee assumed that the various institutions, rather than Lincoln Center itself, would direct artistic programming.

This is evident in a letter from Reginald Allen, executive director of operations for Lincoln Center, to José Limón, the distinguished dancer and choreographer, confirming that the Center's leadership had always planned for contemporary or modern dance concerts as well as classical ballet to be programmed at the Center. In the letter, Allen also explains that "Lincoln Center itself will not produce or underwrite any of the performing arts which will appear on its stages. Our role will be that of a benevolent landlord and catalyst."[14]

The idea of funding the Center was soon on the minds of Exploratory Committee members. In a document regarding the philosophy of Lincoln Center that was distributed to the public early in the Center's planning years, fundraising was presented as involving a challenge to the nation: "Lincoln Center will be a dramatic answer to the charge that Americans are interested only in making and spending money."[15]

Obtaining the financial resources to realize this mammoth project—which was initially pegged at $75 million after some earlier unrealistically lower levels—was of considerable importance to JDR 3rd, not only because the project needed to be funded but also because Rockefeller was deeply concerned that the project leaders would eventually turn to him to bail it out if sufficient financial resources were not obtained. This scenario was anathema to his view of how Lincoln Center was to function.

An amount of $55 million was budgeted for land acquisition and building construction. The remaining $20 million was to cover the development of new productions, support for the Center's educational program, and funding for the creation of a drama constituent and a library-museum."[16]

The Committee on Slum Clearance estimated in 1956 that the cost of clearing the entire "slum area" from Sixty-Second to Seventieth Streets would be about $150 million. Lincoln Center was the largest part of that area. Under Title I of the Federal Housing Act of 1949, New York City would pay one-third and the federal government two-thirds of the cost of buying the land. The land would then be sold at sharp markdowns to private developers.[17]

Independent of governmental funding, other important sources of financial support came from foundations and individuals. Early in the process, major philanthropic organizations provided large grants to the project, including $12.5 million from the Ford Foundation and $10.5 million from the Rockefeller Foundation.[18]

The largest gift from an individual came from someone awfully close to JDR 3d in the person of his father, John D. Rockefeller, Jr., who contributed just over $5 million to the project, almost doubling, at the time, the second-largest individual gift, given by Vivian Beaumont Allen, who provided $3 million for the construction of the Center's repertory drama theater. Clarence Francis, campaign chair, announced that with the Rockefeller gift contributions to the Center totaled $35,526,000, just shy of halfway to the $75 million goal.

It is interesting to note that JDR 3rd soon thereafter solicited his father for a second large gift. Such an aggressive move for the reserved Rockefeller shows his intense need to acquire as much financial support as possible for the project, but he expressed his regret for doing so in a subsequent letter to his father: "I felt badly about our telephone conversation as I thought about it afterwards. I am afraid that I gave the impression of being more concerned about additional amounts later, than the most generous pledge now. This I regret very much as I am deeply appreciative of what you are doing. . . . I am sorry."[19]

Not all residents of New York or citizens of the United States were necessarily in favor of this major new arts center. Litigation to stop the Lincoln Square project began soon after the Exploratory Committee became known to the public. One approach by local residential and commercial tenants in testing the venture focused on the separation of church and state regarding the involvement of Fordham University, a Jesuit institution, in the overall project. In addition, community members expressed concern that the Center's construction would exacerbate the city's housing shortage and the severe hardships realized by the area's displaced residents.[20]

By early 1958, the Lincoln Square sites were acquired by the city and sold to the two sponsors, Fordham University and Lincoln Center for the Performing Arts. Lawsuits were filed against the acquisitions, and the New York Court of Appeals upheld the legality of the condemnation of the redevelopment area on March 3, 1958, with the U.S. Supreme Court soon thereafter declining to consider the constitutionality of the Lincoln Square project, allowing the venture to move forward.

The most problematic legal issue facing the project in its early stage had to do with the proposed Fordham University campus stretching along Sixty-Second Street between Columbus and Amsterdam Avenues. Although the Fordham construction was not officially part of the Lincoln Center project, it was included in the over-all slum clearance initiative overseen by Moses.

The New York chapter of the Americans United for Separation of Church and State vociferously complained, in a pamphlet titled "Lincoln Square: A Slum Clearance Project That Endangers Religious Freedom," that since public funds were being used to support the overall project, it was inappropriate—and illegal—to have the Roman Catholic Church receive such funds.[21] In addition, numerous individuals and quasi-religious organizations wrote to JDR 3rd to condemn in virulently anti-Catholic rhetoric the presence of Fordham in the overall project. Robert Moses expressed to Rockefeller his alarm that groups were coalescing to bring down the overall Lincoln Square complex: "They aim . . . at a national free-for-all church and state showdown. They can't win but they can make a lot of trouble for us at Lincoln Square, not to speak of fomenting intolerance and bigotry throughout the country."[22]

These legal protestations were not new to the project. In November 1956, a group of Lincoln Square residents and activists led by Harris L. Present, chair of the private Council on Housing Relocation Practices and counsel for the Lincoln Square Chamber of Commerce, began litigation to kill the redevelopment of the slum clearance area. Since federal and city funds would be used for land acquisition, Present contended that this action violated the First Amendment's separation of church and state due to Fordham's participation. He threatened to "tie the project up for years in the courts."[23]

Ten months after Present's November threat Rockefeller and Present would cross swords at a public hearing before the City Planning Commission, in September 1957, to review the Lincoln Square project. The City Planning Commission meeting lasted ten hours; twenty-six individuals spoke for the project and thirty-six against it.[24]

Present accused the Center's leaders of ignoring human values and failing to provide alternative low-income housing. He also complained that "there is no sound reason . . . for grouping all cultural activities within a single area."[25] In turn, Rockefeller presented the high-minded precepts associated with the venture from its inception, saying the Exploratory Committee represented a group of citizens interested in "constructive development of our city for the benefit and enjoyment of all its people—also for the maintenance of its position of leadership."[26]

Father Laurence J. McGinley, president of Fordham University, also testified, accompanied by periodic boos from some in attendance; he declared that Fordham "held its door open to every race, creed and nationality and that it numbered among its graduates rabbis, Protestant ministers, nuns in parochial schools and judges."[27] For Lincoln Center's part, JDR 3rd was firmly supportive of Fordham and announced that "Lincoln Center for the Performing Arts is pleased and happy to have them as neighbors."[28]

The *New York Times*, in an opinion piece published two days after the hearing, expressed frustration with the negativity toward the project, and justified the Lincoln Square initiative with a somewhat dismissive argument: "City government simply cannot defer or abandon the rebuilding of New York . . . because some people want to live in a certain house, or a certain neighborhood, or do business in a given location. If the city proceeded—or rather stood still—on that basis, it would never get anything done. . . . [Lincoln Square] is the biggest and the best single improvement touching the culture, the artistic education, aspirations and enjoyments offered to the city in generations, perhaps ever in the long history of New York. What in the world, then, is there to argue about?"[29]

In late 1958, Wallace K. Harrison, as coordinating architect for the project, assembled a team of architects that would design the six dedicated buildings in the $75 million undertaking. By that time Lincoln Center had raised about half the projected cost, so the architectural team was encouraged to develop the Center's buildings as expeditiously as possible.

The six prominent architects who were appointed to design the Center's buildings were Harrison, functioning not only as coordinating architect but as the designer of the Metropolitan Opera House; his business partner Max Abramovitz as architect for the New York Philharmonic's concert hall; Philip Johnson, designer of the dance/operetta theater; Pietro Belluschi, architect for The Juilliard School building, in consultation with Helge Westermann and Eduardo Catalano; Gordon Bunshaft of Skidmore, Owings and

René d'Harnoncourt, director of the Museum of Modern Art, coordinating a meeting of the six original Lincoln Center architects. (Seated, left to right): René d'Harnoncourt (at head of table), *Wallace K. Harrison, Pietro Belluschi, Philip Johnson, Gordon Bunshaft, Max Abramovitz, and Eero Saarinen, ca. 1959–60. (Photo by Dan Weiner; Copyright John Broderick)*

Merrill, designer of the Library-Museum; and Eero Saarinen, designer of the Drama Theater. In his earliest thinking, Harrison had envisioned a "single building with a great common foyer and two separate halls," but that concept was abandoned, although the approach was later used in the design of the Kennedy Center in Washington, DC.[30] Rockefeller and his board colleagues also decided to appoint René d'Harnoncourt, director of the Museum of Modern Art, as an intermediary between the architectural team members and the Lincoln Center board. D'Harnoncourt was particularly adept in this extremely sensitive role and played an important part in coordinating the Center's architectural planning.

In a somewhat whimsical yet perceptive article in the *New York Times Magazine* of February 1959, Harold C. Schonberg, soon to become the paper's chief music critic, compared the task of the six architects sorting out the overall design of the Center to an imaginary gathering of six great pianists—Vladimir Horowitz, Artur Rubinstein, Guiomar Novaes, Rudolf Serkin, Sviatoslav Richter, and Wilhelm Backhaus—who would be asked to come up with a correct and common interpretation of Beethoven's mammoth *Hammerklavier* Sonata. "How many eons would pass? How many wounds would be inflicted? How much blood would be shed?" Schonberg asked.[31]

In the very first design concept of the new arts center, Max Abramovitz noted that "the idea was to build a great unified complex, in which you'd have one big boiler plant. You would have an enormous place for workshops, which would take care of everybody's shops, and you'd have one publicity department; you'd have a big unified group . . . a central organization."[32] According to Philip Johnson, this approach was Gordon Bunshaft's idea, but Johnson went on to say that "the trouble with Bunshaft was that he was his own worst enemy. He undercut himself all the time by yelling and screaming and stamping."[33] However, as each constituent asked for specific elements to be contained within their own building, the unified concept approach disappeared. Unity of design did prevail, however, through the uniform size and mass of each building on the plaza, as well as the adoption of an organizational approach reminiscent of Michelangelo's Piazza del Campidoglio in Rome, "with Johnson's fountain at its heart—[giving] the center a European Plaza, festive and urbane, in the heart of the city."[34]

Aesthetically, although all six architects had their individual approaches to design, collectively they had grown to professional maturity influenced by the so-called International Style (a term coined by Philip Johnson and Henry-Russell Hitchcock, Jr., in 1932), with emphasis on a simplicity of form, a rejection of ornamentation, and a predominant use of steel, concrete, and especially glass as building materials, creating a clean and efficient-looking edifice with clear geometric proportions. This architectural approach was evident throughout the Center, but the Brutalist architectural aesthetic was also present in the final designs, especially Belluschi's concept for the Juilliard building. The Brutalist style was expressed through large, block-like construction using stone or brick (in Lincoln Center's case, travertine marble) as building surfaces. Belluschi's Juilliard building did not feature the wide expanse of glass that the Center's main plaza had. Rather, Juilliard's massive walls, enclosing numerous small windows, created a sense of a looming fortress overlooking Lincoln Center's North Plaza.

The travertine used to clad the Lincoln Center buildings had been utilized around the globe for centuries for the façades of several types of structures. Regrettably, the choice was a significant mistake because the stone disintegrated quickly, eventually requiring that all the constituents spend millions of dollars to periodically replace the façades of their buildings. Frederick P. Rose, a well-known New York City real estate developer and member of the Lincoln Center board, when asked why the stone was deteriorating so quickly, explained that the average winter temperature in New York City at the time was 32 degrees Fahrenheit. Therefore, water trapped in the open veins of the stone goes through a cycle of freezing and thawing for at least three months of the year, causing great damage to the stone.

Harrison garnered the respect of his distinguished colleagues. He stated, "The six of us may have different ideas, but we're united. . . . After all we're on the same side of the fence. We have come up through the modern movement together, and we're looking away from the Puritanism of the International Style toward enriched forms. Johnson saw it differently, stating, "The more meetings we went to, the more fragmented it got. [By the end] we really weren't speaking. I mean, it was ridiculous. Grown-ups. Good architects. . . . The unfortunate thing is that Lincoln Center is design by committee, and the committee didn't have any strength to impose a final solution."[35]

The architectural team expressed concern that the site was too small for all that they wished to accomplish, and they ultimately were forced to propose housing more than one constituent under the same roof (which came to pass with the Library-Museum and the Drama Theater). The architects wished to take land from the area designated for what was to become Damrosch Park, on the southwestern portion of the site, but Moses refused to have the park site diminished.

The mammoth construction project undertaken by Lincoln Center obviously required laborers as well as architects, and Center officials were proactive in cultivating the powerful unions which controlled the City's building trades, as well as in interacting with the unions representing artists.

Victor Borella, vice president in charge of operations for Rockefeller Center, worked closely with JDR 3rd and his Lincoln Center colleagues to engage the city's union leaders in order to minimize labor strife during the long construction period, which stretched from 1959 to 1969. Anna M. Rosenberg, a PR consultant for industrial relations, was hired to create what was called the Lincoln Center Labor Advisory Committee, whose main purpose was twofold: to convince organized labor that they should have a stake in the success of Lincoln Center through providing financial contributions; and to mediate so-called jurisdictional conflicts that might occur with the simultaneous "demolition of houses, the digging of foundations, the erection of buildings and the operating of concerts and operas."[36]

JDR 3rd and his staff also met regularly with powerful union officials such as Harry Van Arsdale, Jr., president of the New York City Central Labor Council AFL-CIO; David Dubinsky, president of the International Ladies' Garment Workers' Union; and Al Manuti, president of the American Federation of Musicians, Local 802.

Lincoln Center was generally successful in maintaining good relations with organized labor: the project received financial contributions from individual unions and help applying political pressure on city and state officials. In fact, Edgar Young once requested of Harry Van Arsdale, Jr., that a "no strike" arrangement be created between the city's labor force and Lincoln Center so that the New York State Theater could be completed on time for the opening of the World's Fair in April 1964. There had been frequent mention of a work stoppage citywide for the summer of 1963, but the unions had agreed not to discontinue work at the fairgrounds in Flushing Meadows. Young argued that the State Theater was part of that "no strike" agreement, writing Van Arsdale, "May we count on your help to resolve the difficulty and to avoid a disastrous delay?"[37] Fortunately, construction on the State Theater was never interrupted by any work stoppages.

Black workers also expressed their concern that they be treated equitably and hired for construction work at the Center. In September 1961, the Emergency Committee for Unity on Social and Economic Problems, an organization representing Black workers, released a report asking that they "be given the opportunity [to] work on all phases of the construction of Lincoln Center . . . [and that] in light of the black man's contributions to all modern American music through his development of jazz [there be built] a Palace of Jazz similar to the Palaces of Opera and ballet etc."[38] Although Black workers did participate in the construction of the Center, the idea of a "Palace of Jazz" would not be acted on until Jazz at Lincoln Center opened its complex at Columbus Circle in 2004.

As the Lincoln Center project was approaching a historic moment, with an elaborate groundbreaking ceremony scheduled in mid-May 1959, a curious occurrence took place which caught JDR 3rd and his colleagues off guard. Although Lincoln Kirstein was always a cantankerous and contrarian presence as part of the Lincoln Center planning process, rivaling the confrontational aura of Robert Moses, he was also an extremely important voice in the development of the Center's philosophy and a critical player in bringing the New York City Ballet, and ultimately the City Center of Music and Drama, into the fold. In addition, JDR 3rd respected Kirstein's counsel regarding how the performing arts worked.

It was therefore distressing, and ultimately embarrassing, for Lincoln Center leaders to learn that Kirstein wished to resign from the board just eight days before the groundbreaking ceremony. In a curt letter of resignation dated May 6, 1959, Kirstein wrote to JDR 3rd that he was "resigning as a member of the Board of Directors of Lincoln Square [sic] for the Performing Arts, Inc."[39] He stated that he had returned all germane documents related to the Center in his possession with "the intent never to speak or write of the reasons for my resignation . . . or my opinion of the project," a promise he would not keep.[40]

The board did, in fact, accept Kirstein's resignation at its regularly scheduled meeting on May 18. Rockefeller wrote that same day to Kirstein, expressing his regrets and saying, "During the last few years we have been closely associated. . . . People are bound to have differences . . . but this should not be allowed to destroy mutual admiration and respect."[41]

In mid-June, Kirstein expressed his intense negativity toward the Lincoln Center project, writing to Young that he had no desire to consult on dance programming at the Center: "It would seem far stranger to those artists with whom I have worked . . . that my name should be connected with a venture which has neither principle, policy nor patronage. . . . As for History: she may deal harshly with those who, out of facile expedience, ignorance or brute power betray the brightest hope for the performing arts in our time."[42]

JDR 3rd attempted to ameliorate the situation in early July by writing to Kirstein.[43] However, Kirstein was not mollified by Rockefeller's goodwill and wrote in mid-December a particularly vitriolic and incisive analysis of what Lincoln Center, in his view, had turned into: "There is nowhere in any thinking that I have so far encountered any notion of what it *takes* to create a work of art, as something that is not a prestige or status-token, something to fill up space and time in expensive real-estate. . . . In a word, it lacks a soul, as I once told you."[44]

Exhibiting a mercurial personality that was frustrating for those who had to work with him, Kirstein reversed course in January 1961 and expressed his support of Rockefeller: "You [JDR 3rd] alone [will get] the credit achieved [in erecting] these buildings. I would like to apologize to you for being so greedy, for asking for so much so quickly. Do not worry about the inclusion of artists on your Board; the Board is no place for them. Just get the buildings up."[45]

Rockefeller would eventually resolve his differences with Kirstein, but the philosophical contradictions that Kirstein raised with him would influence Rockefeller's thinking in the time ahead.

With their work on the architectural, fundraising, financial, personnel, and slum clearance components moving forward, the Exploratory Committee and the board of Lincoln Center set about to create a grand public groundbreaking, choosing May 14, 1959, as the day of the celebration. Since this was a momentous occasion, not only for the city and the state but also for the nation, it was only proper that the president of the United States, Dwight D. Eisenhower, be invited as the honored guest. Due to the good relations that JDR 3rd, as a staunch Republican and one of the richest individuals in America, had with the president and his administration, Eisenhower agreed to speak at the ceremony and to turn over a few shovelfuls of earth to break ground for the Center.

The event was planned to last no longer than one hour, which caused considerable problems for the planners, since various government speakers, as well as musical performances, were under consideration. Planners settled on the following line up of speakers: JDR 3rd served as host, followed by Commissioner Moses, Mayor Robert F. Wagner, Lieutenant Governor Malcolm Wilson substituting for Governor Nelson Rockefeller (JDR 3rd's brother), and President Eisenhower. Each speaker, except for the president, was to limit his remarks to no more than two minutes.

Such a request did not go over well with Commissioner Moses. Writing directly to JDR 3rd in an angry tone reminiscent of Kirstein, Moses minced no words: "I most respectfully decline to speak for one minute. Nothing can be said in one minute. What I have to say can be reduced to about four minutes or a little less. . . . Incidentally, I do not propose to submit my remarks . . . for approval. You may be sure, however, that they will be entirely friendly and in good taste."[46] JDR 3rd dutifully and respectfully responded as soon as he received Moses's letter: "We have felt that we could not limit the President. . . . The ceremonies are to be televised by CBS and ABC; hence it is essential that they [the remarks] may be kept within the one-hour limit."[47] In his typically dyspeptic manner, Moses immediately replied that he would speak no more than four minutes, but then added, "If I followed my natural inclinations, I should not turn up at all. . . . It is just a question of whether or not you want to insult your friends."[48] Moses spoke for about three and a half minutes, two minutes longer than Mayor Wagner, but shorter than President Eisenhower. Moreover, he could not help but include a controversial point in his speech: "We do indeed sympathize with tenants and do everything possible to help them, but we cannot give everybody and his lawyer what they want."[49]

A large, covered stage was built approximately where Sixty-Fourth Street existed before the demolition process began (about two hundred feet west of Broadway). An estimated crowd of twelve thousand was in attendance on a bright, sunny day. Leonard Bernstein conducted the New York Philharmonic and the Juilliard Chorus in a diverse program, including Copland's *Fanfare for the Common Man* (William Schuman would joke that there "wasn't a 'common man' in the crowd"),[50] the prologue from *I Pagliacci* by

President Dwight D. Eisenhower at Lincoln Center's groundbreaking ceremony,
May 14, 1959. Behind the president are (left to right): *John D. Rockefeller 3rd,*
David Keiser, Robert Moses, Manhattan Borough president Hulan Jack,
Mayor Robert F. Wagner, and Lieutenant Governor Malcolm Wilson.
(Photo by Bob Serating)

Leoncavallo featuring baritone Leonard Warren as soloist, the Ha-
banera from Bizet's *Carmen* with mezzo-soprano Risë Stevens, Beethoven's *Egmont* Overture, the "Hallelujah" chorus from Handel's
Messiah, during which President Eisenhower took a chrome-plated
shovel and turned over a few patches of dirt, and Sousa's *Semper
Fidelis* march.

Eisenhower blended political, social, and artistic topics in his
talk, speaking of the Center as an entity that would "develop a
mighty influence for peace and understanding throughout the world
and serve as a stimulating approach to one of the nation's pressing
problems: urban blight." He seemed to enjoy the ceremony and in
fact said to JDR 3rd, "I had a big time. I loved it. It was wonderful

to hear the music." He even playfully quipped regarding the quality of the acoustical experience, "If they can do this well under a tent—why the square?"[51]

JDR 3rd wrote in a note of thanks to Eisenhower after the event, "You went much further than being with us as the head of our Government. Your enthusiasm . . . your spontaneous response to the musical numbers, your warmth and friendliness . . . lifted the whole occasion above the normal routine of a ground-breaking ceremony."[52] In turn, Eisenhower responded to Rockefeller, "In the tireless efforts of yourself and your associates, once again is demonstrated that one of the great strengths of America lies in our willingness—even desire—to share the good things of life with all our citizens."[53]

Even Moses felt the event was a rousing success, writing to Rockefeller on May 21, "The Performing Arts ceremony was not only a success, it was damn near perfect. I have never seen a thing of this kind run more smoothly and with more dignity and inspiration."[54]

The person showered with the most accolades at the conclusion of the ceremony was the very deserving John D. Rockefeller 3rd, the project's true creator and visionary leader. In a laudatory "Man in the News" column appearing on the day of the ceremony, the *New York Times* editors praised JDR 3rd's tact, vision, and civility. The fifty-one-year-old Rockefeller was described in modest hyperbole as "a rangy six-footer with a lean, jutting chin that is slightly cleft at the tip and deep-set eyes[,] dark blue with a hint of gray and green. His straight hair, which he parts far on the left[,] is still plentiful."[55]

The article suggested that Rockefeller's commitment to the Lincoln Center project was born from plans never realized by his father, JDR, Jr., to build a new Metropolitan Opera House in Rockefeller Center. JDR 3rd's travels in East Asia for the Institute of Pacific Relations were also noted, crediting him with a strong "feeling of the significance of the cultural side in a nation's life. His efforts in the reconstruction of Colonial Williamsburg [also] gave him a taste for cultural institutions."[56]

As the glow of the groundbreaking began to dim, JDR 3rd and his colleagues leading Lincoln Center now had to guarantee that their grand plans would come to fruition.

CHAPTER THREE

No Longer a Dream but a Reality

THE IDEA OF APPOINTING A CHIEF executive officer to oversee the administration of Lincoln Center was raised quite early in the deliberations of the Exploratory Committee. JDR 3rd had met with the executive search firm of Rogers, Slade & Hill in May 1956 to discuss the search for an executive vice president reporting directly to Rockefeller, who would continue to hold the title of president.[1] Day & Zimmermann had suggested that a Lincoln Center CEO, who would also be a major fundraiser, could come from the ranks of academia: "A retired university president . . . might have more appeal to potential donors [than] would a businessman, since the university man has spent his life in the world of cultural ideas."[2]

This suggestion generated a giant question mark penciled in the report's margin, which can be assumed to have been written by Rockefeller himself. A retired college president was not who Rockefeller envisioned to lead this project so dear to his heart. Rockefeller showed that his greatest comfort level concerning senior employees centered on individuals in high corporate positions or retired members of the military. Retired Major General Otto L. Nelson, Jr., would eventually oversee the entire project as executive director for construction, and retired Colonel William Powers would report to Nelson on related matters.

It was not surprising, therefore, that Rockefeller would seek out a former military officer to ensure competent overall leadership of the undertaking, as he hoped it would increase the chances the venture would be realized on time and on budget. He picked one of the most respected soldiers of his generation, retired General Maxwell Davenport Taylor. JDR 3rd announced Taylor's appointment as president and chief executive officer of Lincoln Center, as well as member of the Lincoln Center board, on October 30, 1960. In turn, Rockefeller stepped down from the center's presidency to become board chair and senior officer of the Center.

Taylor came to Lincoln Center with impeccable credentials. He was fourth in his class at West Point, and eventually commanded the 101st Airborne Division, parachuting into combat with his troops and becoming the first American general to land in Normandy on D-Day. In 1945, he was appointed superintendent of the U.S. Military Academy at West Point, and he then commanded forces in Korea. He became U.S. Army chief of staff in 1955 and retired from active service in 1959. In addition to his military accomplishments, he was also a respected author and educator, overseeing a major overhaul of West Point's curriculum. After leaving the army, he became chair of the Mexican Light and Power Company in Mexico City.[3]

By late September 1960, Taylor's employment arrangements were finalized, providing a five-year contract that would extend to the second and final year of the New York World's Fair. For the remainder of 1960 Taylor would visit New York frequently to become familiar with the various intricacies of his new position. Upon his appointment Taylor said, "Lincoln Center is not only a cultural project of great importance to our people but the reflection of an image of America to all parts of the world."[4] He began his new job as the second president of Lincoln Center on January 1, 1961.

Regrettably, his tenure was distressingly short due to world events that would wash over the idealistic goals of an arts center in New York City. On April 17, 1961, the Central Intelligence Agency clandestinely launched an invasion of Cuba in the Bahia de los Cochinos (Bay of Pigs) area by a force of 1,400 American-trained Cubans, many of whom had fled Cuba when Fidel Castro seized power on January 1, 1959. The invasion was one of the great debacles in American military history, with 114 killed and over 1,100 captured. The new American president, John F. Kennedy, quickly asked Taylor to return to Washington to lead a committee investigating the invasion. Kennedy had been impressed with Taylor's 1960 book *The Uncertain Trumpet*, which criticized America's strategic planning and organization, and which reinforced the president's lack of confidence in the members of the Joint Chiefs of Staff.

A leave of absence with pay from the presidency of Lincoln Center was authorized on April 24, 1961, so that Taylor could take on this "temporary assignment. . . . It was mutually understood that the anticipated study would not require more than two months."[5] As it turned out, Taylor's White House appointment was not in the least "temporary." Kennedy was so pleased with Taylor's committee work that he appointed him "Military Representative at the White House," a newly created title and position. Subsequently, Taylor would be appointed chair of the Joint Chiefs of Staff, where he would develop a policy of expanded U.S. military involvement in Southeast Asia, leading to the Vietnam War, another debacle in American history.

In a press release of June 26, 1961, JDR 3rd said, "While we sincerely regret that his service with the Center could not have been longer, our sense of loss is lessened by the knowledge that once again he will serve our government with honor and distinction."[6] Until a successor was appointed, Edgar Young would serve as acting president, as he had during Taylor's leave.

The composer and educational administrator William Schuman became Lincoln Center's third president on January 1, 1962, but in many ways he was the fledgling arts organization's first functioning CEO. As founding president, John D. Rockefeller 3rd appropriately focused his leadership on mission, financing, philosophical concepts, and, of course, the beginning of construction. General Taylor focused primarily on bringing a sense of order to the giant construction project, with little emphasis on artistic matters.

Conversely, William Schuman presented a quite different profile. A prolific and distinguished American composer and president of The Juilliard School of Music from 1945 to the last day of 1961, at the age of fifty-one he was poised to lead Lincoln Center into the future and brought with him an exceedingly clear artistic point of view.

In a letter to the Juilliard faculty dated September 12, 1961, one day before the official announcement of his new position at Lincoln Center, Schuman wrote, "It is my conviction that Lincoln Center can be and must be a dynamic and constructive force for music, drama, and the dance not only in the New York City area but for the entire nation, and internationally as well. . . . It can lead to a vastly increased interest in and support for the performing arts. . . . We owe a duty to make its highest promise a reality."[7]

Although Schuman enjoyed a work schedule at Juilliard that allowed him ample time to compose, this would not be the case at Lincoln Center, where Schuman's vice president for programming, Schuyler Chapin, once described the work environment as "poisonous."[8] Schuman had been instrumental in persuading Rockefeller and the other members of the Exploratory Committee that The Juilliard School of Music should be the educational constituent of Lincoln Center. Therefore, JDR 3rd and Schuman knew each other well and quickly developed an effective professional relationship.

The working environment Schuman inherited was populated by artistic professionals employed by the constituents who had long labored to create and present dance, drama, and music events at the highest standard of excellence. In addition, he needed to manage a strong-willed board. Schuman once commented regarding the members of Lincoln Center's board, "Those business relationships were always at the backs of their minds, and the conflicts that came up did not necessarily produce the best results for Lincoln Center."[9] Schuman often said that in the arts "our goal was not the usual bottom line; our goal was to lose money wisely."[10] From Rockefeller and his Lincoln Center board, Schuman was to learn how naive that approach really was.

Ominously, some of Schuman's closest friends, including the well-known Broadway composer (and boyhood pal) Frank Loesser as well as Leonard Bernstein, counseled him not to take the Lincoln Center presidency, but Schuman ignored their advice. The agenda for the new president was sizable, including oversight of the construction program, beginning the first efforts to bring the constituents together by emphasizing the "Lincoln Center concept" of all

*A distinguished group of Lincoln Center artists and administrators in
a* Look Magazine *photo of January 19, 1960. Grouped around an
early model of the Center are* (left to right): *prima ballerina Alicia
Markova, Martha Graham, William Schuman, soprano Lucine Amara,
Juilliard violin student Dorothy Pixley, Rudolf Bing, the Center's
executive director of operations Reginald Allen, New York Philharmonic
managing director George E. Judd, Jr., Leonard Bernstein, actor Julie
Harris, and Repertory Theater producer Robert Whitehead. (Photo by
Arnold Newman / Arnold Newman Collection via Getty Images)*

working together for the good of the entire community; planning
for summer presentations in the anticipated empty new halls of
the Center; nurturing new constituents in drama, musical theater,
and modern dance; developing a film festival; and dealing with the
acoustical problems of Philharmonic Hall and the completion of the
New York State Theater for the opening of the New York World's
Fair in 1964. In addition, designs needed to be completed for the
Drama, Library-Museum, and Juilliard buildings. It seems of little
surprise that Schuman's compositional activities fell off dramatically
during this period.

In the first months of his presidency, Schuman's most pressing responsibility was to oversee the elaborate plans for the opening of
Philharmonic Hall, slated for September 23, 1962. The inauguration of this first Lincoln Center venue was a historic event for all

the right reasons. Its realization showed that Lincoln Center was no longer a dream but a reality. Leaders of the city, state, and nation were well represented at the occasion. Arthur Gelb of the *New York Times* wrote that the hall's opening "will be chronicled as a symbol of the cultural coming-of-age of the United States."[11] JDR 3rd echoed this high-minded rhetoric when he said from the stage at the inauguration ceremony that the Center now moved away from planning and "into the world of performance. Now and in the years ahead, only the artist and his art can fulfill the aspirations of the planners and exalt the labors of the builders."[12]

The energy of the inaugural evening was heightened considerably by the arrival of the First Lady, Jacqueline Kennedy. She stayed for only the first part of the program due to scheduling issues, but did see Leonard Bernstein backstage at intermission and told him that he looked ten pounds lighter than the last time she had seen

*John D. Rockefeller 3rd, First Lady Jacqueline Kennedy, and Leonard Bernstein
at the opening of Philharmonic Hall, September 23, 1962.
(Photo by Ralph Morse / The LIFE Picture Collection via Getty Images)*

him, to which the maestro replied that "he had sweat[ed] it off during the first half of the concert."[13]

Such a retort by Bernstein validly reflected a prodigiously demanding program that included the Gloria from Beethoven's *Missa solemnis*, the premiere of Aaron Copland's *Connotations* (the composer's first dodecaphonic work, which caused a good deal of consternation for the audience), the *Serenade to Music* of Ralph Vaughan Williams, and part 1 (*Veni creator spiritus*) of Mahler's enormous Symphony No. 8 (Symphony of a Thousand), presented by the New York Philharmonic, all with Bernstein conducting. It included such distinguished vocal artists as Eileen Farrell, Shirley Verrett, Jennie Tourel, Jon Vickers, Richard Tucker, and George London. The Schola Cantorum of New York, the Columbus Boychoir, and the Juilliard Chorus were also part of the performing forces.[14]

The principal acoustician for the hall, Dr. Leo L. Beranek, commented that Bernstein drove the performing forces to louder and louder levels during the evening, causing a perceived distortion in the hall's sound.[15] The two-hour-plus inaugural concert was broadcast in prime time by CBS. Alistair Cooke hosted, and the program was directed by Kirk Browning, who would oversee many *Live from Lincoln Center* broadcasts in the ensuing decades.

The grand opening concert of Philharmonic Hall was only the first of thirteen concerts collectively presented as the "Opening Week of Lincoln Center for the Performing Arts, September 23–30, 1962." The handsome program booklet for the festive week contained programs for all the concerts, which included appearances by not only the New York Philharmonic but also the Boston Symphony Orchestra, Erich Leinsdorf conducting; the Philadelphia Orchestra, Eugene Ormandy conducting; the Cleveland Orchestra, George Szell conducting; the Metropolitan Opera Orchestra, soloists and chorus, Ernest Ansermet conducting; and the Juilliard Orchestra, Jean Morel conducting.

Additional performing groups included the respected early music ensemble New York Pro Musica, directed by Noah Greenberg, the Juilliard String Quartet, and the duopianists Gold and Fizdale. Reflecting the organizers' dedication to new compositions created by American composers, world premieres of commissioned works by Aaron Copland, Virgil Thomson, Henry Cowell, Vincent Persichetti, Samuel Barber, Walter Piston, and William Bergsma were presented during several concerts. The soloists for various concerts also featured such American artists as Van Cliburn, John Browning, Isaac Stern, and Leonard Rose, with Adlai Stevenson, the two-time presidential candidate, as narrator in Copland's *Lincoln Portrait*. As a programming novelty, the Metropolitan Opera delved into a bit of esoterica with an all–Manuel de Falla evening (performed twice), including the American premiere of his dramatic cantata *Atlántida*.

A notable postponement in the performance-week schedule was the inaugural organ recital to be performed by E. Power Biggs, Catharine Crozier, and Virgil Fox. The organ—which had been built by the Aeolian-Skinner Organ Company of Boston and had 98 ranks and 5,498 pipes—was positioned directly behind the hall's stage. Regrettably, workers neglected to install a filter over the organ's air duct and debris and dust were sucked into the instrument, rendering it temporarily unplayable.[16]

Although the new concert date for the inauguration of the organ was set for December 15, 1962, the history of the instrument in Philharmonic Hall was not a happy one. The organ was removed in 1976 during a major hall renovation and rebuilt for installation in the Crystal Cathedral in Garden Grove, California. Since that time there has never been a permanent pipe organ in the hall.

With the cornucopia of musical attractions that came to Philharmonic Hall for its opening week, this special series of events also involved one very prominent artist who did *not* perform. In late August 1961, JDR 3rd personally wrote the great Spanish cellist Pablo Casals, inviting him to participate in the gala opening week of Philharmonic Hall. Specifically, Rockefeller asked Casals to perform in a program of instrumental chamber music on September 28, where he would be joined by his colleagues and friends Isaac Stern and Rudolf Serkin in a concert of piano trios. Rockefeller wrote to Casals that his presence "would lend our undertaking a sense of history which we deem more important than any cornerstone. Not incidentally, it would give hundreds of American music-lovers the great privilege of hearing you in person for the first time."[17]

Casals responded in one month's time indicating that he could not accept Rockefeller's invitation due to his personal pledge that he would not perform in the United States while it still recognized the regime of Francisco Franco in Spain.[18] Rockefeller continued to pursue his prized guest after Casals's historic performance in the White House East Room on November 13, 1961, hosted by the Kennedys. Despite Casals's political stance regarding the United States, he agreed to this performance as a gesture of admiration and respect for the new president.

The extended saga of bringing Casals to New York ended when he telegraphed Rockefeller saying he was not available in September 1962 due to previous commitments in Europe. The episode showed both how personally dedicated Rockefeller was to the success of Lincoln Center and his exceptional respect for a true artist of conscience.

Regrettably, the negative response to the hall's acoustics marred the opening festivities. Harold C. Schonberg, the *Times*'s chief music critic, was lukewarm, at best, on the subject, writing that "the sound was clear, a little dry, with not much reverberation and a decided lack of bass."[19] This "lack of bass" criticism would be a consistent complaint that would last well into the twenty-first century.

As the Center's president as well as a distinguished composer, Schuman quickly addressed the acoustical properties of the hall. He reported to his board in June 1962, well before the September opening, that, in general, the acoustics were acceptable, and claimed that both Leopold Stokowski and Bernstein had been "favorably impressed with the hall's acoustical properties."[20] These "acoustical properties" were of enormous importance to the hall's architect Max Abramovitz and the acoustical firm of Bolt Beranek & Newman, with Leo L. Beranek as the lead acoustician for the project, assisted by his young colleague Russell Johnson, who became a respected acoustician in his own right. The Lincoln Center board, in fact, authorized $250,000 on June 28, 1962, to "tune" the hall further, but the venue needed more intense improvement.

The prevailing attitude toward the hall's acoustics is illustrated by a famous anecdote: when George Szell and the Cleveland Orchestra had a dress rehearsal in the new hall, they played for just fifteen minutes before Szell turned to Lincoln Center officials awaiting his opinion and said, "Tear it down."[21] The process of improving the acoustics of Philharmonic Hall would, over time, be reminiscent of the trials of Sisyphus and his boulder. Leo Beranek, in particular, came in for a good deal of criticism for his firm's acoustical design. The greatest controversy centered on the panels or "clouds," as they were called, above the stage, which, due to their construction and placement, caused a deficiency in low-frequency tones or bass, an unacceptable level of reverberation, and a perceived stridency of tone. In addition, musicians said that they could not hear each other well on stage, that there was a consistent imbalance between strings and brass, and that an echo occurred when sound bounced off the hall's rear wall.

For Beranek's part, he believed that his acoustical design had been sabotaged by Abramovitz's agreement to add more than 200 seats to the hall's capacity, going from 2,400 to more than 2,600. When this increase in seats took place, according to Beranek, many other components of the acoustical plan were abandoned. He recalled, "It ended up worse than the architect's plans because they cut out his motors [to move acoustical "clouds" above the stage], they cut out the wall irregularities [for diffusion], they painted the thing blue and all kinds of things. They lost confidence in Max and hired an interior decorator for the interior of the hall. More foolishness."[22]

Schuman and his advisers decided to engage a panel of distinguished acousticians in the fall of 1962 to evaluate the state of the hall's acoustics and to recommend practical solutions which would not require major structural changes or a large financial outlay. Vern O. Knudsen, the American acoustical physicist, was chosen as coordinating consultant and was joined by Heinrich Keilholz, Paul Veneklasen, and Manfred Schroeder of Bell Labs, who was serving as an independent source of scientific information. This group was to work with Beranek on the evaluation.

Knudsen's group faulted Beranek for the "cloud" design, which was known to create a low-frequency distortion. The committee authorized the acoustical reconstruction work to begin immediately while the hall was unoccupied during the summer of 1963. Regrettably, the problem was not completely resolved even then, making the faulty acoustics of Philharmonic Hall a disturbing leitmotif for its entire existence.

The acoustical problems of Philharmonic Hall were exacerbated by a competitor that Lincoln Center officials had assumed would no longer exist. In the spring of 1955 Robert E. Simon, Jr., the head of the organization that owned Carnegie Hall, located on Seventh Avenue and Fifty-Seventh Street, had decided to raze the famous hall and sell the land to a developer. This news was the precipitating factor in having the New York Philharmonic become a founding member of the Lincoln Center project. A forty-four-story office tower clad in red porcelain enamel designed by Pomerance & Breines was to sit where the old hall had been, which sparked public protests from architects, critics, and artists.

One of those concerned artists was the violinist Isaac Stern, who led the charge to save the hall. He was a highly effective advocate as chair of the Citizens Committee for Carnegie Hall who, along with politicians and civic leaders, persuaded the New York State Legislature in May 1960 to pass a bill, eventually signed by Governor Rockefeller, that would enable the City of New York to acquire the hall for leasing to a private, nonprofit corporation.

All of this transpired as Lincoln Center officials looked on with concern and disbelief, fearing that the continued existence of Carnegie Hall would put the viability of Philharmonic Hall into question. In an ominous memo to JDR 3rd, Reginald Allen, director of operations for Lincoln Center, expressed his worst fears regarding the continued presence of Carnegie Hall in New York: "The announced demolition of Carnegie Hall was the cornerstone of the Lincoln Center building program. When Lincoln Center decided to build a concert hall, the sole operational objective and problem was to replace and succeed Carnegie Hall. . . . It will be literally disastrous to operate the new Philharmonic Hall except at utterly unthinkable rental fees or at a mountainous deficit. [Allen then makes the draconian suggestion that Lincoln Center leadership consider] suspend[ing] indefinitely the completion of Philharmonic Hall."[23]

Rockefeller and his board colleagues realized that any direct public effort to deter support for Carnegie Hall would be counterproductive, and the enabling legislation to save Carnegie passed expeditiously. Allen's dreaded fears concerning a revived Carnegie Hall's negative impact on Lincoln Center also did not come to pass.

One of the greatest challenges for Lincoln Center officials during this formative time was to resolve which of the various artistic components of the New York City Center of Music and Drama, located on Fifty-Fifth Street just east of Seventh Avenue, would become part of Lincoln Center. City Center was the home of not only the New York City Ballet but also the New York City Opera, dubbed the "people's opera" by Mayor Fiorello H. La Guardia for its reasonable prices and a clientele that differed markedly from the high-society patrons of the Metropolitan Opera. In addition, a drama and light opera company under the leadership of Jean Dalrymple performed at the Center.[24]

Lincoln Kirstein, as general director of the New York City Ballet as well as a charter member of Lincoln Center's Exploratory Committee, had always assumed that a theater in support of the artistic vision of George Balanchine would be built by Lincoln Center for City Ballet's use. That theater, located on the Center's southeastern corner—originally called the "Theater for Dance and Operetta"—became the New York State Theater. Philip Johnson designed it with a particular sensitivity to the needs of classical ballet, making the sounds of the dancers' footfalls on stage barely audible to the audience. This was a perfect environment for dance, but acoustically it presented many challenges for the performance of unamplified opera productions. In turn, Schuman and his colleagues planned to create constituents in musical theater and modern dance that would use the New York State Theater when City Ballet was not performing.

The role of dance at Lincoln Center was first addressed in early 1957 by an "Exploratory Committee on the Dance" chaired by George D. Stoddard and included Charles M. Spofford, Edgar Young, dance critics John Martin of the *New York Times* and Walter Terry of the *New York Herald Tribune*, and, of course, Lincoln Kirstein. There was agreement that a sizable dance audience existed in New York City based on the considerable number of ballet performances at City Center (with an average attendance of over two thousand) and the public's demonstrated interest in touring "name companies." The basic question before the committee was whether to merge an existing dance company into the Center or create a completely new organization—a question the Center's leaders also had to address in education and in drama.

In addition to the New York City Ballet, requests for inclusion in the Center included the Ballet Russe de Monte Carlo and Ballet

Theatre (soon to become American Ballet Theatre). Modern dance leaders were also intent on finding a permanent place at Lincoln Center. These leaders noted the inclination of the Center's leadership to favor classical ballet. In a letter of May 25, 1960, to JDR 3rd signed by well-known modern choreographers—including José Limón, Anna Sokolow, Hanya Holm, Sophie Maslow, and Charles Weidman, among others—they proposed the creation of a permanent modern dance company, comprising as many as thirty-five dancers, to develop a repertory of new works and revivals.[25]

Prominently missing from the letter was Martha Graham's signature, although a line had been provided for her. In a letter from Graham to JDR 3rd, the choreographer and dancer had explained that she did not believe it was appropriate for her to sign the letter since she was a member of the Lincoln Center Advisory Council on the Dance. She ends her letter by writing, "Furthermore, and this is really the truth of the matter, my concern is that the best of dance have every opportunity to be shown at Lincoln Center, whether it be ballet or contemporary dance, or any other form the art might take."[26] Although a noble position on her part, it was also the case that Graham was a fierce protector of her company; a new contemporary dance organization based at Lincoln Center would certainly be a competitor for her, if realized.

As the Center's officials continued to work on what exactly would be presented in the Theater for Dance and Operetta, both Governor Nelson Rockefeller and Robert Moses, who now added the presidency of the New York World's Fair to his many duties, settled how the theater's construction would be paid for. The approximate $30 million of funding came from budgeted resources to build the World's Fair campus in Flushing Meadows, Queens, as well as lesser financial support from the city. Governor Rockefeller required that the theater be ready for opening in April 1964, at the time of the opening of the Fair, since the theater represented "the performing arts angle, the performing arts expression of the World's Fair."[27] The official name of the new venue would be the New York State Theater.

The completion of the New York State Theater was tied to an agreement regarding City Center's potential move to Lincoln Center and the development of its constituent status, a direction that had been deferred by the Lincoln Center board in 1956. Negotiations between Lincoln Center and City Center continued, driven primarily by Kirstein's fervent desire to bring City Ballet to a grand new home. Newbold Morris, chair of City Center, had proposed to Rockefeller in late 1962 that all the companies within City Center (i.e., New York City Ballet, New York City Opera, and the drama and light opera programs) come in one group to Lincoln Center. In this proposal, the Fifty-Fifth Street property would be sold to offset further costs for the State Theater construction.

Morton Baum, City Center's powerful finance committee chair, was an experienced practitioner of the hardball politics of New York City, and he became Schuman's nemesis in the extended negotiations to bring City Center to Lincoln Center. One of the first issues that surfaced concerning the City Center proposal was that the Metropolitan Opera had absolutely no desire to have another opera company as a Lincoln Center constituent. The Met had always assumed that it would be the only professional opera company on campus.

Baum also further complicated matters by insisting that City Center be a tenant of New York City in the State Theater, as it had been on Fifty-Fifth Street. Although City Center hoped to maintain the autonomy it had earlier enjoyed, such a request was a clear deal breaker for Lincoln Center officials and therefore was rejected.

Negotiations continued as the new year of 1963 was celebrated. Schuman was in the unfortunate position of having to negotiate with both the tough-minded Baum and the highly manipulative Kirstein. This tension-filled environment was confirmed by Schuyler Chapin, who stated that Kirstein once became so angry during a telephone conversation that he "ripped the entire telephone off the wall, wires, everything. . . . Lincoln was a madman at times."[28]

Kirstein also had a good deal of influence over the design of the State Theater. In a highly sophisticated and surreptitious move, he was able to realize one of his aesthetic desires by installing in the theater two enormous statues, each comprising two female figures, initially conceived by the Polish American sculptor Elie Nadelman, called *Circus Women* and *Two Nudes*.

The enormous sculptures were re-created by an anonymous Italian artisan who carved the large statues based on the smaller, four-foot versions made of plaster and paper that were originally created by Nadelman. According to the City Ballet, "Kirstein arranged to have the immense artworks brought into the Theater just before the fourth and final wall was closed up and before the Lincoln Center leadership could order their removal, which, in fact, they did; but the statues could no longer be removed."[29] (A photo of these sculptures appears in chapter 5.)

Schuman's plan was to have the City Ballet open the State Theater based on the specific request of Governor Rockefeller, but he was also committed to creating a constituent for music theater headed by the legendary Richard Rodgers, which would perform musicals and operettas when the City Ballet was not performing. In addition, the City Opera had to be fit into the theater's schedule.

Negotiations with City Center were ongoing and highly problematic. On December 31, 1964, Schuman issued a press release announcing that Lincoln Center was not able to come to an agreement with City Center, "although our invitation to City Center remains open."[30] That opening was filled quickly when JDR 3rd announced that City Center would become a constituent of Lincoln Center on April 12, 1965, bringing with it the City Ballet and the City Opera.

Lincoln Center conceded to City Center's demands with two exceptions: the State Theater would not be run by the government of New York City; and City Center's drama, light opera, and Gilbert and Sullivan companies would continue to perform at the Fifty-Fifth Street theater. City Center also agreed to limit its top ticket price to $4.95, continuing a hallmark City Center tradition. Lincoln Center made available to City Center $200,000 from the Lincoln Center Fund for Education and Creative Artistic Advancement to commission new works for the City Ballet and to subsidize student tickets.

Whatever reciprocity may have been realized at the end of the turbulent negotiations between City Center and Lincoln Center, the level of rancor generated by the difficult discussions was a significant watershed in the history of the arts center. The cantankerous Morton Baum wrenched the decorous meetings of the Exploratory Committee chaired by JDR 3rd into the bare knuckles arena of New York City politics. This mean-spirited environment also presaged the difficult relationships that were developing between Lincoln Center and the constituents, specifically those who saw the

Center's leadership not as that of a benign landlord but rather that of an artistic competitor.

Baum even went after JDR 3rd himself in his efforts to protest the Lincoln Center concept. Baum had no qualms about publicly criticizing the founding father of Lincoln Center, saying that "the Rockefellers have a great possessive quality. Mr. Rockefeller [John D. Rockefeller 3rd] is the iceberg of which you only see a tenth. He is the power. Nobody on the board will cross him. They'll never get reconciled to our independence. There will always be resentment toward them on the part of the constituents."[31]

CHAPTER FOUR

You Have Made Something
That Will Last

ALTHOUGH THE CITY CENTER negotiations were lengthy and bruising for all participating parties, with several details still to be finalized, there had been resolution regarding the future of the City Center drama component. Rockefeller and his board colleagues believed that City Center's drama program was not at the standard needed for the new Lincoln Center and decided to create a drama constituent from scratch. Owing to prior discussions and conferences focused on drama at Lincoln Center, the Center's leadership decided to commit to creating a drama constituent that would function as a "repertory theater," with a core group of actors and a diverse array of plays presented on a revolving basis each week of the season.

The early investigation of a drama constituent was begun before Schuman's arrival by an exploratory subcommittee chaired by George Stoddard, then chancellor of New York University, and included the director Elia Kazan, the producer Robert Whitehead, and the critics Brooks Atkinson and Walter Kerr. Independent of the subcommittee, the well-known actor, director, and teacher Lee Strasberg, representing his Actors Studio, suggested that he could lead a Lincoln Center drama constituent with both presenting and teaching responsibilities. In addition, Joseph Papp of the Public

Theater wrote to Rockefeller to express interest in his company being the drama constituent, a prescient move that would be re-addressed in the early 1970s. However, the Lincoln Center board stuck to its belief that a new drama organization needed to be created and chose Kazan and Whitehead for the task.

Kazan was a highly celebrated director who had cofounded the Actors Studio and had Academy Awards, Tonys, and Golden Globes to his credit. His reputation had been sullied by his testimony before the House Committee on Un-American Activities in 1952, during which he identified eight former Group Theatre members and colleagues as Communists. Although his testimony alienated him from many colleagues in the profession, it did not hamper his efforts to lead the new theater at Lincoln Center. Whitehead was one of the top Broadway producers of his day whose résumé featured a string of awards and successful productions throughout his long career. He was also deeply committed to the repertory concept and saw the Lincoln Center effort as one that was revolutionary for the presentation of serious drama in America.

A formal exploratory committee was subsequently created to develop a drama constituent, led by George D. Woods, chair of First Boston Corporation, a trustee of the Rockefeller Foundation and of the American Shakespeare Festival and Academy. When the Repertory Theater was authorized to become a Lincoln Center constituent on February 15, 1960, Woods became its board president and worked with Kazan and Whitehead, who oversaw artistic and administrative matters. Initially the new constituent took the name of Repertory Theater Association, but this was changed in 1961 to the Lincoln Center Repertory Company.

Whitehead's enthusiasm for the concept of a repertory theater was intense; he envisioned a company of "seventy, eighty, ninety people and . . . three . . . or four productions a week playing."[1] Not only were Whitehead and Kazan enthusiastic about the theater's potential, but many media outlets around the country commented on the Lincoln Center theater experiment as a new beginning for the American drama profession. Howard Taubman, chief *New York Times* theater critic, wrote, "The Lincoln Center Theater [an abbreviated name for the new dramatic entity at the Center] . . . can be a seminal force in the development of talent and ideas. It can be a help, not a menace, to Broadway. It can be an inspiration to the country."[2] The English theater critic Kenneth Tynan wrote that the new venture could be "the nearest thing to a National Theatre in America."[3]

Vivian Beaumont Allen pledged $3 million in May 1958 as a naming gift for the new drama theater, after a solicitation process led by JDR 3rd. The cost of construction for the building totaled $8.2 million. Eventually the Vivian Beaumont Allen Foundation would give almost $7 million to the repertory company in support of construction and production costs. Vivian Beaumont would pass away in October 1962 before the Repertory Company ever produced a play.

The theater was to open in 1963, but significant construction delays pushed the opening to 1965. Whitehead and Kazan were hell-bent on beginning to produce plays, even if there were no venue at Lincoln Center in which to do so. The team had already signed contracts with actors and committed to the production of certain works. Any further delay would risk losing all they had already put together. As a result, they sought out a way to artistically launch their venture by creating a partnership with the American National Theater and Academy (ANTA) and New York University (NYU), building a temporary theater at 40 West Fourth Street in Greenwich Village. The financial feasibility of such a venture was of great concern to the Lincoln Center board, which backed away from the project and decided not to support the temporary theater construction.

Despite this setback and the lack of support from even his own theater board, Whitehead proceeded with ANTA and NYU. According to Edgar Young, "By mid-February 1963, [Woods] told the Lincoln Center Executive Committee that he had lost confidence in Whitehead."[4] Whitehead, in turn, had significant problems with Woods, saying that "George Woods is totally insensitive to the problems. Very bright, marvelous at running a board meeting and diabolic because of that. Totally lacking in any understanding about the needs of the theater. . . . I bored him."[5]

The "diabolic" comment referred to Woods's tactic of bringing on three new theater board members at the beginning of the meeting where there was to be a vote on the temporary theater structure. Those three new members voted against the new structure and that provided enough votes to bring down the effort. Whitehead reflected that "he [Woods] handled that very skillfully [but] it was dishonest."[6] Through Whitehead's determination, however, he and Kazan persuaded NYU to provide, at no cost, land that the university controlled at Washington Square as the temporary theater site, and the duo also found financing to build the structure, essentially end-running the board's negative vote.

Against considerable odds, the temporary theater took shape, fashioned on the planned venue at Lincoln Center, with a seating capacity of 1,158 enclosed in a steel-supported "tent." John Dinkeloo of the Saarinen firm, which was engaged to design the Beaumont Theater, engineered the temporary structure, and Jo Mielziner, the respected theatrical and lighting designer, created the interior, as he would at the Beaumont. Although the Lincoln Center board would not provide any financial support for bricks and mortar, they did agree to a grant of $500,000 through the Center's Fund for Education and Creative Artistic Advancement to provide seed money for the creation of theatrical productions downtown.

Financing for the construction of the temporary structure came entirely from the First National City Bank, with the loan guaranteed by ANTA. Although ANTA believed it would be able to cover the mortgage through ticket revenue, by December 1964 ANTA had only paid back a third of the total cost of $618,000, causing future severe financial problems for the organization.[7]

After less than a year of construction, on January 23, 1964, the new temporary space opened at 40 West Fourth Street presenting Arthur Miller's new play *After the Fall*, starring Jason Robards, Jr., Barbara Loden (Kazan's future wife), with the budding Hollywood star Faye Dunaway in a small role. It was directed by Kazan, with sets and lighting by Mielziner. The play was Miller's first in about nine years, and there was great anticipation involving the work. Critics took umbrage with the fact that the plot was a clear reflection of Miller's divorce of Marilyn Monroe and her suicide in August 1962. Some critics saw this as Miller taking advantage of Monroe's personal tragedy to develop his play.

In accordance with Whitehead and Kazan's vision of a repertory theater, a production of Eugene O'Neill's *Marco Millions*, directed by José Quintero, opened in February, and a new comedy by S. N. Behrman, *But for Whom Charlie*, was produced in March. The temporary theater space would present plays until November 1965, when it concluded its short life with the original production of the Mitch Leigh musical *Man of La Mancha*. The structure was demolished in 1968.

Regrettably, although ticket revenue for *After the Fall* was acceptable, it was not enough to prevent a financial shortfall for the theater, necessitating a loan of $100,000 provided by Lincoln Center from its New Projects Underwriting Fund to help pay the bills. As the season ended, the theater's annual deficit was calculated at $350,000. In addition to the financial challenges, the Repertory Company also experienced a significant board leadership change when George Woods stepped down from his presidency to become the head of the World Bank in January 1963. He was followed in 1964 by Robert L. Hoguet, Jr., who had been involved in the planning of the Center and came from the banking world as well. According to Whitehead, "Hoguet was a pleasant, socially acceptable fellow who knew less about the needs of the theater company than even George Woods."[8]

By the beginning of the 1964–65 repertory theater season, there was considerable concern on the part of Lincoln Center board leadership that the theater was not moving in the correct direction, either financially or artistically. This was unfortunately confirmed by a less than successful production of the Jacobean tragedy *The Changeling* written by two contemporaries of Shakespeare, Thomas Middleton and William Rowley, directed by Kazan. Critics had been highly negative about the absence of classic plays in the company's first season, to which *The Changeling* was a response.

The cast was populated by several young actors who came out of the new theater's actor training program. Beginning in late 1961, this program involved forty actors who participated in an eight-month training regimen, which resulted in fourteen remaining actors appearing with the professional company.[9] One of the consistent criticisms of *The Changeling* production was the lack of experience of the cast, an inevitable result considering the youth of the actors. The director and critic Robert Brustein provided a particularly poisonous critique of the overall Lincoln Center Repertory Company effort and lambasted the actors from the training group in the *But for Whom Charlie* production as having "marbles in their mouths, [moving] like sleepwalkers and mannered and remote."[10] He continued his critical fusillade by writing that the production of *The Changeling* would have "disgraced the theatre club of South Dakota Subnormal Junior High."[11] Kazan himself understood the debacle of *The Changeling* production, writing in his autobiography, "The disaster of 'The Changeling' had destroyed our defenses, and we were now vulnerable . . . to our corporate bosses. . . . A living sacrifice was being called for to pay for our failures."[12]

This exceedingly negative view of the Repertory Company leadership by both Lincoln Center board members and administrators led to a series of inappropriate and poorly reasoned decisions on the part of William Schuman, causing the first crisis in the history of the new arts center. The unfortunate turn of events began when Hoguet reached out to Schuman in November 1964 to inquire whether something could be done to get stronger administrative leadership for the theater.

Schuman subsequently met with Charles Spofford, a vice chair of Lincoln Center and a member of the board of the Repertory Company, suggesting that Herman Krawitz, an assistant manager at the Met, could be an effective administrator for the theater and put its finances and management on firmer ground.[13] Spofford saw this suggestion as plausible, and Schuman proceeded to mention this strategy to JDR 3rd and speak with Krawitz about the position. All this Machiavellian behavior was taking place behind the backs of Whitehead and Kazan.

Schuman then decided in late November to advise Anthony Bliss, the Met president, of his discussion with Krawitz. Bliss was immediately negative about the proposal since Krawitz was overseeing the building of the new Met opera, which was at a crucial stage of construction. In turn, the Met's general manager, Rudolf Bing, was furious when he learned of Schuman's discussion with Krawitz and decided to go to the press with his concerns. Schuyler Chapin said of the situation that "it was Bing at his insect-biting best."[14]

Another new Arthur Miller play, *Incident at Vichy*, was produced by the Repertory Company and opened on December 4, 1964. However, the real news regarding the company appeared in the *New York*

Times on the next day when a front-page article detailed the controversy and quoted Bing as saying that Lincoln Center was "apparently deteriorating to a free-for-all jungle where constituents can raid each other at will. . . . I am deeply disturbed over the matter . . . because I see in the way it's been handled the breakdown of the Lincoln Center concept, that is . . . of sister organizations . . . who work toward a higher goal of artistic achievement."[15] Schuman was presented by the *New York Times* as interfering in the internal artistic affairs of constituents, which was, to some extent, true, which caused some of the constituents to resent his less than transparent manipulations.

By late December 1964, Whitehead and Kazan had resigned, accompanied by vitriolic comments from American theater icons such as Miller and Maureen Stapleton, saying they would never set foot in the Repertory Company again. From his perspective, the seasoned Lincoln Center administrator and JDR 3rd's amanuensis, Edgar Young, characterized the debacle by saying, "By the end of 1964, the Repertory Theater was left without professional leadership, but with a handsome, new theater nearing completion. Lincoln Center's public image had been badly tarnished."[16]

In his eloquent and sardonic fashion, Chapin summed up the situation by saying, "The Krawitz thing blew higher than a kite. . . . No Whitehead, no leadership, the Beaumont getting ready to open with the company almost bankrupt by virtue of the first season."[17] Lincoln Center's president would soon learn that the problems he experienced in 1964 were just the first steps in a long and arduous journey.

Although 1964 turned out to be an exceedingly challenging time for William Schuman, earlier in the year, on April 23, 1964, he had the comparatively pleasant task of overseeing the opening of the Center's second new building, the New York State Theater. Governor Rockefeller and Robert Moses had put great emphasis on the fact that the State Theater, designated the performing arts venue for the New York World's Fair, had to be functioning at the time of the Fair's opening. The principal venue for the Fair was in Flushing Meadows.

In June 1961, New York State agreed to purchase the completed theater from Lincoln Center for $15 million. In addition, New York City provided another $4,383,000 toward the cost of the building.

Eventually, the city would lease the theater back to Lincoln Center "for a nominal rental."[18]

Unlike Philharmonic Hall, which was built to house orchestral performances, the State Theater was a multifunctional venue, although its primary tenant was clearly the New York City Ballet. The hall's architect, Philip Johnson, worked closely with both George Balanchine and Lincoln Kirstein in designing a theater that would be particularly conducive to the presentation of ballet, and the size of the theater, at 2,729 seats, would accommodate a large ballet audience for City Ballet and international companies.

No matter how ballet-centric the theater was, however, it was also intended as the home of the Music Theater of Lincoln Center and eventually the New York City Opera, even though final constituent negotiations with City Center were not yet completed. Therefore, City Ballet shared the opening night stage with the Music Theater of Lincoln Center. The program included a scene from Rodgers and Hammerstein's *Carousel* featuring John Raitt and Joan Weldon; George Balanchine's *Allegro Brillante*, which the great choreographer said was "everything I know about classical ballet in thirteen minutes,"[19] danced to the music of Tchaikovsky's Piano Concerto no. 3 and starring Maria Tallchief and André Prokovsky; and, finally, selections from the exuberant Balanchine creation *Stars and Stripes* featuring Patricia McBride and Jacques d'Amboise, accompanied by John Philip Sousa marches. The iconic Lincoln Center fountain in the center of the plaza, designed by Philip Johnson, officially opened on April 6, 1964, adding vaporous beauty to the inauguration of the new theater just steps away.

Critical response to the decor and acoustics of the theater was favorable, including its unique feature of using a so-called continental seating configuration, with no center aisles dividing the orchestra section. The cantankerous Lincoln Kirstein expressed gleeful enthusiasm for the new theater, writing to JDR 3rd the day before its opening, "Personally, I want to thank you for your patience and forbearance and suffering along with us. . . . Maybe you have had little enough pleasure, and lots of sweat, blood and tears; but you have made something that will last."[20] Rockefeller wrote back to say that he was deeply gratified by Kirstein's satisfaction with the new theater.[21]

Lincoln Kirstein and George Balanchine overseeing a rehearsal
of New York City Ballet dancers, 1960. (Photo by Martha Swope
© The New York Public Library for the Performing Arts)

Regrettably, the joy of the theater's opening became a bit muted
a few weeks later when spoken drama was presented for the first
time through plays presented by the august Royal Shakespeare
Company. The company first put on their production of *King Lear*
starring Paul Scofield and directed by Peter Brook. It had always
been planned that the production would be amplified, but the company declined to conduct a dress rehearsal or even a sound check. In
particular, Brook exhibited a certain level of arrogance when he dis-
missively rejected any need for a rehearsal: "Our actors know how to
deal with any conditions, we won't have any problem."[22]

Such hubris did little to make the actors understandable to the
audience, due, in part, to the quick tempo of their speech. Also,
Lear's elevated set covered all the microphones, blocking access to
the amplification system. Fortunately, in subsequent performances
the frustrated British actors slowed the pace of their speech, allowing the text to be more understandable. Brook spoke to the press the
day after the opening and added fuel to the fire when he remarked
upon slowing the verbal tempo of his actors, "we might just as well

have played at Radio City."[23] Schuman was once again faced with an acoustical problem in a Lincoln Center hall, but the State Theater issues were not as problematic as those of Philharmonic Hall.

In addition to the elaborate opening of the New York State Theater to celebrate the World's Fair, a summerlong World's Fair Festival was inaugurated, utilizing Philharmonic Hall, the New York State Theater, and the old Metropolitan Opera House. Philharmonic Hall hosted well-known American and international orchestras; the State Theater had City Ballet performances in April and May followed by Music Theater of Lincoln Center shows and selected visiting dance and drama troupes; and the Metropolitan Opera finished its 1963–64 season in their house on Thirty-Ninth Street as part of the festival.

Of all the various artistic ventures conceived for inclusion in the new arts center, the one with the weakest roots was the constituent dedicated to American musical theater. From the very beginning of architectural planning for Lincoln Center, there was always a goal of building one theater dedicated to ballet and operetta. Once negotiations with City Center were completed, both ballet and opera performances were planned in the new theater. So why did President Schuman and his advisers push to create a musical theater program within this crowded space?

Without doubt, a driving force was the reality that this constituent would be led by the most prominent and distinguished musical theater composer in history, Richard Rodgers. Schuman and Rodgers were close personal friends, often socializing with their wives, and to have Rodgers oversee this venture augured well for success.

The precipitating factor in presenting musical theater at Lincoln Center, however, may well have been the New York State Theater's role in the New York World's Fair. Having a series of musicals to complement the City Ballet's presentations added a popular element that would attract a new and large audience to Lincoln Center.

Several months before the Fair's opening, the concept of the Music Theater of Lincoln Center was officially presented to the public (under its original name, the New York Music Theater). Its purpose was to present operettas and musical plays.[24] The new constituent would produce established plays, but eventually would develop new works as well. Each show was slated to run for a period of five to six weeks, after which it would tour the United States for nine to ten months. It was announced that bookings had already been confirmed in Boston, Detroit, and Toronto following the first summer season in 1964.

It was emphasized that Rodgers would serve "without compensation in the dual capacity of President and member of the Board of Directors [and that he would be] primarily responsible for selecting works to be performed and [would] actively supervise all artistic aspects of each production."[25] The other officers of the Music Theater were Hoyt Ammidon, chair of the United States Trust Company, as chair of the board, and Robert L. Hoguet, executive vice president of First National City Bank, as treasurer, while also serving as president of the Repertory Theater.

The Theater leadership created a strategy that box-office receipts at the New York State Theater and on tour would cover all operating expenses and would, in addition, generate a profit during the 1964–65 season of approximately $750,000."[26] This optimistic plan seemed to be somewhat realistic due to the positive results realized through the first two productions of the venture: Rodgers and Hammerstein's *The King and I* in July and Franz Lehár's *The Merry Widow* in August. Reviews of both productions were positive.[27] By the end of *The King and I* run in mid-August, the show had total receipts of $438,866, and the highest-grossing revenue for one week at $95,200, establishing a record for a musical in New York.[28]

Unfortunately, the Music Theater of Lincoln Center was short-lived, plagued by inadequate fundraising, declining ticket revenue, and the inevitable competition from Broadway shows.[29] Its overly optimistic financial projections never came to pass. The theater's board, with the agreement of Richard Rodgers, decided to cease operations in 1970.

After the debacle of the departure of Kazan and Whitehead as heads of the Lincoln Center Repertory Company in late 1964, the Lincoln Center and Repertory Company boards moved quickly to appoint a new artistic/administrative team for the theater. On January 25, 1965, it was announced that Herbert Blau and Jules Irving would assume their new duties on March 1. The two had cofounded the San Francisco Actor's Workshop in 1952, which presented a classic mix of plays from Aristophanes and Shakespeare to Eugene O'Neill, Samuel Beckett, and Sean O'Casey, as well as more contemporary works. Their first season at Lincoln Center included four plays: *Danton's Death* by Georg Buechner, *The Country Wife* by William Wycherley, *The Condemned of Altona* by Jean-Paul Sartre, and *The Caucasian Chalk Circle* by Bertolt Brecht.

The official opening of the Vivian Beaumont Theater at Lincoln Center took place on October 14, 1965. In 1967, plays would be presented in the Theater's 299-seat venue, initially called the Forum, and eventually named the Mitzi Newhouse Theater after the prominent New York philanthropist.

Lincoln Center leadership had long harbored serious concerns about the cost overruns for construction of the Beaumont Theater and the Library-Museum. The Theater construction had been budgeted at $8.2 million (completed at $9.6 million) and the Library-Museum at $7 million (completed at $8.1 million).

Architecturally, the Beaumont Theater and the Library and Museum of the Performing Arts shared the same building in a unique configuration. Eero Saarinen and Associates designed the interior of the Theater, with Jo Mielziner as collaborating designer. Skidmore, Owings & Merrill, with Gordon Bunshaft as lead architect, was responsible for the Library-Museum design.

Sadly, during the design process, Eero Saarinen died from unsuccessful surgery to remove a brain tumor. He was fifty-one years old and one of the best-known architects in the world, celebrated for such projects as the TWA Flight Center at New York International Airport and the American Embassy in London. His firm would complete the architectural design.

One feature of the design of the large theater which became a source of conflict in ensuing years was that it could function with either a proscenium stage or an open stage of extreme thrust.[30] The house was to seat 1,140 patrons when in the proscenium position and 1,083 with the extreme thrust stage.

The formal dedication ceremony for the Beaumont in 1965 included as speakers JDR 3rd; Schuman; Josephine Pope, daughter of the late Vivian Beaumont Allen; Robert L. Hoguet, president of the Repertory Theater; as well as Blau and Irving. Vivian Beaumont Allen's $3 million gift to house a drama repertory company was the first to carry the privilege of having a personal name on a Lincoln Center structure, a tradition that would continue well into the future.

As the theater/library complex opened, the Lincoln Center leadership was able to take stock of the success of its fundraising campaign, which in 1965 had a goal of $160.7 million, more than twice the amount of $75 million budgeted for construction of the Center in the first stages of the venture. As of late September 1965, Lincoln Center's own fundraising apparatus had raised $157.7 million, showing contributions from individuals, city and state governments, urban-renewal funds from federal grants-in-aid, foundations, corporations, and foreign governments.[31]

Lincoln Center's founders always had an idealistic approach to the creation of the mammoth arts center, and the inclusion of a Library-Museum on campus certainly was a manifestation of that philosophy. The Library-Museum would stand as an entity devoted to intellect, addressing both the life of the mind and the life of the stage.

In the case of this constituent, the Center's leaders wished to establish a partnership with the New York Public Library, whose musical collection was both substantial and distinguished, but languishing in cramped quarters at the main branch on Forty-Second Street, as well as in off-site storage, making access to the materials difficult. By June 1959, the library trustees had approved, in principle, the establishment of the Library-Museum at Lincoln Center.

The library's collection focusing on music, dance, and drama had been acquired over the past hundred years and included musical manuscripts ranging from the fifteenth to the twentieth centuries, as well as close to fifty thousand sound recordings. The dance collection also held priceless items rich in manuscripts, drawings, photographs, and printed materials. Drama was represented by more than sixty thousand books and scripts of famous productions.[32] The museum also planned to present exhibits focusing on aspects of the performing arts and make them available to the public at no charge. In November 1965, a $1 million gift was given to the Library-Museum for support of exhibits named after the donor, Shelby Cullom Davis, a financier and eventually ambassador to Switzerland under Presidents Richard Nixon and Gerald Ford.

In addition to the traditional services provided by a research library, there were also performances planned within a small recital hall, eventually named the Bruno Walter Auditorium, in honor of the great conductor, who was frequently on the podium at both the Metropolitan Opera and the New York Philharmonic. The organization was seen as a unifying force for the Center, bringing together the public with performers, scholars, and students to explore the intellectual and emotional elements of the performing arts.[33] The Library-Museum officially opened its doors on November 30, 1965, having been designated a constituent just a few days earlier, on November 26.

The new constituent organizing committee was chaired by Gilbert W. Chapman, president of the New York Public Library. JDR 3rd commented on this addition to the Center by stating, "The Center must be more than performance halls. . . . To be a true cultural Center for the performing arts, Lincoln Center should embrace the trilogy of education, creative scholarship and performance. For these reasons, we have believed from the very beginning that the Library-Museum is an essential element of the Center which we are all working together to build."[34]

The construction of The Juilliard School, the last scheduled building to be finished on campus, had perhaps the most circuitous route to completion in the early saga of the Center. From the time that The Juilliard School of Music agreed to join the Lincoln Center project in February 1957, the placement of the new Juilliard building on campus was a bit of a moving target. The earliest design put Juilliard on the southern side of Sixty-Fifth Street, but that was quickly changed when the Center was given access to land on the northern side of the street stretching to Sixty-Sixth Street and bordered on the east by Broadway.

By early 1961, the Juilliard architect, Pietro Belluschi, had presented revised plans for a smaller building.[35] In addition to planning for a smaller building, Lincoln Center also had to persuade the Board of Estimate and the Board of Education to release the land occupied by the old High School of Commerce, which occupied the western end of the proposed Juilliard site. The diplomatic assignment of persuading the Board of Estimate to give such authorization fell to Edgar Young, who in 1965 was executive vice president of Lincoln Center and chair of the Center's building committee.

Young was quite effective in presenting this complex real estate issue when he testified before the city's Board of Estimate on June 11, 1965. He argued that any further delay on the part of the city would cause Lincoln Center to end its plans and commitments for the building of The Juilliard School. In turn, Juilliard would be forced to cancel its commitment to sell its current School building, located at 122nd Street and Claremont Avenue, to the Manhattan School of Music.[36]

Ultimately, the city surrendered the "old wing" of the High School of Commerce to make way for the Juilliard building, but the high school's "annex" was retained and renamed the Brandeis Annex, providing additional space for students who were assigned to the new Louis D. Brandeis High School at Eighty-Fourth Street and Amsterdam Avenue. The annex stood, although for many years without students, until it was razed to build the Samuel B. and David Rose Building, which opened in 1990. After numerous delays, the new Juilliard School opened on October 26, 1969.

According to the Center's initial schedule, the Metropolitan Opera House was to open in 1965, but the omnipresent construction problems and budget overages caused a delay. By 1966, the Met's construction budget had ballooned to $45.7 million, approximately $9.5 million above the 1962 budget. Both Young and Schuman were pressured by their board to resolve the Met's problems. Inevitably, the blame for these problems fell on the Met's architect, Wallace Harrison. Earlier, serious discussions took place with JDR 3rd, Devereaux Josephs, Young, and Anthony Bliss raising the idea of replacing Harrison. The Center's leaders perceived a lack of conviction on Harrison's part, as he upset budgeting and schedules by continually inserting design changes in his plan.[37]

JDR 3rd had problems with Harrison as early as 1959, when Rockefeller met with the architect and suggested that he confer with the Center's other architects to ensure that the three buildings on the fountain plaza would have a uniformity of architectural approach. Rockefeller reported in his confidential notes that "it has become evident that he [Harrison] is anxious to do the Opera entirely on his own without consultation with any of the other architects for the Center in terms of its relationship to their buildings."[38] Several months later JDR 3rd again brought up the issue of working with other architects, this time suggesting consultations with either Gordon Bunshaft or Eero Saarinen, but according to Rockefeller "Harrison reacted very strongly against this."[39]

Ultimately, it was understood that Harrison's removal would be a highly upsetting turn of events for Robert Moses, a close friend of the architect. The Center's leadership opted to allow the architect to complete the project. However, cost-cutting did take place, involving the eventual deletion of an opera tower of about fourteen stories high, including office space for the Met and rentable areas to generate revenue.[40] Even with this huge deletion, the new Met represented a massive building, boasting a seating capacity of 3,788, made available to the Met on a long-term lease from Lincoln Center, free of debt.

Relations between the Met and Lincoln Center were strained well before the Met gala opening in 1966. Aside from its reaction to the notorious "Krawitz affair," the Met was perceived by JDR 3rd as not being a "team player," namely by underappreciating the benefits of belonging to the Lincoln Center community: "[The Met's approach] is somewhat disappointing and, I will have to admit, annoying. . . . They are still not fully appreciative of the value to them in the public association with us."[41]

This "disappointment" on Rockefeller's part would linger for years to come in the minds of future Lincoln Center administrators, but his plan of bringing a disparate group of arts organizations to operate on one campus, with all its inherent challenges, still represented the most audacious project in support of the performing arts in America's history. He would push forward to ensure that his vision be realized in the next three years.

CHAPTER FIVE

It Was Not a Matter of Friendship but Principle

T
HE NEW METROPOLITAN OPERA HOUSE opened with great glitter and panache on Friday, September 16, 1966. Although it was already the fifth new venue to be opened since 1962, the Met was, by far, the most anticipated hall at the new arts center.

"Lady Bird" Johnson, the First Lady, represented her husband. She was accompanied by the First Lady of the Philippines, Imelda Marcos, who attended with her husband, Ferdinand Marcos. Four days later, JDR 3rd would host a dinner honoring President Marcos at the New York Hilton Hotel, praising him for the "wise and vigorous statesmanship he is bringing to his own country and its part of the world."[1]

Life Magazine declared the opening "the single biggest theatrical event in all of human history. . . . Nothing less than the cultural super-event of the culture center of the cultural capital of the civilized world."[2]

The *New York Times* continued the hyperbole, announcing that the opening night audience included "virtually every member of New York's predictably elegant diamond brigade . . . assorted Great Society over-achievers were among the 3,800 persons who produced a record $400,000 gross—more than 12 times what the Met usually

Opening night of the Metropolitan Opera House, September 16, 1966.
Pictured standing on the Center's Plaza (left to right): *chair of the*
Metropolitan Opera board G. Lauder Greenway, President Ferdinand Marcos
of the Philippines, Rudolf Bing, Imelda Marcos, First Lady "Lady Bird"
Johnson, and John D. Rockefeller 3rd. (Photo by Jack Manning /
The New York Times / Redux Pictures)

gets for a sellout—and the kind of glamour the nation has come to associate with New York on a good day."[3]

The inaugural event even allowed time to fit in an opera, with the world premiere of Samuel Barber's *Antony and Cleopatra* starring Justino Diaz and Leontyne Price in the title roles, Thomas Schippers conducting, Alvin Ailey as choreographer, and the highly expansive Franco Zeffirelli as librettist, director, and designer. Barber was a natural choice to receive the Met's opening-night commission. Already established as one of America's most distinguished composers, he had enjoyed an earlier Met success in 1958 with his opera *Vanessa*, which earned him a Pulitzer Prize.

Harold Schonberg savaged the new opera production, writing in the *New York Times* that the work was "a big, complicated package: big, grand, impressive and vulgar. . . . Sets nobly and ponderously arrived from the rear, slowly and majestically, like a Sherman tank passing over a wheat field. . . . And, it must be confessed, sometimes so vulgar: artifice masquerading with a great flourish as art. . . . Almost everything about the evening, artistically speaking, failed in total impact."[4] The architectural critic of the same newspaper, Ada Louise Huxtable, was somewhat less florid but still negative in evaluating the new structure: "The architecture sets no high-water mark for the city. . . . It is average rather than adventurous or avante-garde."[5]

It was Robert Moses who gave the most piquant evaluation of the new Met in a message written to his friend Harrison after touring the almost completed building in 1965: "Wally: you know I'm not given to slobbering, so mark my words for once as a chum. . . . I was enormously impressed . . . by the Met Opera House. . . . In spite of differences and shortcomings, Lincoln Center will be regarded as a triumph of citizenship. It makes me proud of the town when I begin to despair of it. . . . Make [the opening] Aida. Bring on the elephants, crashing symbols [*sic*] and dancing gals."[6]

The Barber opera did not enjoy the success of *Aida* and had only a meager life after its premiere. The composer withdrew the work after the Met opening and presented a revised version in 1983. Leontyne Price, however, would often reprise one of the work's major arias, "Bring Me My Robe," at her concert performances.

The days before the Met opening were made that much more tense by the labor unrest fomented by the Met orchestra's musicians, who had been working without a contract for the past two years. The high-stakes opening of the new hall provided the musician's union, Local 802 of the American Federation of Musicians, with an extremely effective pressure point for pushing the Met management to provide a generous contract for the orchestra.

The orchestra agreed to perform on opening night, but the rest of the season was still in question. In a dramatic coup worthy of a Verdian plot turn, the negotiations successfully concluded at 8:00 p.m. on opening night—during the second intermission the orchestra voted in favor of the new contract. An exultant Rudolf

Bing announced the good news from the apron of the stage at the beginning of the third act, which garnered much applause from the audience.

In addition to the performing art of opera appearing onstage at the Met, the visual arts were also admirably represented in the new building through the work of distinguished international artists. Perhaps the most striking commission went to the Russian-born French artist Marc Chagall, who was invited to create two mammoth murals facing Lincoln Center Plaza, each thirty feet wide and thirty-six feet high, flanking the main stairway of the Grand Foyer. The commission had been facilitated by Mrs. August Belmont,[7] the first woman to serve on the Metropolitan Opera board and the founder of the Metropolitan Opera Guild, who reported to JDR 3rd that a gift of $1 million could go to the Met in support of art in the new opera house.

Looking into the lobby from the street, Chagall's mural appearing to the right of the main staircase is titled *Les Sources de la musique* and the one to the left *Le Triomphe de la musique*. Art critic Patricia Boccadoro wrote of the murals, "The yellow panel that is *The Sources of Music* shows King David in double profile as he plays the harp surrounded by musicians, animals and angels, while the red panel that is *The Triumph of Music* represents a victorious angel blowing a trumpet in the midst of a whirlwind, sweeping up musicians, orchestra, and phantasmagorical animals in its wake."[8]

Originally, Chagall had envisioned placing the murals vice versa from how they are displayed today, but they were inadvertently installed incorrectly before the artist arrived in New York. Upon seeing the murals in their reverse state, he said, "[I] yelled as I never have before. My mother, when she gave birth to her children, didn't yell as much. I could doubtless be heard all over Lincoln Square."[9] But Chagall decided he could live with the incorrect placement.

The works were commissioned by the Henry L. and Grace Doherty Charitable Foundation. Chagall also designed a groundbreaking Met production of *The Magic Flute* for presentation later in the season. In addition, works by Raoul Dufy, Aristide Maillol, and Wilhelm Lehmbruch were either commissioned or displayed in the new house.[10]

Marc Chagall standing before his mural titled Le Triomphe
de la musique *in the Metropolitan Opera House lobby,*
1966. (Photo by Rose Callahan / Met Opera)

The Lincoln Center founders had addressed the larger issue
of acquisition of art for the entire campus in early 1960 through a
memorandum authored by trustee Arthur A. Houghton, Jr., which
reviewed ways of accepting objects of art as gifts but also authorized
each architect to engage qualified professionals to assist in choosing the type and placement of works of art in each of the Center's
buildings. By mid-decade, the Art Committee of Lincoln Center
was created, chaired by Frank Stanton, president of the Columbia
Broadcasting System. The choice of art for the Center was an internal process unless the work was to be placed on land owned by New
York City, which was the case for all the plazas and parks on campus.

It is thus that the eternal question of "What is art?" came to Lincoln Center through a work by the American sculptor Alexander Calder, named *Le Guichet* (The Box Office). In June 1964, Howard W. Lipman, the financier, distinguished collector, and eventual chair of the Whitney Museum of American Art beginning in 1977, and his wife, Jean, approached JDR 3rd to commission a Calder sculpture for the Center.[11] Lipman recommended that the artist create a stabile that would sit permanently at the Center. He would cover all costs of the commission and installation, which were to result in a contribution of $20,000.

Rockefeller accepted the gift with enthusiasm and the process of bringing the work to Lincoln Center began. The placement of the sculpture was determined to be in an open space surrounded by the Metropolitan Opera, the Library-Museum, and the Beaumont Theater buildings, which was designated as city land. In order for the sculpture to be placed on that site it had to be authorized by the city's Art Commission, but it first had to be forwarded to the commission by the city's Parks Department, which at that time was overseen by Newbold Morris, former City Center chair and well known to Lincoln Center community members. Unexpectedly, Morris did not think much of the sculpture and refused to pass on the authorization process to the Art Commission.

This "tempest in a teapot" had an energy of its own that was of great interest to the New York press, with Morris writing confidentially to Edgar Young in March 1965, "My duty is to stick to certain standards, which may be based in part upon my own taste, and to resist the use of park property for artistic experiments. . . . I happen to be the brother of an abstract painter and sculptor . . . [but] City property must be used for the benefit of the great mass of people, not for the esoteric half of one per cent who live at the top. . . . The word 'stabile' is new to my vocabulary, but I guess it means a piece of immovable metal or concrete, which is not art."[12] Morris finally suggested in the letter that the work be moved to non-park land, such as the lobby of the Metropolitan Opera House.

Gentle pressure was applied to Morris to change his decision, both by Rockefeller and William F. R. Ballard, chair of the City Planning Commission. The final successful pressure point, however, was activated by Mayor Wagner, who was persuaded by Alfred H.

(Left to right): *Alexander Calder,* Le Guichet *(The Box Office),*
1963; Henry Moore, Reclining Figure, *1965; and Elie Nadelman,*
Two Circus Women, *1931, adapted in 1964, viewed by William*
Schuman (right) *and two guests. (Calder and Moore photos courtesy*
of Stephanie Bazirjian; Nadelman photo by Bob Serating)

Barr, Jr., the distinguished director of museum collections at the
Museum of Modern Art, that this was not an appropriate action to
be taken by a city as supposedly sophisticated as New York.

In addition to the work by Calder, the British artist Henry
Moore was commissioned by the Albert A. List Foundation to create the largest piece in Moore's series of "reclining figures." Moore
regarded the Lincoln Center piece as the "end result" of this series
dating from 1959, and he described the sculpture as "a leg part and
a head and arms part."[13] The six-ton sculpture was created in two
sections and stood sixteen feet high and thirty feet wide. It was also
to be placed on city-controlled land in the center of the North Plaza
reflecting pool.

Morris allowed the commission to vote on both the Calder
work and the Moore sculpture. The city's Art Commission, which
ruled in July 1965 by a five to four vote, allowed both works to
occupy city property at Lincoln Center. Asked to make a comment after the meeting, Morris said, "I'm 62 years old. If I were
40 years younger, I'd go sit on a park bench and cry. Do I have to
say more?"[14]

After all the criticism, financial and logistical challenges, and pe-
ripheral distractions, the opening of the new Metropolitan Opera

House was a watershed moment for Lincoln Center. The opening of five major venues in only nine years of planning ensured that this idealistic venture was well positioned to succeed in the future.

As the construction of buildings moved toward completion, the idea of creating new constituents also surfaced. Lincoln Center had presented its first International Film Festival beginning on September 10, 1963, showing both domestic and international cinema. Schuman was a great champion for the creation of a Lincoln Center constituent in film. When he brought up the idea, Anthony Bliss of the Metropolitan Opera complained that film was "not a live art," to which Schuman retorted, "It's a hell of a lot livelier than the Metropolitan Opera."[15]

By 1966, Lincoln Center had made it clear to William F. May, Lincoln Center Film Committee chair, that the Center would fully finance a film program for the 1967–68 season, but it would reduce its support beginning with the fiscal year 1968–69. May pledged that his committee would raise up to $100,000 by the end of 1967 and $275,000 in the next year, thus making it possible for the Film Society to become a constituent.[16]

May reinforced the status of film at Lincoln Center by stating, "Lincoln Center considers film to be a performing art that ranks equally with music, opera, theater and dance. Film is the only new art medium created and developed during the 20th century. In spite of this relatively short history, it has produced an impressive body of acknowledged masterpieces."[17] The film department was directed by Amos Vogel. Its activities included the annual New York Film Festival, a yearly National Student Film Awards Competition, and other film programs, such as a series of films presented during each year's Lincoln Center Festival.

The Film Society of Lincoln Center became a constituent on June 19, 1969, with May as chair and Martin E. Segal as president. Schuyler G. Chapin, who had served in leadership positions at Lincoln Center during the Schuman years, was appointed the new program's executive director. The Seventh New York Film Festival, which took place in the fall of 1969, would use the newly opened Alice Tully Hall for its screenings (switching from the event's previous venue, Philharmonic Hall).

Perhaps the greatest early success of the Film Society occurred in 1972 when the organization decided to honor Charlie Chaplin, who attended the event after not setting foot in the United States for twenty years due to his anger over criticism in the 1940s and 1950s of his politics, artistry, and personal life. The British-born actor was branded a Communist by Senator Joseph McCarthy's House Un-American Activities Committee, as a result of which he was put on an FBI blacklist in 1948 and therefore no longer able to make films in Hollywood. The "Salute to Chaplin" was chaired by David Rockefeller, Jr., and organized by Segal. The honorary committee for the event included a "who's who" of financiers, artists, and socialites from throughout the world, generating much-needed funds for the Society's programs.

One proposed element of the new arts center fascinated many planners: a "mall" stretching between Lincoln Center and Central Park West, which would allow an unobstructed view of Central Park from the Lincoln Center buildings. The concept was first developed by William F. R. Ballard, an architect and chair of the city's Planning Commission. In Ballard's view, the mall would improve the neighborhood's aesthetics and also provide much-needed underground parking for up to one thousand cars, generating revenue for the project.

The city's administrator of recreation and culture, Thomas P. F. Hoving, and Donald H. Elliott, chair of the city's Planning Commission, were charged with determining the feasibility of the concept for review by Mayor John V. Lindsay, who was said to be "very interested" in the plan. However, the Ballard approach would necessitate the razing of most of the buildings on the block bounded by Broadway, Central Park West, and Sixty-Third and Sixty-Fourth Streets. Included on the block were two major institutions, the West Side YMCA and the meeting house of the New York Society for Ethical Culture, both of which had supported the creation of Lincoln Center in the late 1950s.

Only a week after the first public announcement of the mall concept, on December 5, 1966, an alternative, less disruptive approach was presented by Hoving in which, instead of razing the entire block, many new buildings would be constructed, connected by elevated, interlocking walkways so that pedestrians would have "unobstructed access between the Park and Lincoln Center. . . . The walkways would run past fountains and shrubbery, and along rows of art galleries, book stores and coffee houses, designed to create an 'Old World' atmosphere."[18]

Both Harrison and his partner Max Abramovitz strenuously objected to the Hoving proposal. They claimed that it was "incompatible with any plan to enhance access to the arts center or to provide an organic pattern of urban design for the West Side."[19] Such a bold and visionary project brought out supporters and detractors in droves, but it was the respected *New York Times* architecture critic Ada Louise Huxtable who sealed the fate of the project with her scathing evaluation of the mall. Huxtable wrote that the "two conflicting versions . . . [offer] non-solutions to the problems of one of the more critical, transitional areas of the city in the throes of social and economic renewal. One is a showy plunge back into planning's dark ages [the Ballard design] and the other is a fashionable leap onto the bandwagon of current clichés [the Hoving design]."[20]

Putting the proverbial "nail in the coffin," Huxtable concluded her piece by challenging Mayor Lindsay, the final arbiter of the mall concept: "For once the Mayor is not on the horns of a genuine dilemma. It is more like a genuine boondoggle, and he can go on to more serious matters."[21] In addition, Philip Johnson reported that Commissioner Moses "refused to do [the project] point-blank. He said, 'Look what I got you. Now shut up.'"[22] Unable to surmount the various challenges, the mall concept collapsed, though it has remained a distant dream for some city and Lincoln Center officials who have looked longingly east toward Central Park and tried to envision what could have been.

By the end of 1966, a serious rift had developed between William Schuman and JDR 3rd. Perhaps the split was inevitable. Schuman was a self-made person who overcame various societal and financial challenges to become a successful educator and composer. Rockefeller was American royalty, the quintessential patrician, whose wealth came with the understanding that he was to be a responsible member of American society. His philanthropy was strategic, rational, and slow-paced.

It is clear in several letters to Schuman from Rockefeller that it was anticipated Schuman would serve as the Center's president until 1975, when he would have reached the traditional retirement age of sixty-five. Schuman, however, was uneasy and impatient with his task of bringing together a highly recalcitrant group of constituents to make Lincoln Center more than the sum of its parts.

As one of the very few Jewish members of the Lincoln Center board at the time, and certainly the only artist, Schuman would express frustration with the background of his board colleagues and resented their insistence on becoming involved in artistic issues of the Center. He commented, "Way down deep, it [Lincoln Center] was WASP-controlled, society-controlled, money-controlled. Yet I would not say for a minute that these were not dedicated men. . . . But they had political axes to grind. . . . There was an interweaving of personal, professional, financial lives with their views as volunteer directors."[23]

In addition to the financial and societal challenges Schuman experienced at Lincoln Center, he also had a great passion to become involved in programming artistic events. Initially the Center's founders believed that Lincoln Center, Inc., would have to program events in the campus's halls only when constituents were not using them, primarily in the summer. Schuman was thinking far bigger, hoping to create new constituents and develop festivals and special programs during the traditional season stretching from September to early June.

In a strongly worded letter to Rockefeller in June 1967, Schuman was emphatic in objecting to the concept that Lincoln Center itself should not be in programming, writing, "What happens to the dream of cross-fertilization and all the other beautiful statements we made? . . . I now ask your help in finding some way to reach a rededication of these principles on the part of our Board."[24] The Lincoln Center constituents were not pleased with this approach and ultimately neither was Rockefeller.

At the same time, Schuman presented four new artistic or educational initiatives that he wished to create: a chamber music organization and a film institute, both of which became constituents; a modern dance company based at the Center; and a teacher's institute. Except for a modern dance presence on campus, the other three initiatives came to fruition, with the board, at the time, expressing no concerns with any of the ventures.

These initiatives, plus the Center's ongoing summer festival, however, caused considerable friction among the constituents. The New York Philharmonic saw the creation of a chamber music constituent as a potential competitor for ticket revenue, and the Met was troubled by the Hamburg Opera's place in the 1967 summer festival and the potential performances of the Rome Opera in the 1968 summer festival. Both companies paid higher fees than the Met to star performers, which put the Met in an awkward negotiating position in developing its own productions.

By early 1966, the New York press, and in particular Harold Schonberg of the *New York Times*, became quite critical of Lincoln Center and Schuman's leadership. According to a confidential memo to the file from John W. McNulty, Lincoln Center's director of public relations, who met with Schonberg in December 1965, the critic minced no words regarding the organization and its president, saying that Lincoln Center "hasn't lived up to its ideals. . . . [Blau and Irving of the Repertory Theatre] are not professional—[they are] out-of-town hicks. . . . Press relations are bad—unimaginative— Schuman won't be frank, open—too cagy."[25]

But Schonberg's worst criticism was that there was no artistic leadership at the Center. "Music Theater [is a] showcase for Dick Rodgers, nothing new and exciting. . . . Lincoln Center has no standing with the 'intellectual establishment.' Schuman, who should have it, has lost their respect."[26]

JDR 3rd traditionally wrote end-of-year evaluation letters to the heads of all the eleemosynary organizations he chaired. His December 30, 1966, letter to Schuman was one that the Lincoln Center president saw as a "bombshell" and a signal that his position as the CEO of the Center was in a fragile state.[27] Rockefeller expressed plainly that Schuman's actions in producing events were incompatible with the general environment Rockefeller envisioned for the Center, and emphasized that due to Schuman's artistic ventures the constituents saw Lincoln Center, Inc., as a competitor.[28]

Schuman's creative initiatives also came with a price, and Rockefeller and his board were in no mood to raise large sums of money beyond what was already needed to pay for the burgeoning construction overages. More funding for new programs, festivals (the deficit for the Lincoln Center Festival '67 was conservatively projected at $535,000), and the creation of new constituents all ran counter to what Rockefeller saw as prudent leadership. Although Midsummer Serenades—A Mozart Festival (the precursor to Mostly Mozart, which would officially take on that name in July 1972) began on August 1, 1966, to a modicum of both artistic and financial success, and was notable as the first indoor music festival in New York City within an air-conditioned hall, its positive presence on campus was offset by the very large deficits generated by Schuman's festivals.

Rockefeller believed that the constituents viewed Lincoln Center as having unlimited funding for its artistic programming, making relations with them that much more difficult. Rockefeller's financial concerns were exacerbated by a speech Schuman gave in December 1966 at the Princeton University Conference on the Performing Arts: Their Economic Problems titled "The New Establishment," which referred to the newly created entity of the performing arts center. In his talk, Schuman argued that artistic goals overrode prudent financial planning. The coup de grâce line of the speech, which certainly caught Rockefeller's attention, was this: "Basic to our problem is not that our deficits are too large, but that they are too small."[29]

Schuman would go on to presumptuously ignore Rockefeller's admonitions and proceed to undertake new projects, including a chamber music constituent, to which Rockefeller responded in February 1967, "It is not a question of merit, not a question of importance [of a chamber music constituent], but rather the future of Lincoln Center as a whole. . . . Neither you nor I want to preside over the liquidation of Lincoln Center. My belief is that we are moving in that direction unless we stop now the making of new commitments for programs involving substantial amounts of money."[30] Remarkably, Schuman refused to back down, responding in March, "Lincoln Center was to be more than buildings. . . . The buildings of Lincoln Center stand, but each day their justification must be proved anew by what goes on the stages."[31]

The proposed Chamber Music Society (CMS) Rockefeller alluded to was one of Schuman's top priorities. As a distinguished composer, he saw chamber music as a pillar of Western art music, and he also believed that the new hall in the Juilliard building would be an ideal home for a constituent dedicated to this genre.

The concept of a chamber music constituent was not one that Rockefeller rejected philosophically. He simply believed that a new constituent—no matter what discipline—would cost the Center money it did not have. However, in 1965, when a potential donor for the naming of the new chamber music hall surfaced, Rockefeller authorized Schuman to explore the matter, which concerned a potential grant from a cousin of the Philharmonic chair, Arthur Houghton.[32]

The cousin in question was Alice Tully, a serious singer when she was in her twenties, a daring aviator, and one of the heirs to the Corning Glass Works fortune. The proposed thousand-seat hall would be located in the far eastern part of the new Juilliard building but administered by Lincoln Center. Members of the Houghton family had already committed $850,000 to the Lincoln Center campaign, and thought was given to naming the new venue Houghton Hall.

Schuman approached Arthur Houghton about facilitating a meeting with Miss Tully to see if she was interested not only in putting her name on the hall but also in supporting the new chamber music constituent. Schuman and Tully had a productive meeting on December 6, 1965, after which Schuman wrote to her, "I was more than delighted—I was encouraged. The spirit of dedication and genuine involvement which was apparent in everything that you said about *our* [emphasis mine] chamber music project was deeply appreciated."[33] Tully wrote two months later that "my own especial joy is the thought that each day that passes brings our cherished dream of a Chamber Music Center nearer to realization."[34]

Planning and discussions progressed throughout the winter and, on May 10, 1966, it was announced that the chamber music recital hall would be named for Alice Tully. The Tully naming gift totaled $1.3 million, based on the assumption that the entire cost of the hall would be $2.6 million.

By April 1967, Lincoln Center authorized the creation of another exploratory committee, this time to create a chamber music constituent, with Tully as chair. Earlier, Schuman had said, with a

(Left to right): *John D. Rockefeller 3rd, Alice Tully, and
John W. Mazzola, ca. 1969–70. (Photo by Bob Serating)*

clever turn of phrase, that he wished to create "a repertory theater of
chamber music."[35] As the committee began to work on developing
the new constituent, Schuman reached out again to Tully, this time
obtaining a three-year, $300,000 grant that would be used to plan
and support the various artistic and administrative elements of the
venture. Soon new board members joined, including Frank Taplin as
president, to assist Tully as chair.

Charles Wadsworth, pianist and, at the time, artistic director of
chamber music at the Festival of Two Worlds in Spoleto, Italy, became the first and long-tenured artistic director of the new organization. Artistically, the new group moved quickly, commissioning composers such as Samuel Barber, Pierre Boulez, Carlos Chavez, Alberto
Ginastera, Olivier Messiaen, Darius Milhaud, and John Corigliano
to create works to be performed during the first season. Structurally,
Schuman pushed hard for his concept of a chamber music "repertory company," which to him meant a group of approximately eight
musicians who would form the core of instrumentalists to be mixed
and matched in the presentation of chamber music repertoire.

Schuman proposed that the Society could either manage Alice
Tully Hall on its own or allow Lincoln Center to oversee the venue,

as was the case with the New York Philharmonic and Philharmonic Hall. The latter formula was finally adopted, but the question of Juilliard's access to a hall in its own building for the School's chamber music and orchestral concerts still needed to be resolved.

Amid the many complex challenges Schuman was facing as the Center's president, he suffered a serious heart attack on May 10, 1968, which kept him away from his duties until mid-autumn. In his absence, John Mazzola, a lawyer originally from the firm of Milbank, Tweed, Hope & Hadley who had worked with JDR 3rd during the Center's formative years and was now its secretary and general counsel, was appointed chief executive officer. Mazzola immediately began to work with the Lincoln Center board to reduce the annual deficit and to set a leadership direction that diverged from Schuman's approach. In a tenuous state of health and coming up against an increasingly fiscally conservative board, Schuman found his position weakened as 1968 was coming to an end.

In November, after Schuman's return from medical leave, Edgar Young forcefully lobbied JDR 3rd not to proceed with further efforts to make the Chamber Music Society a constituent. Young also suggested that Miss Tully be persuaded that creating such a body during this difficult financial period would not be prudent. In a confidential memorandum to JDR 3rd, Young wrote that "Miss Tully . . . is much more interested in the use and success of Tully Hall than in the formation of a new institution [a chamber music constituent]. She had gone along with WS [William Schuman] on his plan for the new group but has no personal conviction as to its necessity. I believe she would welcome a frank review of the situation."[36] In his confidential memorandum, Young goes on to say, "Attainment of the musical objectives of Tully Hall does not require formation of a new performing group. . . . The Artistic Director (Charles Wadsworth) is a controversial figure. The Chairman (Frank Taplin) is weak and ineffective. He has a record of failure. . . . Plans are moving inexorably to commitments with artists. All of this will create a situation from which retreat will be impossible. . . . The blame for any such failure will be on Lincoln Center."[37]

Motivated by Young's memos, JDR 3rd wrote Miss Tully on December 11, 1968. He began his letter deferentially with "Dear Alice (if I may call you that)" and shared with her a scathing evaluation of the concept of creating a chamber music constituent: "It [the evaluation] is written by a foundation officer knowledgeable in the music field and with a genuine interest in the success of Lincoln Center. The memorandum is frank and outspoken which I hope you don't mind."[38] The report JDR 3rd shared had been written, anonymously, by Rockefeller Foundation officer Steven Benedict, who argued that "the need for a new organization for chamber music at Lincoln Center, on the scale proposed, should be seriously challenged.... The City is bulging with chamber music of very high quality. . . . I [also] find astonishing the notion of initiating an artistic enterprise . . . through the endowment route.... The idea of raising $2.5 million–$5 million for such a purpose, at this particular time, is totally unrealistic."[39]

However, Schuman, who was aware of the deep reservations of Rockefeller and Young concerning the launch of the new chamber music constituent, activated what seems to have been a desperate effort to regain power by sending a press release on December 17, 1968. Titled "New Institution Comes to Lincoln Center," the document presented a complete Chamber Music Society schedule for the upcoming season. The announcement—which was from Schuman, not Miss Tully or Frank Taplin—described an ensemble of eight players led by Charles Wadsworth serving as artistic director and Irwin Scherzer, Miss Tully's frequent escort and close friend, as business manager. The new constituent would perform a twenty-four-week season.

As soon as Young learned of the release, which had already been mailed to the *New York Times*, he contacted JDR 3rd and told him that Amyas Ames, chair of the Lincoln Center executive committee, knew nothing of the release. "Ames feels you must decide in the light of your conversations with Miss Tully whether to let this release go as already issued or an effort should be made to kill it," Young wrote.[40] "Rockefeller called Miss Tully and learned that she had been aware of the release, but was now concerned about the reservations she had learned of from Rockefeller and some constituents. She asked to see if he [Rockefeller] could prevent the release of the statement."[41] JDR 3rd took the extraordinary step of personally calling Arthur Ochs Sulzberger, Sr., publisher of the *Times*, which successfully killed the announcement.

Rockefeller set a meeting for December 20, 1968, to discuss future actions for the Chamber Music Society attended by Alice Tully, Devereaux Josephs, Frank Taplin, Edward Wardwell, and John Mazzola, but not Schuman. Rockefeller graciously "accepted the blame" for the fact that the CMS had been prematurely encouraged by Lincoln Center (i.e., Schuman) to proceed.[42] The members of the CMS board decided to defer engagement of their resident artists for about a year and to delay efforts to raise an endowment. Constituency status would be conferred when the Society could "assure the constituents and Lincoln Center of its financial independence . . . with the Society to open [Alice Tully] Hall in September 1969."[43]

Amyas Ames worked closely with Alice Tully in early 1969 to find a path for the CMS launch without fully embracing Schuman's costly "resident artist" concept. As a result, on March 4, 1969, just a few months after the press release crisis, Charles Wadsworth announced the creation of the Chamber Music Society of Lincoln Center and the scheduling of performances beginning in October 1969. Sixteen regular subscription concerts were planned, down from the earlier concert schedule of twenty-four, grouped in four series of four concerts each. Although there was an initial group of nine musicians presented as "Artists of the Society," many guests also participated. A gala concert took place on September 11, 1969, inaugurating Alice Tully Hall, which featured performances by Chamber Music Society artists. The Chamber Music Society of Lincoln Center would officially become a constituent on January 1, 1973.

Remarkably, throughout all these trials, JDR 3rd still hoped that Schuman's presidency could survive. According to Edgar Young, "John Rockefeller was still trying very hard to help Schuman succeed. John didn't want to see a change occur if it could be avoided."[44]

During Schuman's recuperation that summer, Festival '68 took place and racked up nearly $600,000 in losses. Young also reported that the August Serenades and the Film Festival spilled more red ink for the Center, and officials expressed concern that the Center might soon be forced to declare bankruptcy.[45]

As the year ended, Mazzola was asked to report at the November board meeting regarding his view of the Center's financial status. He ominously titled his report "Analysis of the Disappearing

Net Worth of the Lincoln Center Fund." The board addressed the issue by converting certain long-term assets to more liquid vehicles but also voted to prohibit the creation of any new programs unless funds were guaranteed. Contract authorizations for Festival '69 were rescinded, and the 1969 August Serenades were canceled. Schuman voted to discontinue the Serenades but, in a muted signal that the Lincoln Center president would go down fighting, he abstained from canceling Festival '69.

In a weakened state and overridden by his board on various initiatives he wished to pursue, Schuman resigned on November 25, 1968, effective January 1, 1969. He was given a severance package that provided a monetary payment over three years and the title of president emeritus. Schuman's departure was a disruptive experience for all parties at the Center, but Young contended that it had been necessary "to bring financial reality and to create a situation where they [Lincoln Center] could start almost afresh to raise money for the ongoing operations and purposes."[46] Mazzola commented, "I think Devereaux Josephs [a member of the Lincoln Center Executive Committee] made [the] point better than anyone. [He said] 'All these were terrible mistakes [by Schuman] but they were the kind of mistakes we had to make and we owe Bill Schuman a debt of thanks for making them.'"[47]

Schuman would not be involved in Lincoln Center matters until the opening of the new Juilliard School building on October 26, 1969. Schuman was, of course, the primary force behind bringing Juilliard to Lincoln Center in 1957. He was contacted by JDR 3rd by telephone after many months of silence between the two men and anticipated an invitation to speak at the opening ceremony. However, Rockefeller explained that the chosen speakers would be Juilliard president Peter Mennin, Rockefeller, and President Richard M. Nixon (who never appeared). Rockefeller then added, "Bill, I would like you to write my speech for me."[48]

Schuman was deeply wounded by what he felt was an insensitive request, although he admitted that Rockefeller made it "in no way departing from [his] customary gentlemanly demeanor."[49] He declined the invitation "for reasons both institutional and personal" but did attend the Juilliard opening ceremony.[50] Although not quite as grand as the Met opening three years earlier, it was still an elaborate event.

The ceremony took place in Alice Tully Hall and was broadcast live by CBS, hosted by Leonard Bernstein. The Juilliard Orchestra was the featured ensemble, conducted by Leopold Stokowski and Jean Morel, Juilliard's resident conductor. A recent violin graduate named Itzhak Perlman played the first movement of Niccolò Paganini's Violin Concerto no. 1; the two other alumni soloists were the distinguished mezzo-soprano Shirley Verrett, singing selections from Mozart, Donizetti, and Saint-Saëns, and, to conclude the program with an exciting flair, Van Cliburn playing Franz Liszt's Piano Concerto no. 1.

The tradition of having First Ladies represent their husbands at Lincoln Center inaugurations continued, as Pat Nixon attended, accompanied by her daughter Julie and son-in-law David Eisenhower. Although Schuman would not be speaking at the event, his good friend Bernstein, as the evening's television host, promised he would recognize the role Schuman had played in bringing Juilliard to Lincoln Center. However, any praise of Schuman was prohibited by Mennin, who was the television script's final arbiter.

The regrettable animosity between Schuman and Mennin dated back to the early 1960s when Schuman did not support Mennin's candidacy for the Juilliard presidency. Moreover, when Schuman became Lincoln Center president in 1962 there were serious misunderstandings between the two men regarding the financial responsibility that Lincoln Center had in supporting the dance and drama divisions at Juilliard, which were mandated by the Center. In addition, the issue of cost-free access to Alice Tully Hall, which was located in the Juilliard building but administered by Lincoln Center, was a sore point for the two men.[51] Therefore, Mennin held a considerable grudge against Schuman and felt no great desire to have him participate in the Juilliard School opening.

Nevertheless, Bernstein ignored the prohibition and went off script:

Ultimately, I suppose the most rewarding result [of Juilliard's presence at Lincoln Center] can be the attainment of the Socratic ideal, where teachers learn and students teach, where wisdom is acquired by all from all in an endless, free-flowing exchange of ideas and knowledge. And that's the real meaning and the promise of today's event. . . . I would like to say a word of tribute to a man without whom none of this might have happened. William Schuman, one of America's most celebrated composers . . . through his unique combination of intellect and spirit, he has lent an originality and grandeur of concept to the whole project that it could easily have lacked without him. William Schuman should be a very proud man this Sunday evening.[52]

After the ceremony Schuman thanked Bernstein for both the mention and his friendship, and Bernstein responded, "It was not a matter of friendship but principle."[53]

The deterioration of the Schuman-Rockefeller relationship had much to do with the philosophical divide between sound business practices and the vision of those who live to create art at the highest level of excellence and integrity. Schuman would never forgive Rockefeller and his fellow board members for what he believed was an abandonment of the Lincoln Center mission, which was less about the construction and maintenance of real estate and more about producing high-quality artistic events for the public. He also blamed many of his problems on what he saw as the pettiness of the constituents, who "didn't like my independence, didn't like my building Lincoln Center into its own 'constituency.' . . . The Center is a success because of the symbol it has become. . . . But to me, it is a sellout in terms of what it might have been, success though it is."[54]

His colleague Schuyler Chapin summed up the Schuman years in a slightly different tone: "Those people who serve on Boards of great organizations for the most part are all amateur lovers of what they're supporting. But with the [performing] arts they seem to feel a greater liberty to put forth their desires, on the theory that they're paying the bills. They wouldn't do that at a hospital. . . . I think that time has proven the validity of Bill's point of view, but oh, boy, it was at quite a cost. . . . It was a rough ride."[55] That "ride" would now be overseen by a new team of Lincoln Center leaders.

CHAPTER SIX

Opening Night and Amateur
Night at the Same Time

W ITH THE OFFICIAL opening of The Juilliard School building in 1969, the founders of Lincoln Center took pride in what they had accomplished since their Exploratory Committee first met in late 1955. Lincoln Center was now a functioning organization presenting performances by the Metropolitan Opera, the New York Philharmonic, the New York City Ballet, the New York City Opera, the Music Theater of Lincoln Center, the Beaumont Theater, and The Juilliard School.

In addition, special spring and summer festivals filled the air-conditioned halls, including the successful International University Choral Festival, and new constituents in chamber music and film were under consideration. The public began to understand what Lincoln Center could be, and there was considerable optimism that an ambitious dream had been realized, albeit with a concomitant series of financial and artistic challenges which sobered the mood of the Center's leadership. The overall cost of constructing the Center came in at $185.4 million, 26 percent above the estimate made in 1960.[1] Lincoln Center was out of the construction business for the foreseeable future.

It was therefore not surprising that John D. Rockefeller 3rd would decide that his task as the Center's principal leader had been completed. Rockefeller chose as his successor Amyas Ames, who assumed the Lincoln Center chair on May 11, 1970. Born into a prominent Massachusetts family, Ames attended Harvard College (class of 1928) and then graduated from the university's business school in 1930, after which he entered the finance world at the Depression's lowest point.

As a young boy, Amyas attended concerts of the Boston Symphony Orchestra, became attracted to orchestral music, and even played a bit of saxophone and piano himself. After his graduate studies, he moved to New York to work at Kidder, Peabody and rose to become managing partner and chair of its executive committee. Ames's first involvement with Lincoln Center came through the New York Philharmonic when he joined its board in 1955 and went on to serve as its president and then chair from 1970 to 1983.[2] During Ames's early years at the Philharmonic Leonard Bernstein was the orchestra's music director, and Ames and Bernstein became friends.[3]

Along with Carlos Moseley (the orchestra's managing director and future president) and David Keiser (the orchestra's chair until 1970), Ames helped oversee the engagement of Pierre Boulez as the Philharmonic's music director. Ames showed a particular openness in working with the highly intellectual and demanding French conductor.

Keiser strongly advised Ames that it would be inappropriate for him to take on the Lincoln Center chair while also chairing the Philharmonic board: "Look Amyas . . . you cannot become chairman of Lincoln Center. It is a direct conflict of interest."[4] Although Ames respected Keiser, he felt the advice was a bit heavy-handed: "I knew he [Keiser] was wrong. I knew I could do it, and I knew I wasn't going to take his advice, but I asked two or three directors who were closely oriented to the Philharmonic. They agreed with me, and I accepted [the Lincoln Center chair in 1970], against Keiser's direct advice."[5]

Ames felt that in his role as Lincoln Center chair he needed to unify the constituents who had been alienated during the Schuman presidency. He saw the constituents as exhibiting a "feeling of separateness [which was] there in spades at the Metropolitan Opera. Juilliard was a little empire all by itself; they wanted no part of Lincoln Center's problems. The same thing was true with City Center."[6]

A large part of Ames's strategy with the constituents was to develop a rapprochement focused on reversing Schuman's program of having Lincoln Center function as a separate producing unit that competed with them. Constituent leaders believed that there was a finite number of donors and ticket buyers for Lincoln Center presentations and that the Center's own producing activities, according to Ames, created "a whole new drain of money out of a given pool. The constituents thought 'We created the pool; it's our pool; it's a direct invasion of our existence.' . . . My view—and it's very strong— is that Lincoln Center should not compete with the performing arts [groups] that are brought together there."[7]

Although Ames was a supporter and friend of Schuman's, he did feel that Schuman "made a mistake . . . in dramatizing a separate activity by Lincoln Center before he had accomplished the marriage of Lincoln Center to the separate artistic entities."[8] Ames believed that such cooperation would make each constituent stronger.

He decided to resign from Kidder, Peabody in order to work full-time as chair of Lincoln Center, although he took no salary for that position. Coming from the New York Philharmonic, Ames could make the case to the constituents that he was "one of them" and therefore would be sensitive to their needs and concerns.

Ames made it clear to JDR 3rd that he did not want to find a replacement for Schuman. He suggested that the Lincoln Center presidency remain vacant and that Ames combine the positions of chair and president, acting as the Center's CEO. John Mazzola, who had been associated with the Center since the late 1950s, was frustrated by this new leadership configuration since he saw himself as the heir apparent for Lincoln Center's presidency: "It may have been a mistake, but I said I did not want to be president, I wanted to be general manager. . . . Amyas always thought he was president and I knew I was president, so we would always joke about that. He and I fought a great deal. . . . We were fighting like hell all the time but getting along."[9] Mazzola would hold several senior titles during his years at Lincoln Center: chief executive officer in 1968, managing director in 1970, and president from 1977 to 1982.

Aside from good-natured friction between himself and his colleagues, Ames felt quite positive about his professional relationship with both Mazzola and John O'Keefe, the head of public relations for the Center: "I had with me two very remarkable men [Mazzola and O'Keefe]. They both were natural politicians. . . . They were people-oriented, and they were the ones who did the community work. . . . Mazzola was my right hand. . . . John Mazzola and I probably did as much for Lincoln Center as any pair—John O'Keefe made it three—in molding everything. . . . No man was luckier than I was in being one of a three-man team."[10]

Ames's leadership style during his time as chair brimmed with optimism about what Lincoln Center had realized and what it might achieve in the future. In early 1972, Ames sent a memorandum to the members of the Lincoln Center board titled "Lincoln Center for the Performing Arts—The Second Decade." The multipage document expressed Ames's idealistic belief that Lincoln Center was a unique institution that deserved to flourish and be supported for the good of American society: "Lincoln Center is more than a physical home for the constituents, being also an important center for the performing arts . . . [which] acts as catalyst and coordinator in joining the . . . constituents together in common enterprises."[11]

The memo's primary message, however, was that Lincoln Center and its constituents needed significantly more funding to accomplish their goals. He reported that "the net operating cost of Lincoln Center had been reduced by over $1 million from approximately $2,900,000 in 1968–69 to the budgeted level of $1,800,000 for 1972."[12] A $10 million bequest from the estate of Martha Baird Rockefeller in 1971 helped the Center's endowment fund, but much more was needed in annual fundraising results. Ames ended his message to the board by plainly stating that "the Lincoln Center Concept has been tested and proved in its first decade, but it has been and still is restricted by lack of sufficient on-going support."[13]

The financial challenges Ames alluded to pointed to a crisis that endangered the Center's very existence. Although Lincoln Center leadership had earlier created a $20 million reserve fund to address unexpected financial needs, the entire amount had been used to complete the Juilliard building.

Regrettably for Ames, his decade-long tenure as Lincoln Center's chair coincided with one of the worst economic eras in U.S. history. By 1980, the inflation rate was near 14.5 percent and unemployment was over 7.5 percent.[14] The combination of high inflation and low economic growth created a period of damaging "stagflation." Added to these macroeconomic problems were the heightened intensity of the Vietnam War, the eventual resignation of President Nixon, the repeated energy crises involving oil embargoes, and the quadrupling of crude oil prices during the Carter administration, culminating in the Iranian hostage crisis. During this period such political and economic instability had an inevitable negative impact on all aspects of American society, including the arts.

Even before Ames became Lincoln Center's chair, he was deeply involved in trying to ensure the organization's financial health. In an effort to avert financial crisis and complete its capital fund drive, Ames, acting as chair of Lincoln Center's executive committee in 1969, approached JDR 3rd for yet another gift. He recalled saying to Rockefeller, "John, we are bankrupt. You've got to help us with another $2 million. And he blew up. He said 'Listen, there isn't any way I will give any more money. My family has given $40 million and we are not going to give a penny more. That's all.'"[15] Such an outburst from the reserved Rockefeller must have been a shock to Ames, but JDR 3rd did advise him to see Lawrence Wien to discuss the Center's financial woes further.

Wien, one of the most successful real estate lawyers and developers in New York City, co-owned the Empire State Building as well as such prominent hotels as the Plaza and the St. Moritz. He was also a major philanthropist, and one who would identify a problem and act on it immediately, a style considerably different from JDR 3rd's process-oriented approach. For example, he was upset with the soiled façade of a building on Park Avenue that he passed each day on his way to work. When he learned that the building's owner did not have the financial resources to clean it, he paid for the sandblasting himself.

Therefore, it was not surprising that Wien would insert himself into the financial discussion, saying to Ames, "Look, you just don't know how to talk to John Rockefeller. I will do it."[16] In one week the problem was solved: JDR 3rd contributed $1.25 million and Wien provided the same amount, adding up to $500,000 more than the previous ask to Rockefeller. The two contributions enabled Lincoln Center in 1969 to successfully end its thirteen-year capital campaign, which raised $184 million. [17]

Ames also believed that government funding for the arts was a necessary part of a healthy American arts environment. Through President Lyndon B. Johnson's support, legislation was passed in 1965 which authorized the creation of the National Endowment for the Arts and the National Endowment for the Humanities, reflecting the prevailing belief that the arts play an important role in the nation's spiritual and intellectual health. Ames, along with John Mazzola and John O'Keefe, created organizations on the state and national levels aimed at generating support for the arts. These types of initiatives were new ventures for Lincoln Center and showed that the Center now had a reputation that allowed its leaders to influence local and national artistic issues.

The Lincoln Center Corporate Fund was created during Ames's leadership. At the time, corporations, mostly based in New York City, chafed against the continuous solicitations that came from the individual Lincoln Center constituents. In response, Ames suggested the idea of creating a unified Lincoln Center fund drive, hoping that this approach could raise more money for the constituents. In a rare moment of unanimity, the constituents agreed to the plan based on the idea that the receipts from the fund would be divided using a formula to be determined. This effort succeeded, and total gifts did exceed individual constituent contributions from corporations. Constituents were still permitted, however, to solicit corporations for support of specific projects such as tours or benefits.

Perhaps the greatest fundraising success for Ames during his time as chair occurred serendipitously and addressed one of his great financial challenges: the annual deficit associated with Philharmonic Hall. In 1973 Mazzola was contacted by an accountant, known to him only as Mr. Silverberg, who said he represented a potential donor, but the donor would first need to review the Center's recent audited financial statements before any gift could be discussed.

After a subsequent meeting with the accountant, Mazzola contacted Carlos Moseley, president of the New York Philharmonic, and said, "This [representative of the] anonymous donor showed up . . . and we would rename the building [Philharmonic Hall] for $10 million [based on his proposal]. . . . Carlos said, 'It sounds marvelous.'"[18]

Soon after, Ames and Mazzola met the mystery man, one Avery Fisher, who had been completely unknown to either of them. Fisher explained that he was the head of Fisher Electronics and had amassed $40 million (Fisher sold his firm for $30 million in 1971 to Emerson Electric Company of St. Louis). He had recently decided to make a major gift to Lincoln Center because classical music had been so important to him. He was particularly fond of orchestral music and wanted to have his name on a building at Lincoln Center where such music was performed.[19] Initially, Fisher asked to fund the construction of an entirely new building on campus, but that was not a realistic proposal. The renaming of Philharmonic Hall would be the best way to recognize his enormous gift.

Avery Fisher was a native New Yorker and had graduated from NYU. His company, founded in 1937, was known for state-of-the-art high-fidelity sound components for home use. He was also an avid amateur violinist who had a passion for performing the string quartet repertoire. He owned a Stradivarius violin made in 1692 (now known as the "Fisher Stradivarius"), which he donated to The Juilliard School at the occasion of his eighty-fifth birthday in 1991. Ultimately, Fisher agreed to provide a gift of $10 million to Lincoln Center, which transformed Philharmonic Hall into Avery Fisher Hall.

Based on the deed of gift, 80 percent of the grant was to be invested, and the revenue was to be used to help offset the hall's annual operating deficit, which amounted to about $500,000 in 1973. The remaining 20 percent would also be endowed to create the Avery Fisher Fellowship Program to support the career growth of young American solo musicians. This program would eventually evolve to support small chamber ensembles as well and would divide awards between Career Grants to emerging artists and the Avery Fisher Prize awarded to an established performer for exceptional achievements.

At the time of the announcement, Fisher referred to the financial success he had realized through the sale of high-fidelity equipment by saying, "I owe it all to live music and live musicians. They made everything possible for me." Fisher also defended the acoustics of his newly named hall: "Many of the [negative] comments about the hall made today are unjustified. . . . Much of the chit-chat is like the stories about UFOs—mass hysteria, almost. It's like athlete's foot, the way it spreads from toe to toe, from cocktail party to cocktail party, and gets all out of proportion."[20] However, Fisher was well aware of the hall's acoustical deficiencies and had already agreed to join Amyas Ames, Pierre Boulez, and Carlos Moseley to plan for a major hall renovation.

The Fisher gift was the largest single donation from an individual in the history of the Center at the time. Lincoln Center officials explained to him that the hall would require extensive renovations to remedy the acoustical problems. Ames said, "This is where Avery Fisher is such a remarkable man—he faced squarely . . . the fact that it [the hall] was a total lemon."[21] Fisher agreed to use half of the gift, $5 million, to renovate the hall and contributed another $500,000 for the renovation.

The hall's sound issues were identified soon after its opening as Philharmonic Hall in September 1962. At that time, Lincoln Center officials quickly addressed the problems. The distinguished German acoustician Heinrich Keilholz was part of a small group of international acousticians who provided solutions. In the summer of 1964, it was announced that acoustical alterations would be confined to the stage of the hall and that no renovations were planned in the auditorium. Generally, there was positive critical response to the change.

However, by April 1965 Lincoln Center believed that it needed to take additional steps to solve the remaining acoustical problems, which included complaints from orchestra members that they could not hear themselves or other players on stage and that there was little rapport between performers and audience members, with applause sounding strangely muffled. Once again, in August 1965, Keilholz was asked to provide solutions, which included placing sound reflectors on the smooth walls of the auditorium and correcting the sound absorbency of the seats.

The next episode of this acoustical melodrama began in 1968 when there was strong demand from the musicians of the New York

Philharmonic to improve the stage acoustics and correct sound problems in the auditorium. Leonard Bernstein, William Steinberg, and Rudolf Serkin all expressed great concern that the acoustical problem was a serious one. The New York Philharmonic and Lincoln Center came together to address it: the Philharmonic pledged to supply $300,000 and Lincoln Center added $178,000 toward paying for a renovation, which was estimated to cost approximately $900,000. The renovations were slated to take place during the summer of 1969, with the acoustical "clouds" above the stage disappearing and further work being done on the acoustics of the stage and the auditorium. Harrison & Abramovitz would return to the hall as the architects overseeing the project, and Keilholz once again oversaw the acoustics.

As scheduled, the New York Philharmonic opened its 1969–70 season in a renovated hall on September 24, 1969. The response from critics was generally positive. The *New York Times*'s Harold C. Schonberg, a severe and constant critic of the hall's earlier acoustics, stated that the hall "has a new look, a new sound, and there was a feeling of success in the air. Philharmonic Hall from now on is going to be a happy auditorium."[22] Schonberg reinforced his glee in an October review that brought up the recent World Series win by the New York Mets: "The Philharmonic and Keilholz have pulled off the greatest miracle since the birth of Tom Seaver. Listening to music in the Philharmonic Hall is no longer an ordeal. It is now a pleasure, a real pleasure."[23]

Unfortunately, the enthusiasm surrounding the hall's renovation dissipated quickly, and Philharmonic musicians once again complained about not hearing each other clearly on stage. Pierre Boulez, in 1976, was highly negative about the acoustics, commenting before the beginning of the next renovation, "I am happy to see this hall disappear."[24]

Adding to the persistent tensions caused by the hall's acoustical problems was consternation regarding a strike by the New York Philharmonic musicians that began on September 20, 1973. The orchestra members demanded higher wages and improved pension and health insurance benefits, but the negotiations were complicated considerably by the recently completed labor negotiations with the Chicago Symphony Orchestra, which had made that ensemble the highest paid in the world. The New York players wanted at least parity with Chicago. In addition, the highly respected Carlos Moseley suffered a heart attack on September 17 and could not participate in negotiations, a circumstance that hampered further discussions without his goodwill and experience.

The strike impacted the Fisher gift because the orchestra committee complained, in the words of orchestra violist Ralph Mendelson, that "it seems strange to us that the money [the Fisher gift] went to the landlord, Lincoln Center, and not to the Philharmonic."[25] The New York musicians also complained that the strike was caused, in part, by the fact that Amyas Ames was chair of both the New York Philharmonic and Lincoln Center, thus creating a conflict of interest. The ten-week strike was settled in late November 1973, and the first post-strike concert took place on December 6, 1973, conducted by Georg Semkow. Boulez returned to conduct on December 13. The controversy regarding the Fisher gift slowly faded, but Fisher was not pleased to be dragged into a labor dispute after he had just committed $10.5 million in the hopes of assisting both the orchestra and the Center.

As the strike ended, Ames could focus on the ensuing hall renovation. He felt strongly that an entirely new architectural and acoustical team had to be assembled beginning in the summer of 1976. He approached the well-known acoustician Cyril Harris, who had already realized significant success at the Center with his acoustical design of the Metropolitan Opera House. Harris was not enthusiastic about the offer and even interrupted Ames's invitation mid-sentence to say, "Look, don't go any further. I won't do it. . . . I am very proud of my profession. That [the hall renovation] is a hopeless situation. . . . I'm not going to touch it."[26] Ames persisted, and Harris agreed to at least review the existing hall's plans.

The following day Harris contacted Ames and said, "Look, I've found out something I didn't know. The interior cube of Philharmonic Hall is of such a shape and size [a rectangle] that either the auditorium of Boston Symphony Hall or the hall I built in Minneapolis . . . will fit inside. If you agree to take the hall down to the supporting beams and give me a free hand to go ahead, I'll go."[27]

With Harris on board, Ames invited Philip Johnson, the architect of the New York State Theater, to lead the renovation design,

Philip Johnson (left) *and acoustician Cyril Harris* (right) *present their plan for the renovated Avery Fisher Hall to Avery Fisher, John W. Mazzola, and Amyas Ames, ca. 1975. (Photo provided courtesy of Lincoln Center for the Performing Arts Archives / Susanne Faulker Stevens, Photographer)*

moving on from the original architect of the hall, Max Abramovitz. Ames said that the decision was made for the following reason: "How do you get an architect to tear his own building down?"[28] In addition, Abramovitz had been involved with the unsuccessful 1969 renovation. According to Abramovitz, no one from Lincoln Center advised him of the architect choice: "[They] were not in consultation with me. It was a surprise to me. . . . It behooves an architect to tell the other architect."[29]

The gala opening concert of the renovated hall took place on October 19, 1976, with Boulez conducting the second and fourth movements of Mahler's Symphony no. 9 and excerpts from Stravinsky's *Firebird*, two works which tested the hall's dynamic range, from the hushed pianissimo at the conclusion of the former to the bombastic conclusion of the latter. Amyas Ames was a proud man that evening and extolled the beauty of sound at the end of the Mahler: "Remarkable. I don't believe I have ever heard a pianissimo quite like that anywhere else in the world."[30]

Upon the renovation's completion, "victory" was once more declared. Perfectionist Pierre Boulez wrote in a personal letter to Fisher in October 1976, "It took not only a great deal of generosity but a great deal of courage to take the decision and make this decision possible. You have made the life of the Orchestra much happier and much easier than before. I am very grateful for that, and I wanted to tell you personally."[31]

Gratitude was also expressed by Ranier C. DeIntinis, the secretary of the orchestra committee and a member of the horn section, who, in a handwritten note, said, "Mr. Fisher, on behalf of the members of the Orchestra I want to thank you for all you did and do. . . . We have something we can live with for years and years to come with the gratifying feeling that people who come to listen to our concerts are truly hearing something worthwhile."[32]

The encomiums to Fisher continued, with the acerbic Philip Johnson gushing, "Of all our clients, I know of few patrons. You are number 1 in my book. Thoughtful . . . respectful and decisive; clear in your own orders but flexible in your judgments. Thank you for being our #1 architectural assistant. . . . Anytime you want a job . . . "[33]

Nonetheless, positivity soon returned to negativity regarding the hall's acoustics, as musicians again complained that they were not able to hear each other on stage and audiences noted a lack of perceived bass overall in the hall. As a result, modifications to improve acoustics continued for decades to come.

One experience related to the acoustics of Avery Fisher Hall was the creation of the Rug Concerts, which opened on June 12, 1973, several months before the orchestra strike and the announcement of the Fisher gift. The Rug Concerts idea came from Carlos Mosely and was enthusiastically embraced by Pierre Boulez. The hall had been initially designed to accommodate a temporary flooring that would cover the orchestra seats, thus allowing tables to be placed there for Andre Kostelanetz's Promenade Concerts, which were a type of "pops" series fashioned on the Boston Pops. The summer "pops" series ran until 1976 and was never revived in its original state, since the orchestra seats had become permanent and the temporary flooring was discarded during the 1976 renovation. However, while the temporary flooring still existed, rugs and cushions were placed on the floor for comfortable audience seating during the Rug Concerts. The New York Philharmonic was placed on the main floor with the audience, although there were listeners in the loges and terraces as well.

The audience was described by Donal Henahan of the *New York Times* as "young, alert, enthusiastic, quietly attentive. . . . The music itself could not have been more happily received. . . . Acoustically, the eccentric placement of the orchestra and the addition of rugs and risers for the audience caused no great difficulties. Moving everyone closer to the players may even have improved matters, psychologically, at least. . . . Few concerts that Mr. Boulez has conducted here can have given him so much satisfaction, one would guess."[34] The improved perception of the hall's acoustics was no doubt due to bringing the orchestra closer to the audience and having them play on the temporary floor, which provided a resonant space underneath.

Although the Rug Concerts continued only until the summer of 1977, just after Boulez had stepped down from the Philharmonic directorship to be replaced by Zubin Mehta, the concept of placing the orchestra closer to the audience is one that would be enacted in the third decade of the twenty-first century.

Perhaps the most persistent challenge facing Ames and his team was the need to find a successful path for the Beaumont Theater. By the time Ames took over the Lincoln Center chair in 1970, the Beaumont had already experienced a significant series of crises, namely the departure of the Whitehead-Kazan duo in 1965 and the collapse of Jules Irving's leadership in 1972.

The history of the failure-plagued Beaumont Theater would rival an ancient Greek tragedy in its continuous challenges, which manifested themselves in artistic, logistical, and financial problems. By the time Ames became Lincoln Center chair, Herbert Blau had already resigned in 1967 as codirector of the Beaumont, and Jules Irving stayed on to run the theater by himself. Robert Hoguet was chair of the theater board, but, due to his almost complete ignorance of how a theater worked, he failed to provide the leadership the Beaumont needed.

The Blau-Irving team realized a modicum of success with their earliest New York productions, but each season was accompanied by incessant negative banter from critics concerning the choice of repertoire, the acoustics and sightlines of the theater, the quality of the acting and scenic design, and the view that the Beaumont was not functioning as a true repertory theater, as it lacked a core roster of actors and did not utilize a revolving repertory system in the weekly presentation of plays.

Critics were particularly negative in reviewing the opening-night production of the Blau-Irving regime, on October 20, 1965, of Georg Büchner's play *Danton's Death*, directed by Blau. Walter Kerr wrote, "Lincoln Center has arranged to have opening night and amateur night at the same time. . . . What passed on the stage for passion was noisy hysteria; what offered itself as dramatic color was the garish surface posturing of penny dreadfuls."[35] Richard Gilman wrote, "As I look back [on opening night of *Danton's Death*], I think my feeling of shame and embarrassment was greater that night than it had been at the opening of Kazan's *The Changeling*. . . . So complete was the debacle . . . that I found it impossible to take comfort in the thought that Büchner's play was, after all, extraordinarily difficult to stage well."[36] In addition to this failure, the Beaumont was stalked by the financial challenges involved with running a highly inefficient theatrical physical plant and the lack of a successful fund-raising effort.

Like so many issues facing the Beaumont, the reasons for its problems were convoluted and complex. By early 1971, Ames sent a memo to his executive committee in which he indicated that the Beaumont would most likely be unable to continue operations due to a lack of funds.[37]

Ames concluded his memo by writing that a reorganization of the Beaumont Theater must take place and that the theater space was even being considered for office rentals, an idea that was wisely put aside. His grand plan was one in which Lincoln Center would partner with the City Center of Music and Drama to expand the

City Center Cinematheque activities in unused Beaumont space. The chair of City Center, Richard Clurman, also expressed interest in such an initiative. According to Ames's memo, "Dick Clurman, as a member of the Executive Committee [of Lincoln Center], was asked to study the possibility of converting the Vivian Beaumont to a multi-purpose house, including the transfer of the Cinematheque to the Vivian Beaumont building, and correlating the activities of the Lincoln Center Film and City Center Film."[38] Clurman was on record that he found the Beaumont "an economic monstrosity."[39]

This plan was codified on February 11, 1971, during a meeting of Ames, Mazzola, Clurman; Norman Singer, City Center's executive director; and Robert Brannigan, City Center's director of production, and resulted in the development of various action items that would be overseen by City Center. Included in the strategy was the reconstruction of the Beaumont Theater, for which City Center would assume the cost, with considerable help from the city. City Center would operate the building, and the Repertory Theater and the new film organization would become subtenants of City Center. The Repertory Theater would be guaranteed at least twenty-eight weeks of performances on the main stage and at the Forum Theater.[40] The administration of the Beaumont was also asked to provide a draft of a reorganization plan "in such form that it can be used for presentation to foundations."[41]

Although this plan was seen by some as draconian and highly unorthodox, by August 1971 the New York City Planning Commission adopted an amendment to the 1971–72 capital budget to acquire and remodel the Beaumont. In this agreement, Lincoln Center agreed to sell the Beaumont building, which cost $8.2 million, to the city for one dollar. In turn, the city agreed to provide $5,182,000 to support the remodeling costs. Management of the theater would be assumed by City Center.[42]

As had been expected by informed participants, this strategy generated a "civic tempest," as the *Daily News* labeled it.[43] Jo Mielziner, who shared in the design of the Beaumont with Eero Saarinen and his colleagues, was plainspoken when he said that the redesign of the theater would be "a rape of a beautiful place. . . . I think it is an outrage that a building dedicated to an art form [drama] is to be chopped up to meet the whim and fancy of somebody that feels a film museum is going to be the solution to keeping repertory theater alive."[44]

Clurman responded later in the same newspaper by positively stating that the renovation "will cause the Beaumont to become the busiest most popular theater at Lincoln Center—a people's theater—and thus will further democratize the audiences at America's leading cultural center."[45] One of the problems that Clurman admitted had not yet been resolved was the ongoing issue of relocating the Forum Theater. Irving had considered that venue as the innovative center for the entire Repertory Theater, and its disappearance or transformation was seen as a fatal blow to Irving's plans for his venue.[46]

This elaborate and quixotic plan came to a crashing halt when, at an October 7, 1971, City Council finance committee meeting Jules Irving testified that he opposed the plan, after which Clurman withdrew City Center's offer. At the meeting, theater leaders such as Joseph Papp and the critic Clive Barnes spoke against the City Center plan, but it was Irving's impassioned statement that supplied the initiative's deathblow. According to theater scholar Saraleigh Carney, "He challenged Amyas Ames and Lincoln Center for refusing to support the one organization born directly of the Lincoln Center idea and ideal. He challenged Richard Clurman and City Center for their lack of reasons behind the decision to destroy the Forum and the conversion of the Beaumont building."[47]

Irving let out all the frustrations that had been festering in him for the past seven years:

> We have been strangled by constant penny-pinching since our inception, and I and my staff are sick and tired of it. . . . We were told point-blank to agree to the plan or get out of the Beaumont. . . . There *are* alternatives. Where is—I ask— our civic pride? What a terrifying world we have created that a cultural center supported by the city it serves feels a rationale and a justification in eating the child it gave birth to. . . . There must be a better way to make theater flourish at Lincoln Center. There has to be another way.[48]

On November 24, 1971, Ames notified the Lincoln Center executive committee that "since [we] are all agreed that the plan should not go forward, it is appropriate to notify the City that the [Lincoln Center] offer of the building under the plan is withdrawn."[49] There remained a lingering negotiation between City Center and Lincoln Center as to which entity was responsible for costs incurred in developing the plan, but those issues were quickly resolved.

A few months after the meeting, Clurman recalled:

> An extraordinary thing happened [at the hearing]. . . . Jules stood up . . . and said, "Dick Clurman is a liar; Amyas Ames is a liar; we are solvent, we are not going bankrupt. . . . The whole thing is a lying plan on the part of Lincoln Center and City Center to stamp us out." When he said that to the total bewilderment of the City Council Finance Committee, I stood up and said, "Gentlemen, if they don't need it, I would be inclined to withdraw the plan," which took place on December 1, 1971.[50]

In October 1972, after seven years of fighting with critics, Lincoln Center officials, and financial naysayers of all stripes, Jules Irving resigned as the Beaumont's artistic director, citing insufficient funds to support an upcoming season at the Forum Theater. Clarke Coggeshall, the Beaumont board's president, expressed disappointment with the Irving decision; although several board members attempted to dissuade him, Irving stuck to his resignation. Many board members found a level of irony in the fact that the theater was at the start of what promised to be one of its more interesting seasons, with an upcoming production of Maxim Gorky's *Enemies* directed by Ellis Raab and a Samuel Beckett Festival featuring Hume Cronin and Jessica Tandy, including the world premiere of Beckett's *Not I.*

Ames openly admitted that he had no great interest or expertise regarding matters of the theater, but he also understood that he could not allow the Beaumont Theater building to remain empty— not only for the significant negative financial results of such a closure for both the theater and the Center, but also because another setback for the Beaumont would be seen as a failure for Lincoln Center overall. Even though Ames felt that as chair he should not interfere in the internal matters of a constituent, he decided to act aggressively and recruit a person, in his opinion, who could lead the Beaumont with vision and energy. That person was Joseph Papp.

CHAPTER SEVEN

The Cursed Inheritance

THE APPOINTMENT OF JOSEPH PAPP as the Beaumont's artistic director was not an unexpected decision for either Lincoln Center or the Repertory Theater. Papp had expressed interest during the Center's earliest years in running the Beaumont, and his aggressive, abrasive, but successful leadership style made him a highly visible member of the American theater community in the early 1970s.

Joseph Papp was born Joseph Papirofsky in 1921 in Brooklyn. His mother was from Lithuania and his father from Poland. Papp founded the New York Shakespeare Festival in 1954 and three years later was given access to Central Park to present free productions of Shakespeare plays. In 1967, he created the Public Theater, located in the old Astor Library on Lafayette Street in the East Village, where he frequently produced new plays. His most prominent successes, which all transferred from the Public to Broadway, included *Hair*, *The Pirates of Penzance*, *For Colored Girls Who Have Considered Suicide / When the Rainbow Is Enuf*, and the mega-hit *A Chorus Line*, featuring music by Marvin Hamlisch and directed by Michael Bennett. Papp kept the producing rights to *A Chorus Line*, which turned it into a cash cow that helped fund his future productions.

After discussing the idea of approaching Papp with the Lincoln Center's executive committee and the Beaumont board, Mazzola and Ames met with him "and challenged him a little bit with what

Joseph Papp (left) *speaks with Amyas Ames and donor Mitzi E. Newhouse at a news conference in New York, May 30, 1973. (AP Photo/Ron Frehm)*

he could accomplish for theater by coming to Lincoln Center. He bought it and came."[1] Before accepting, however, Papp asked to meet with Lincoln Center's executive committee, theoretically to be assured that he had a free hand to do what he believed was necessary to achieve success. Ames knew that Papp considered most of the members of the committee to be quite "stuffy," and therefore to tweak the committee he said that his first play would be one "in which nobody had any clothes on at all. . . . There was sort of an appalled silence, and I [Ames] broke in with, 'Joe, as a matter of interest, would that be a short play?' He [then] said, 'Yes that's a short play.' I said 'Well, what would you put on with it?' . . . And before we got through, we got Joe talking about all his other ideas. I think he was baiting. He had expected an explosion."[2]

Such an expectation was warranted because Papp had earlier publicly berated the handling of the Beaumont Theater and said that if he were offered the post as the theater's artistic director "I would tell the board to resign."[3] The idea that Papp would come "uptown" to the Beaumont did not sit well with his board or his colleagues at the New York Shakespeare Festival, who were antagonistic toward the entire venture and felt that he was deserting his urban, downtown roots for the "elitism" of Lincoln Center.[4]

In a long, revealing letter to Shakespeare Theater vice president LuEsther Mertz, Papp expressed great optimism that he could succeed in leading the Beaumont and overseeing the Public Theater, writing that a constant criticism of his leadership came in the form of the questions "Are we biting off more than we can chew? Are we spreading ourselves too thin?"[5] Papp saw the move to Lincoln Center as consolidating the gains of the Shakespeare Theater "to grow and mature as a theater . . . located in the city where theater, as it has existed in the past, is in the throes of profound change."[6]

According to Robert Marx, president of the Fan Fox and Leslie R. Samuels Foundation, instead of moving uptown into the Beaumont the New York Shakespeare Festival continued to be administered out of the Public Theater offices downtown. "It was just an added venue for Papp. . . . Joe was deeply uncomfortable at Lincoln Center. I remember him telling me how embarrassed he was by Lincoln Center's unwelcoming back wall of travertine that faced Amsterdam Avenue and the [housing] projects. For him THAT was the symbol of Lincoln Center, not the eastward-facing open plaza," Marx recalled.[7]

Bernard Gersten, Papp's lieutenant, reinforced the point regarding Papp's discomfort; according to him, Papp viewed Lincoln Center as "the establishment. The bourgeoisie. The high bourgeoisie. . . . I don't think Joe ever felt comfortable at the center. . . . Joe struggled over a three-year period to conquer Lincoln Center. . . . And ultimately, he returned to where he was more comfortable, more in command."[8]

In retrospect, it seems clear that one of Papp's goals in taking on the Beaumont was to support his work at the Public Theater. Mel Gussow of the *New York Times* wrote that Papp "saw it as the best way to save his Public Theater from bankruptcy. Lincoln Center would give him [an establishment position] from which he could raise large sums of money."[9]

On May 21, 1973, the New York Shakespeare Festival became a Lincoln Center constituent, and the festival board replaced the

Repertory Theater board. Repertory Theater of Lincoln Center ceased to exist as an administrative and artistic entity. An annual authorized deficit level for the new theater administration was raised from $750,000 to $1.5 million.

In a series of sarcastic, playful, yet revealing comments at the press conference announcing his appointment, Papp stated that he was coming to Lincoln Center "for personal aggrandizement and to establish a cultural power base here in New York so as to take over the rest of the repertory theaters in the country, and to create a liaison with China and Russia."[10] Papp had often spoken of the development of a national theater, an idea that had been bandied about for close to a century. In typically dyspeptic fashion, Robert Brustein, the omnipresent naysayer regarding all things Beaumont, wrote, "When the Lincoln Center management was inevitably offered to Papp, it was perhaps inevitable that he would accept it, in magnificent hubristic defiance of the cursed inheritance which, like some merciless phantom, grips the throats of all who would embrace it."[11]

Papp, intent to squeeze as much money as he could from his Lincoln Center board—which had been supplemented by members outside the Shakespeare Festival community—was as aggressive in this area as he was in running his theater. He did enjoy remarkable success with Mitzi E. Newhouse, who donated $1 million so that her name could grace the Forum Theater, the problematic venue that was to be moved and transformed under the failed City Center plan.

Papp's first season, in 1973–74, was a mixed bag generating mostly negative reviews. The biggest hit was Miguel Pinero's play *Short Eyes*, although David Rabe's *In the Boom Boom Room* starring Madeline Kahn and Charles Durning and August Strindberg's *Dance of Death* each garnered some critical success. Three Shakespeare plays were also produced in the Newhouse: *The Tempest*, *Troilus and Cressida*, and *Macbeth*, once again to mixed reviews. Subscriptions dropped from "27,000 in the first season, to 22,000 in the second and Papp saw the possibility that for the third season the figure might go to as low as 10,000."[12]

By 1976–77 the Papp regime was unraveling. The burden of running the Public Theater, Shakespeare in the Park (at the Delacorte Theater in Central Park), and the Vivian Beaumont Theater promised to exhaust the finances of Papp's artistic empire. As John Mazzola reported to the Lincoln Center board on July 13, 1977:

> In essence, using all his available funds—including all of the profits it generated by three companies of *Chorus Line*—the total activities of the three locations had a two-year life expectancy. However, if the New York Shakespeare Festival withdrew from the Beaumont and made some adjustment in the financing of the Delacorte Theater . . . there would be available funding for at least five years of continued operations in the Public Theater and Central Park. . . . Mr. Papp's primary responsibility was to the continued life of the New York Shakespeare Festival.[13]

In a news release from the Public Theater announcing its withdrawal from Lincoln Center, Papp tried to defend his tenure artistically and to present the inevitability of the financial failure of his time at the Beaumont. He argued that his productions "had played to an average of 80% to 90% of capacity [and] that three of the new plays presented had been honored by the Drama Critics as 'Best American Play' (*Short Eyes* by Miguel Pinero, 1974; *The Taking of Miss Janie* by Ed Bullins, 1975; and *Streamers* by David Rabe, 1976)."[14]

Robert Marx remembered that "for the first time, the whole building seemed alive with top-rank work—even visionary work—and sold-out performances. And then, as soon as Joe proved that the Beaumont could be a viable, exciting theater, he quit. The problem wasn't just financial. . . . He truly hated being there. So, he declared victory, and got out—to wild consternation and shock, because after 1976–77, nearly everyone expected more seasons just like it."[15]

The final straw that caused Papp's departure from the Beaumont was, in fact, the financial exigencies of running the two theaters at Lincoln Center. Papp said, "Financially . . . supporting the Beaumont operation is impossible. . . . In our four years at Lincoln Center, we incurred a total deficit of $3,655,000. Next year . . . we will incur a deficit of $2 million. While a *Chorus Line* might possibly be able to cover this for a year, what would we do thereafter?"[16]

A statement by Ames on the Shakespeare Festival's departure cast blame not on Papp but rather on the lack of support for the arts in America: "It [Papp's departure] is one more example why there is a national need for an American way of support for the arts."[17] Soon thereafter, Ames held a confidential meeting with the Beaumont's bête noire, Robert Brustein, visiting him at his home on Martha's Vineyard just two months after Papp's departure from Lincoln Center (in fact, Ames and his wife, Evvie, were old friends of the Brusteins).[18]

While meeting with Ames, Brustein softened his stance on the Beaumont. He admitted that while he had been a severe critic of its acoustics and design, its existence was a boon to theaters throughout America.[19] Ames concluded his notes from the chat by writing, "He [Brustein] is obviously very keenly intellectually interested in our problems and their solution but has given me no indication of any personal interest."[20] Ames seemed inclined to consider Brustein taking over the leadership of the Beaumont, but that would not come to pass.

The Lincoln Center board addressed the problem of the leaderless Beaumont with great speed, and in the summer of 1977 John Mazzola presented some alternative strategies to keep the building operational. These approaches included subleasing the theater to an outside operator—either profit or nonprofit, straight booking of the venue, and use by an existing or new institution. However, it was quite clear that keeping the Beaumont "dark" would "throw a further central service (HVAC, garage, security, etc.) burden on the constituents."[21] Regrettably, the problems of the Lincoln Center Theater would not be resolved during the tenures of either Amyas Ames or John Mazzola.

Although the earlier City Center initiative involving the Beaumont could only be categorized as a debacle, difficulties between Lincoln Center and City Center leadership had calmed considerably since that effort was abandoned due to, in Ames's colorful language, "A big red woman who is Beverly Sills.... She was dominant at City Center.... That great hulk of a woman, who comes across on television and on the stage ... so marvelously, is as smart as a whip.... We had a smooth working relationship."[22]

It is unlikely that Beverly Sills would have approved of the term "big red woman," but Ames was correct in characterizing the out-sized power that Sills had over the New York City Opera during her years as the company's reigning diva. In fact, it was clear that the City Opera's subscription base was supported by Sills's appearances through the simple strategy of including a Sills performance within a subscription, thereby guaranteeing that ticket buyers would pur-chase the entire package in order to be guaranteed access to a single appearance by the charismatic diva.

Sills had made her City Opera debut in 1955, but her break-through moment came on September 27, 1966, with her legendary performance as Cleopatra in George Frideric Handel's opera *Giulio Cesare*. The opera was conducted by Julius Rudel, directed by Tito Capobianco (a favorite of Sills's), designed by Ming Cho Lee, and featured bass-baritone Norman Treigle as Caesar. Sills herself said that her second act aria was "the single most extraordinary piece of singing I ever did."[23] Sills was so intent on taking on the Cleo-patra role, which had originally been promised to Phyllis Curtin, a long-standing and respected member of the City Opera company, that she threatened to perform *Giulio Cesare* at Carnegie Hall at the same time as the City Opera production. Rudel agreed to the cast-ing change, and Curtin never forgave him, Sills, or the company for this egregious decision.

Rudel, as City Opera's principal conductor and general director, adroitly presented *Giulio Cesare* around the same time as the Metro-politan Opera's grand opening on September 16, 1966, of Barber's *Antony and Cleopatra*, which garnered mostly negative reviews. The Handel production was the New York stage premier of the work, and its enthusiastic critical response made the Met look enviously at its neighbor at the State Theater.

By 1969 Sills was a household name, thanks to an appearance on the cover of *Newsweek* and a guest spot on the *Tonight Show Star-ring Johnny Carson*. She was seen as "'The People's Diva' for 'The People's Opera'—it was a perfect pairing."[24] In early 1979 Sills ended her performance career, followed by her decision in July to take over the City Opera as the institution's general director. She would func-tion in that role during the 1980s as a prodigious fundraiser and an effective administrator for the financially struggling opera company,

Beverly Sills in a New York City Opera production of Handel's
Giulio Cesare, *1968. (Photo copyright © Beth Bergman)*

and in the years ahead she would occupy other major Lincoln Center leadership positions.

As the 1970s came to an end, Lincoln Center's financial condition had not improved since earlier in the decade, exacerbated by a stagnant economy and a problematic inflation rate. Ames and his board continued to weather a series of financial storms which endangered the arts center's existence. Collectively, the Center's constituents operated at a net deficit of $3.7 million in fiscal year 1973, and the following year's deficit was expected to balloon to $6.9 million. The Center's perilous position was blamed on increasing costs and spiraling inflation. The Yom Kippur War also triggered a 48 percent drop in the stock market in 1973, affecting endowments all over the world and triggering an international oil crisis.

Although revenue invested in the Center's endowment fund from the Fisher gift helped the bottom line for Lincoln Center, it did not have a direct positive impact on the individual constituents' finances. In fiscal year 1973, the Metropolitan Opera operated at a $2.8 million deficit, while Juilliard's deficit was $1.5 million. In fact, all the other constituents' budgets ran at a deficit—in lower amounts, but still significant in proportion to the annual budget of each organization.[25] As a result of such dreary financial results, Ames proposed in 1973 the creation of a campus-wide drive called "The Fund for the Living Arts at Lincoln Center" with a goal of $57 million, but constituent infighting scuttled the effort.[26]

During this period, Ames encountered considerable problems with the constituent that enjoyed the largest budget, the Metropolitan Opera. It seems that the Met, led by its chair William Rockefeller, a great-grandnephew of John D. Rockefeller, Sr., had pressured Lincoln Center to discontinue all fundraising except the joint corporate fund, based on the reasoning that "Lincoln Center cuts into the Opera's fund-raising ability as an individual institution . . . [and due to] the Opera's deficit situation [which] is so drastic that the Opera is disposed to take any action . . . [the Opera asked Lincoln Center to step away from fundraising] to improve its individual solicitation."[27] Ames had realistic concerns that the Met might need to close if its financial state did not significantly improve.[28]

Ames wrote to William Rockefeller in 1976 to challenge the Met's skeptical position on the usefulness of Lincoln Center's activities regarding the constituents: "It is clear that more money has been raised because of the multiple approach on all fronts to the subject of fundraising."[29] Martin E. Segal would address the same problem with Rockefeller a few years later.

By 1977, Ames reported to the Lincoln Center board that the Center's financial problems had not improved and were, in fact, getting worse. He wrote that funds had not been adequately raised and "the depletion of working capital is serious—at one time this year, we were forced to borrow $400,000 to cover current operations—[and] . . . any further reduction of unrestricted endowment funds, now at the $7 million level, will be detrimental to the operations of Lincoln Center, Inc."[30] Ames and his colleagues were now facing a funding environment entirely different from the organization's halcyon days, which would present a challenge to the Center and its constituents well into the next decade.

Although Lincoln Center faced difficult financial challenges, to the credit of Ames and his fellow board members, there was strong support to create new entities which would address the community's needs and produce artistic events of high quality. On August 20, 1974, the Community/Street Theater Festival, which had functioned since 1971, morphed into Lincoln Center Out of Doors, initially a two-week summer festival led by Leonard de Paur. Many of the presentations took place on Lincoln Center Plaza or at Damrosch Park and featured an eclectic mix of performances, ranging from Ballet Hispanico to string quartet concerts.[31] All performances were free and open to the public during the summer months.

The *Live from Lincoln Center* series on PBS was launched on January 30, 1976, with a live performance featuring the New York Philharmonic conducted by André Previn, featuring Van Cliburn as soloist in the Grieg Piano Concerto. Other broadcasts followed, notably the New York City Opera's performance of Douglas Moore's opera *The Ballad of Baby Doe* on April 21 and the American Ballet Theater's performance of Tchaikovsky's *Swan Lake* on June 30. John Goberman served as executive producer of the series from its beginning to 2011.

The series broke through the rating ceiling on February 12, 1978, when Luciano Pavarotti performed a solo recital at the Metropolitan Opera House, ending the evening with a final encore of his signature aria from Giacomo Puccini's *Turandot*, "Nessun dorma," drawing uproarious applause from the audience and distant cheers from television viewers all over the world. *Live from Lincoln Center* made Lincoln Center known to arts aficionados all over the country and established it as a national artistic force.

In 1972 Sir Rudolf Bing, one of the artistic founders of Lincoln Center who began his long tenure as general manager of the Metropolitan Opera in 1950, stepped down from his position. Bing was a product of pre–World War II Vienna, and his traditional artistic values and keen intellect made the Met the world's most prominent opera company during his time with the company. He also had a significant impact on the arts in Great Britain, where he helped found both the Glyndebourne and Edinburgh festivals.

Bing had a sharp tongue and a quick wit. Although his humor did not surface during his contretemps with William Schuman in the mid-1960s, in one self-deprecating comment he said, "Don't be misled. Behind that cold, austere, severe exterior, there beats a heart of stone."[32] Perhaps his most famous barb concerned the conductor George Szell, with whom he had difficult relations over the years. When told by a colleague that Szell was his own worst enemy, Bing's cutting response was "Not while I'm alive."[33] He died in a nursing home in the Riverdale section of the Bronx at age ninety-five. His stern leadership style and quest for excellence at the Met helped shape the early values and ethos of Lincoln Center.

His intended successor, the Swedish intendant Göran Gentele, was tragically killed in a car crash in the summer of 1972. A former Lincoln Center official, Schuyler Chapin, took on the general manager's position and served from 1972 to 1975. Anthony Bliss, an attorney and Met board member, soon thereafter assumed leadership of the company.

Perhaps the most complex venture focusing on community outreach was the creation of an educational organization overseen by Lincoln Center which would address K–12 arts education, in juxtaposition to the professional performing arts education program provided by The Juilliard School. Through the leadership of Mark Schubart—who was Lincoln Center's director of education and formerly the dean of the Juilliard School of Music during William Schuman's Juilliard presidency—Lincoln Center enlarged its educational program and, through a grant from the Carnegie Corporation, completed a study that pointed to the creation of a new type of arts institution, "one dedicated solely to meeting the needs in the arts of schoolteachers, leaders of community agencies, artists interested in working with young people and young people themselves."[34]

Inaugurated on May 20, 1974, this new entity, the Lincoln Center Institute, set out to "prepare students—not only those majoring in the arts—to make critical choices, realize their own abilities in making esthetic judgments and to relate these abilities to other judgments."[35] The Institute would also serve as the umbrella organization for all of Lincoln Center, Inc.'s educational programs. Francis Keppel, former dean of the Harvard Graduate School of Education and U.S. commissioner of education, would serve as the Institute's chair, and Mark Schubart would be its director. The plan flourished and eventually involved schoolchildren throughout the tristate area and as far away as Australia. The Lincoln Center Institute would be one of the most successful and long-lasting programs developed during Ames's time as chair.

The 1970s was the first time that the artistic activities of all the constituents could be evaluated outside of the tumultuous work to complete the complex construction projects during the Center's earlier years. Lincoln Center–produced events included Joan Sutherland and Luciano Pavarotti singing together at Avery Fisher Hall in a historic performance and live telecast and Vladimir Horowitz's first solo recital at Fisher Hall after his many years of exclusivity at Carnegie Hall. In addition, the individual constituents were now producing new events which garnered popular and critical success.

The innovative and audacious creativity of Balanchine's New York City Ballet Stravinsky Festival of 1972 stands as a stellar example of constituent excellence in programming and is worth further mention. Igor Stravinsky had died a year earlier, and the artistic relationship between him and George Balanchine was deeply significant for the dance world.

Balanchine insisted that the works he wished to present for the festival be compressed into one week. As Kirstein saw the festival, it was Balanchine's vision to "display a panoply of Stravinsky representative scores, some without staging; from first to last recognizing his entire range in one compact, monumental week. . . . Balanchine insisted on the imploded fusion of one big bang. The point of a feast was to gorge, not nibble . . . a state banquet in a State Theater."[36] The festival would run in the New York State Theater from June 18

George Balanchine (center) *and Jerome Robbins* (to his left)
with New York City Ballet dancers in a rehearsal of Pulcinella
for the Stravinsky Festival of 1972. (Photo by Martha Swope
© *The New York Public Library for the Performing Arts)*

to June 25, 1972, and involve thirty-five Stravinsky scores and thirty-one ballets, twenty-one of which were premieres.[37]

The June 18 opening night featured two Stravinsky works never intended to be choreographed: the Violin Concerto, featuring Joseph Silverstein, concertmaster of the Boston Symphony Orchestra, as soloist; and the Symphony in Three Movements. The festival was a sensation, so much so that the *New York Times* covered the concerts as a news event on its front page. The festival finished with the Symphony of Psalms of 1930 for chorus and orchestra, but with an innovative twist. According to Kirstein, "It was not danced; our dancers, staff, ballet masters sat to listen on the stage floor encircling the orchestra, now set within the proscenium. Above them Rouben Ter-Arutunian [the scenic designer] had hung a glowing suggestion of silver and ivory organ pipes. . . . With the still resident final DOM-I-NUM vibrating in the ears and heart, every looker-and-listener was handed a slug of vodka to speed him on his way."[38] Such brilliant artistry and creativity shed a bright light on a proud Lincoln Center constituent, leaving one observer only able to utter "Amen."

Amyas Ames, looking back at the decade with satisfaction, said, "No other center in the world has the constituent strength of Lincoln Center. And the independence of the constituents is the wisest thing in the structure of Lincoln Center. It's their show."[39]

As the decade ended, the Lincoln Center community and the nation were shocked by the sudden death of John D. Rockefeller 3rd, who was killed in a head-on automobile crash on July 10, 1978, near the Rockefeller estate in Westchester County, north of New York City. Police reported that the sixteen-year-old driver of the car that struck the Rockefeller car also died in the accident. A secretary to JDR 3rd was driving the car and survived. Rockefeller was seventy-two years old.

Lincoln Center community members were deeply saddened by the founder's tragic death. A memorial service was held at the Riverside Church on July 13. In keeping with the dignity of the deceased, the ceremony was a simple one, punctuated by the music of J. S. Bach and Johannes Brahms, traditional hymns, and an arrangement of the Lord's Prayer sung by Leontyne Price. Speakers included his son John D. Rockefeller IV, governor of West Virginia at the time; JDR 3rd's nephew Steven C. Rockefeller; Dr. Sherman E. Lee, director of the Cleveland Museum of Art; and the church's senior minister, William Sloane Coffin.

Governor Rockefeller summed up his view of his father by saying, "He was a gentle person—dignified, modest, some said shy— but yet a man of bedrock strength and perseverance. He spent his entire life in service to others—to his community, to his country, and to the world. But he never thought of himself as a 'do-gooder.' He was not self-indulgent. He was not self-satisfied. He was serious, purposeful, idealistic, realistic, totally dedicated.... You have blessed and touched this world in good ways that will last forever."[40]

According to his will, JDR 3rd left $3 million to Lincoln Center, which was placed in the Lincoln Center Endowment Fund. Ames wrote to Rockefeller's executors, J. Richardson Dilworth and Donal C. O'Brien, Jr., that a special plaque would be created for donors to this endowment fund and that "it will be with great pride that we will start the list of these donors with the name John D. Rockefeller 3rd."[41]

JDR 3rd's death closed a chapter in the Center's history. Leaders of Lincoln Center looked to the future with a realistic perspective that the heady days of the arts center's founding, with its attendant belief in the transformative power of the arts, had passed, with little sense of how the arts would be supported in America in the years to come.

CHAPTER EIGHT
It's Called Accountability

W ITH THE CLOSE OF THE 1970s, a certain segment of the American population wanted to return to a sense of societal calm or "normalcy." The past decade had seen the tumult of the Vietnam years, the governmental instability caused by President Nixon's resignation, the interregnum of Gerald Ford, and the tentative presidency of Jimmy Carter. The government of New York City, an important source of financial and political support for Lincoln Center, also saw hard times, best captured in the famous *Daily News* headline of October 30, 1975, concerning a potential federal bailout of New York: "Ford to City: Drop Dead." Fortunately, New York City and its economy rebounded.

Beginning in the early 1980s, Lincoln Center benefited from a robust fundraising environment, though a severe recession in 1982 caused discretionary contributions to slow for a short period. Perhaps most important, the work of the Lincoln Center constituents developed with a new artistic spirit that allowed them to put down roots on the Lincoln Center campus.

In March 1981, during this period of comparative optimism and growth, Martin E. Segal (known to all as Marty) was unanimously elected by the board of Lincoln Center as its new chair, and he began serving in June. He succeeded Amyas Ames, who continued to serve as chair of the New York Philharmonic. John W. Mazzola remained as Lincoln Center's president. Segal was publicly presented as Ames's choice to succeed him, although Mazzola contended that Ames's first choice was Norma Hess. "She's smart as hell. She was a woman . . . tons of money, great leadership," according to Mazzola.[1] However, Norma's husband, Leon Hess, the head of Hess Oil Company, shunned the spotlight and did not want his wife to be the focus of public attention. Therefore, she never pursued the position.

Ames had worked with Segal at the Center when Segal was vice chair of the Lincoln Center board and chair of the Lincoln Center Fund, which had succeeded in providing vital endowment and operating support for the Center's artistic activities. Segal oversaw the donations of an additional $20 million to the Lincoln Center endowment, which brought the fund's total to $32 million in 1981. Segal was also one of the founders of the Film Society of Lincoln Center.

The patrician lineage manifested in the lives of both Rockefeller and Ames differed significantly from Segal's heritage. As one board member commented on Segal's personal energy and manner at the time of his election as chair, "It's going to be a *different* chairmanship, no doubt about it."[2] Martin E. Segal was born in Vitebsk, Russia (now Belarus), in 1916 and left Russia for Poland with his parents in 1918 to escape the Russian Revolution, moving to Belgium and then, in 1921, to the United States. Segal was fond of telling the story of his arrival in America, which revealed a good deal about his imagination and self-deprecating humor. He would often reminisce and say, "I will never forget looking from the deck of the boat and seeing the Statue of Liberty," at which point his father, if within earshot, would interrupt him and say, "Marty, we entered America through the port of Boston."[3]

Segal was the quintessential self-made man: he started his first full-time job when he was eleven and later dropped out of Brooklyn's Erasmus Hall High School in 1931 to run away on a far-flung journey that took him as far north as Canada and south as Florida, hitchhiking all the way. He returned to Brooklyn after his extended odyssey to begin another full-time job at the age of sixteen for the Manhattan Life Insurance Company. Eventually he would start his own business in 1939, the Segal Company, providing consulting and actuarial services in the employee benefits field. He sold the business to Wertheim & Company in 1968 but remained on its board, all of which netted him a handsome financial return. Segal would always arrive at Lincoln Center perfectly attired, with his trademark red tea rose placed in his jacket lapel.

It was reported at the time of the press announcement that neither Ames, Segal, nor Mazzola envisioned any "alteration of Mr. Ames's basic policies or diminution of Mr. Mazzola's role as president."[4] That soon proved inaccurate. Segal hoped that his new position would allow him to create a New York "International Festival of the Arts," a project he had been developing during his time as chair of the Mayor's Committee on Cultural Policy and as chair of the Commission for Cultural Affairs, a position he held from 1975 to 1977. He would have to wait until the end of his Lincoln Center tenure to create the festival he had envisioned.

Segal also noted that he would try to develop greater support for the arts through the Reagan administration. He argued that the arts brought great financial benefit to New York City, which he reinforced by often saying, "You don't go to New York City to ski."[5]

Segal's leadership and negotiating style was often manifested in Manichean terms, unlike the more nuanced and congenial style of Ames. Although Segal was too sophisticated to use the term "take it or leave it," that was often the circumstance faced by a Segal opponent.

Even during his time as chair of the Lincoln Center fund drive he exhibited a steely approach to negotiations, as seen in an incident involving William Rockefeller, then chair of the Metropolitan Opera. Rockefeller told Segal, as he had told Ames regarding fundraising in general by Lincoln Center, that the Met no longer wished to participate in the Lincoln Center Corporate Fund. The response to the Met's proposed departure was the classic Segal approach to such a challenge. "Fine," Segal said. "But you know, we don't have a swinging door. If you leave, you can't come back for a minimum of five years," a regulation Segal created specifically in response to the Met's decision.[6] Segal continued, "Well, you don't think we're just going to sit by and let people experiment as to what is best for them for the moment, regardless of what's best for everybody else. . . . So, you're free to leave, we wish you well. . . . But you can't come back for a minimum of five years."[7] Rockefeller called back the next day and said, "Well, in the interest of congeniality . . ."; Segal cut him off and said, "Whatever your reasons are, Bill, I am glad you decided to stay. It makes sense."[8]

Segal used the same approach with his president, John W. Mazzola, a seasoned Lincoln Center leader who assumed the presidency in 1977. Mazzola had an ebullient personality and a deep knowledge of the Lincoln Center community. He once quipped that his job was "to be responsible for everything that goes wrong."[9] Regrettably, something went exceedingly wrong for him in 1982 when an internal audit showed that he had used Lincoln Center credit cards to charge $18,000 for personal expenses. Those purchases were not paid back until after the audit became known to the Lincoln Center board. Mazzola announced his resignation on August 31, 1982, and indicated that he would leave the presidency at the end of the year. Mazzola said after his resignation that the charges were "errors in judgment."[10] Although Mazzola's actions were wrong, there were members of the Lincoln Center board who felt that his behavior did not warrant his forced resignation in light of his many years of dedicated service. The entire Lincoln Center staff was quite public in their disappointment over his resignation.

Mazzola's departure was a bitter experience for him, which he described later as "extremely painful."[11] When his financial indiscretion was made known to the Lincoln Center board, it was Segal who pushed to have him removed. Mazzola said many years later that "all these terrible stories came out, which were all controlled by one person, Martin Segal. . . . Should I sue him? . . . The only trouble [suing him] is you're just spreading the story further."[12]

With Mazzola's resignation, Segal had a clear field to choose the next Lincoln Center president, but, in a rare act of acquiescence, he allowed the board's executive committee to find Mazzola's replacement, remarking that "the board was very concerned that, here I had come in as chairman and suddenly I was without a president. . . . So, a selection committee, whom I think would prefer not to be part of history, picked [Glenn] Ferguson, when they sort of felt I needed help."[13] Peter Paine, Juilliard's chair, headed the search committee.

The appointment of Glenn W. Ferguson as the fifth Lincoln Center president took place on February 7, 1983, five months after the Mazzola resignation. Ferguson brought to the Center a wide array of high-level employment experiences, including serving as chancellor of Long Island University; president of Clark University, the University of Connecticut, and the American University of Paris; chief executive officer of Radio Free Europe/Radio Liberty; and U.S. ambassador to Kenya. He was described as a "low-keyed, pleasant man who got along with people."[14]

Segal, never comfortable with Ferguson, commented that he was concerned Ferguson "had an awful lot of jobs in a short time . . . [and] he was busy going to see individual board members . . . telling them about all the changes he wanted to make—none of which I knew anything about—and under the by-laws, the chairman is the CEO. So, he didn't last very long."[15] In fact, Ferguson announced his resignation on December 1, 1983, just a few days short of ten months after he became president. He provided a convoluted reason for his quick departure: "I feel I should pursue the career objectives with which I was associated before coming to the center. . . . [I] found performing arts a very challenging field [but he added] that there was nothing negative at all [about his position at Lincoln Center]."[16]

Although both Segal and Ferguson stated that there had never been any personality clashes between the two of them, Segal was not pleased with Ferguson's autonomy as president. He was anxious to appoint a new president who would understand the relationship Segal wished to have with those who reported to him—that is, Martin E. Segal was in charge and others would defer to his wishes.

It therefore seems curious that Segal chose as the next president Nathan Leventhal, who had a long and successful track record in New York City government and had cut his teeth in the rough-and-tumble environment of City Hall. Leventhal grew up in Forest Hills, Queens, graduated from Queens College, and went on to earn a law degree from Columbia University, where he was editor of the *Law Review*. He was soon working in city government and held a series of important positions, eventually at the commissioner's level, and served as chief of staff to Mayor John V. Lindsay, as deputy mayor to Mayor Edward Koch, and as Mayor David Dinkins's mayoral transition committee chair.

Segal and Leventhal had known each other professionally for years, and Segal often gave career advice to his young friend. Soon after Mazzola left the Center's presidency, Segal asked Leventhal over lunch if he would be interested in being considered for the Lincoln Center presidency. At the time, Leventhal was Koch's deputy mayor and wasn't entirely ready to leave City Hall. Leventhal remembered, "I sort of hemmed and hawed and played it cozy."[17]

Much to Leventhal's chagrin, the next thing he knew he was reading the *Times* announcement of Glenn Ferguson's appointment as the new president of Lincoln Center. Leventhal was furious with himself and said, "That's it. I blew it. This guy [Ferguson] will be there for the next 15 years like John Mazzola was. I blew my chance for this job. I'm a real schmuck."[18]

However, as fate would have it, Leventhal would soon learn that Ferguson had resigned. Leventhal jumped on this unexpected opportunity: "So this time I did not sit back. . . . I sent Marty a two-and-a-half-page letter . . . saying all the reasons why he should appoint me to this job. [Segal responded by telephoning Leventhal and said] Now that I've gotten your letter, now for the first time I really feel you want the job."[19] Leventhal was interviewed by the search committee and offered the job. He triumphantly commented many years later, "I got the job because I demanded the job. . . . I didn't wait for him [Segal] to come after me a second time."[20]

The process of appointing Leventhal was nearly scuttled by a consistent yet unspoken issue at Lincoln Center since its creation: the place of Jewish leadership in the organization. In the Center's formative years, there were very few Jews on the exploratory committee or the board. Obviously, the highly visible appointment of William Schuman would change the perception of Lincoln Center being a "Waspy" institution, but not to the extent that one might surmise. Schuman was a nonpracticing German Jew who saw his religious roots as more a cultural characteristic than a religious one.

According to Segal, there were two problems in shepherding Leventhal's appointment through the search committee: "The first problem was that he was from government. The second problem, which was never articulated, was that he was Jewish. I was the first Jewish chairman . . . and the question was 'we [have] a Jewish chairman for the first time, also a Jewish president, how come?' . . . That was a unique development at Lincoln Center."[21] For his part, Leventhal, representing another generation, believed that being Jewish within the Lincoln Center community was never a concern. Commenting after eight years as president, Leventhal said, "The issue has never come up. I've never felt at all uncomfortable about it."[22]

Although the nation sustained a robust economic climate for much of the 1980s, the Center's financial position upon Leventhal's appointment in March 1984 was poor. In the early 1980s, Lincoln Center "was running deficits as large as $1.3 million a year on a budget at that time of maybe $20 million. That's a big deficit," according to Leventhal, who gave Segal credit for working to change course.[23] "Marty Segal really put a lot of things in place that solved the problem [of the deficit]. . . . I took a lot of the credit, as it turned out, for having eliminated the deficit, but I think most of it goes to Marty," said Leventhal.[24]

Leventhal was a wise practitioner of City Hall politics, and he used that experience to develop a strong working relationship with Segal. Leventhal was realistic about the fact that Segal had to be in charge—or at least *feel* that he was in charge—in order for their professional relationship to survive. Leventhal commented, "Marty ran the institution and everyone else was somewhat intimidated by him. He's a wonderful man but he's not a delegator and he's not somebody who can have somebody else in charge. He told me I would be in charge. I wasn't really in charge when Marty was here."[25] As he worked with Segal, Leventhal felt progressively more insecure in his new job and often questioned his own judgment.[26]

Before Leventhal became president, Segal was already immersed in an important renovation of one of Lincoln Center's largest halls. Although acoustical and structural problems at Lincoln Center were usually related to Philharmonic Hall and the Beaumont Theater, the environment for producing operas by the New York City Opera at the New York State Theater had never been considered acceptable either.

As a result, a $5.3 million renovation of the New York State Theater, headed by Philip Johnson, took place in the summer of 1982 to improve the acoustics and address other issues that had not been dealt with since the theater's opening in 1964. The renovation was funded by a $4 million grant from the Fan Fox and Leslie R. Samuels Foundation, a $500,000 gift from the Helen Huntington

Hull Fund, and $763,000 from New York City. Work began soon after July 4, 1982, with the construction of a new proscenium, the enlargement of the orchestra pit, and the installation of new seats. Carpets were also replaced, new paint applied, and a new curtain installed.

Johnson and his partner John Burgee worked with the acoustician Cyril Harris on the project, as they had done for the renovation of Fisher Hall.[27] Johnson provided a rare self-deprecating comment on the project when he remarked, "I have nothing to say except that, as the architect who designed the theater the first time around 20 years ago, I have to admit what architects seldom admit, that theaters are much too important to be left to architects."[28]

The initial response to the renovation was positive, based on the season-opening production of Franz Lehár's *The Merry Widow* by the New York City Opera on September 7. Donal Henahan of the *New York Times* commented that the renovation created "significant improvements, chief among them an increased smoothness of the overall tone. The hard edge has been taken off the sound, which now projects with greater clarity and definition."[29]

Beverly Sills, general director of the City Opera, was thrilled with the work.[30] At *The Merry Widow* opening, Sills came out on stage hand in hand with Mayor Koch to thank him for the city's support of the project, and in turn the mayor proclaimed her "a national treasure."[31] Such encomiums, however, did not prevent the theater's acoustics from being maligned once again at the beginning of the twenty-first century.

Of the countless occurrences that have taken place on the Lincoln Center campus over the years, there is only one that can only be described as both tragic and macabre: the event that came to be known as the "Murder at the Met." With the notable exception of a nonfatal bomb explosion at Avery Fisher Hall that took place on December 29, 1978, perpetrated by an anti–Fidel Castro group called Omega Seven that was protesting the appearance of Cuban musicians at the hall, violence on campus had been rare.

According to press reports, on the evening of July 23, 1980, thirty-one-year-old violinist Helen Hagnes Mintiks was hurled to her death from the Metropolitan Opera House roof into an air shaft below during the intermission of a performance by the Berlin Ballet at the Met. Mintiks, a member of the ballet orchestra accompanying the performance, was a Canadian citizen and had studied at The Juilliard School. Her nude body was found the next morning in the third-floor air shaft.

About five weeks after the murder, Craig S. Crimmins, a twenty-one-year-old stagehand at the Met, was charged with Mintiks's murder. He admitted to trying to rape Mintiks in a backstage elevator; he claimed that on the night of the murder he was drunk and had also used marijuana for the first time. Crimmins was convicted of the murder and is now serving twenty years to life in a maximum-security prison in Wallkill, New York. Every two years since 2000 he has applied for parole, which has been denied every time.

Since its earliest days, two ongoing problems plagued the Center's leadership: the acoustics of Philharmonic/Fisher Hall and the failures of the Beaumont Theater. Of the two continuous problems, the Beaumont quagmire seemed the most intractable, since not only was artistic success an elusive goal, but the theater's physical structure also caused considerable problems for those who produced plays in the space as well as those who had to find the financial resources to keep the theater functioning.

As the new chair of Lincoln Center, Segal initially viewed the solution to the Beaumont problem as just staging a few plays each year that would be "hits" with the public and critics. However, Segal was soon to learn that such a simple solution would not resolve the deep-seated problems that stalked the theater. By the time Segal began his tenure as chair in 1981 there were already three distinct artistic/administrative teams that had tried to tame the Beaumont: Kazan and Whitehead, Blau and Irving, and Joseph Papp and his colleagues from the New York Shakespeare Festival. Soon after Papp's departure, a fourth leadership team came on the scene, led by John S. Samuels 3rd, a successful businessperson from Texas who remarkably was chair of four Lincoln Center constituents at once: City Center, the City Opera, the City Ballet, and the Beaumont. This arrangement existed because City Center had always been the nonprofit umbrella organization overseeing the Opera and Ballet; and City Center had made a valiant but failed effort in the early

1970s to oversee the Beaumont Theater after Jules Irving resigned as its head.

Closely linked to Samuels was a young theater producer from Virginia by the name of Richmond Crinkley, who had moved to New York City in 1977 after working in Washington, DC, at the Folger Theater and the Kennedy Center. Crinkley's claim to fame in New York was his production of Bernard Pomerance's play *The Elephant Man*, which realized success on Broadway after a critically acclaimed run in London. Crinkley had been recommended for the Beaumont position by Roger Stevens, the successful Broadway producer who was also chair of the Kennedy Center in Washington, DC, at the time.

According to Robert Marx, who had contemporaneous discussions with both John Mazzola and Crinkley about the appointment, "In a never-publicly-announced plan, [Stevens and Crinkley were to] functionally merge three organizations: ANTA (American National Theatre and Academy), the Beaumont and the Eisenhower Theater in D.C. ANTA held the federally authorized—but never funded—'American National Theatre' charter [and Crinkley and Stevens were both on ANTA's board]. From the beginning, the plan was to turn the troubled Beaumont into a proscenium theatre so that its stage would be compatible with the Eisenhower stage at the Kennedy Center. Productions would then be co-produced and move between the two cities as a new American National Theatre."[32] The Stevens-Crinkley plan eventually collapsed, but Stevens went ahead with a modified plan in DC to create his own American National Theatre at the Kennedy Center with Peter Sellars as artistic head. This venture lasted for only two seasons in the mid-1980s.

In 1979, two years after the Papp departure, Samuels and Crinkley announced the creation of an artistic committee or "directorate" for the Beaumont that would include six distinguished individuals: the playwright Edward Albee, the opera conductor and director Sarah Caldwell, the theater directors Liviu Ciulei and Ellis Raab, the British actor and director Robin Phillips, and the film director, screenwriter, and playwright Woody Allen. This group would essentially be the artistic leadership of the new Beaumont regime, Crinkley would coordinate their performance plans, and Samuels would oversee the financial side of the enterprise.

The theater community was not enthusiastic about the announcement of this new artistic/administrative structure. The concept of a "committee" being able to develop a focused artistic vision for the Beaumont was viewed with intense skepticism, if not outright derision, by professionals in the field.[33] Crinkley triumphantly announced that the members of the directorate "know and like the Beaumont theaters in their present configurations and do not believe that major architectural or structural changes are needed or desirable."[34] In addition, Crinkley clarified that "I'll be producing the Beaumont season. The directorate is responsible to me while I'm responsible to the board."[35]

The artistic result of this new leadership structure was a three-play season that began on November 5, 1980, with Philip Barry's comedy *The Philadelphia Story*, staged by Ellis Raab; followed by Shakespeare's *Macbeth* directed by Sarah Caldwell, which was the only play she ever directed in her life, realizing disastrous results for all involved; and Woody Allen's semi-autobiographical new play *The Floating Light Bulb*.[36] None of the plays received any level of critical praise, and the Crinkley-Samuels-directorate season was ultimately seen as a failure. Unsurprisingly, the directorate concept soon thereafter fell apart.

Perhaps in response to the plays' negative reviews, Crinkley and Samuels placed a good deal of the blame for the failed season on the theater's physical structure, a complaint that had plagued the venue since its opening in 1965. With Amyas Ames still Lincoln Center chair, in April 1981 both the Beaumont and Lincoln Center announced an aggressive renovation plan that would address structural, sight line, and acoustical problems, all of which had been well documented in the past.

In this plan, the thrust stage would be replaced by a permanent proscenium structure. The renovation, amounting to a cost of $6 million, would be funded by a $4 million challenge grant from the Fan Fox and Leslie R. Samuels Foundation, including the proviso that $2 million be raised by the Beaumont. A gift of $1 million from Beaumont board member Fred Koch was also pledged, on the condition that I. M. Pei be hired as lead architect for the project, with an additional $500,000 pledged from Beaumont president Jerome L. Greene, who would soon replace John Samuels as chair of the Beaumont board. With only $500,000 more to raise to meet the Samuels Foundation challenge and the eventual retention of Cyril Harris as acoustician for the project, all looked bright in the Beaumont community.

Sadly, the "cursed inheritance," as Robert Brustein called the Beaumont, reared its ugly head. With the ascendancy of Segal as the new chair of Lincoln Center in June 1981, the Center's leadership environment changed demonstrably, from the affable and low-key style of Ames to the brash toughness of Segal. To make matters worse, by February 1982, I. M. Pei had resigned from the project over continuing conflicts with Cyril Harris regarding the renovation's appropriate design.[37]

As a result of Pei's departure, Fred Koch withdrew his gift. The optimistic plans of only a year before came crashing down when Leslie R. Samuels (no relation to John Samuels) advised Segal that he was withdrawing his $4 million pledge. According to Segal, Samuels said, "Look, Fred Koch has withdrawn his grant. . . . I understand nothing is happening. The Beaumont has not met my conditions of having $2 million in matching funds, so I'm withdrawing my grant."[38]

For Segal's part, he saw little benefit in undertaking an expensive renovation of the Beaumont's physical plant when there was no artistic plan in place for the theater. Segal commented that "they were really quite taken with themselves—the board and Richmond Crinkley . . . and they kept saying that they had to renovate the theater. Finally, we said, 'You're not going to renovate the theater and spend $3 or $4 or $5 million unless we know what your purposes are artistically.'"[39]

Generally, the New York theater world did not look kindly on the fact that the theater was constantly closed or Crinkley's contention that he could not produce new seasons in the theater until the renovation question had been answered. Concurrently, certain members of the Beaumont board believed Segal was sabotaging their fundraising efforts. John Samuels stated at the time that "I think Marty just decided that Richmond had to go."[40]

In typical fashion, Segal would not let such barbs pass when his integrity was being impugned, and replied that the Beaumont's accusations of sabotage were "really tawdry stuff": "Is there lack of confidence? Yes. For promises made and not kept. For representations made that are untrue. For introductions of representations that are not relevant. And for the absence of performance for which you are paid and for which you are established. Those are all reasons for lack of confidence."[41]

Much to the chagrin of Segal, the Lincoln Center board passed a motion in April 1983 supporting the Beaumont renovation, but Segal quickly outmaneuvered the Beaumont– Lincoln Center leadership by becoming a theater producer in his own right. Segal had received a phone call from the well-known producer Alexander Cohen saying that the British director Peter Brook wished to stage his adaptation of Bizet's opera *Carmen*, titled *La Tragédie de Carmen*, in the Beaumont. The production had already garnered critical praise in Paris, and such a show, if successful, would prove to the world that, in fact, a physical renovation of the Beaumont was unnecessary.

Although Segal was not legally authorized to lease the Beaumont to an outside user (only the Beaumont board could do that), he obtained a signed contract from Cohen along with a deposit of $150,000. Crinkley and the New York theater community became aware of this Machiavellian plan, and the *New York Times* even inquired whether Crinkley, not Segal, was putting this production together. When Segal learned of the *Times* inquiry he was furious since he wanted full credit for bringing the Brook production to Lincoln Center. As a result, he decided to force the Beaumont's hand.

Segal was invited to attend a Beaumont board meeting on July 12, 1983, ostensibly to review architectural models of the proposed theater renovation, but all he wished to discuss was the Brook production of *Carmen*. When asked to review the architectural models, Segal blew up and said, "You're going to show me a model? . . . For God's sake we're talking about the real world. What are we, schoolchildren playing with Tinkertoys?"[42]

Instead, he immediately presented the Cohen-Brook proposal, which was the first time many of the Beaumont board members had heard of the project. Segal insisted that the Beaumont board at once agree to authorize the production. When Crinkley complained that he needed more time to discuss it, Segal said, "I think this story might leak to the press."[43] One Beaumont board member commented after the meeting, "A lot of people on the board did not know Martin Segal. He was really laying into [Crinkley]. It was a performance that was shocking. I looked around the room and began to laugh because the reaction to his performance was so stunning."[44]

There was also a prevailing rumor within the Beaumont community that Segal was planning to replace Crinkley with director Peter Hall. John Samuels decided to investigate and wrote Hall about what was happening. Hall replied, "I had been approached by people highly placed in the Lincoln Center organization for informal talks about the possibility of joining the organization. You must know that this is true, so I really do not understand why you wrote the letter."[45] The Beaumont board ultimately authorized the *Carmen* contract, but in the aftermath of the meeting, individuals resigned from the boards of both Lincoln Center and the Beaumont.

Segal proceeded aggressively: On August 23 the Lincoln Center board prohibited the Beaumont from using the name "Lincoln Center Theater Company" and discontinued the Theater's access to either distributions from the Lincoln Center Corporate Fund or its own portion of garage revenues. Segal was staunch in his position, saying, "Friends, do as you please. Use your own money and not ours. It's a primitive idea, but a wholesome one. It's called accountability."[46]

This Lincoln Center decision would cause the Beaumont to lose approximately $500,000 in needed annual revenue. Crinkley responded by saying that "the actions of the chairman of the board of Lincoln Center seem ill-advised and probably illegal."[47]

As Segal had hoped, the Brook *Carmen* production was a critical success and showed that the Beaumont Theater could house a "hit show." With an undisguised level of glee, Segal crowed, "It [*Carmen*] was a piece of luck, but it also made the point that the theater, if used appropriately by someone who had vision and imagination and competence, could do very well."[48]

Segal decided to leave no stone unturned and persuaded both the Beaumont's chair, Jerome L. Greene, and its president, W. Barnabas McHenry, to resign from the Beaumont board as a show of solidarity with Lincoln Center. Convincing them was not difficult, because the Beaumont board had met on July 20, 1983, without

Greene or McHenry present, and extended Crinkley's contract for two years. The gathering was the definition of a "rump meeting," with only nine of the nineteen board members present.

Idle from 1977 to 1984 and chastened by the success of Brook's adaptation of *Carmen*, a committee comprising members of the Beaumont and Lincoln Center boards came together in April 1984 to negotiate a resolution to the persistent problem. By this time, Nathan Leventhal was able to play a role in developing the agreement for the Lincoln Center side, working with Richard Shinn, a respected member of New York's business community and a member of the boards of both Lincoln Center and the Metropolitan Opera. Linda Janklow, acting chair of the Beaumont, and Richmond Crinkley were the lead negotiators for the theater. Lawrence A. Wien, a Lincoln Center member of the committee, said, "The creation of a new theater will not solve the artistic problem. We are not considering a physical change in the theater at present or in the immediate future. We believe that the Beaumont board will have to be reorganized."[49]

On June 4, 1984, a formal Beaumont reconciliation agreement with Lincoln Center was signed. The accord, seen as a victory for Lincoln Center, included several specific items including the appointment of a "committee of experts" to decide whether the theater should be renovated, the election of a new chair, the appointment of an "artistic manager" reporting to the board, and the creation of a new theater mission statement.

In turn, Lincoln Center would release money to the Beaumont from its Corporate Fund and garage revenues, and the theater could once again use the title "Lincoln Center Theater Company." The theater had until November 30, 1984, to meet all the agreement's requirements. Crinkley stated that he was "excited and enthusiastic [about the agreement and] we are all going into this with enormous goodwill."[50] Linda Janklow said that Crinkley would remain as executive director, but the mandate to appoint an "artistic manager" essentially deleted Crinkley's ability to lead the Beaumont. Crinkley would never again produce anything at Lincoln Center.

This extended and highly disruptive saga ultimately resulted in a victory for Martin E. Segal, who prevailed over a constituent in resolving an ongoing problem which negatively affected the entire

Center. In short order, he would move on to other pursuits and allow the troubled drama constituent to continue on its own.

There was considerable tension on campus due to the trials of the Beaumont and the financial challenges of the early 1980s. However, there was also a vast array of high-quality performances which reinforced Lincoln Center's position as the preeminent arts presenter in America. In addition to the daily concerts, operas, and dance presentations by the New York Philharmonic, the Metropolitan Opera, the New York City Opera, and the New York City Ballet, Lincoln Center also produced many notable events as part of its Great Performers series, which brought to New York a colorful mix of repertoire and ensembles.

These events included recitals by cellist Lynn Harrell, accompanied by James Levine, and solo piano concerts in February 1981 featuring Claudio Arrau, Emanuel Ax, and Peter Serkin. Chamber groups like the Emerson Quartet and the Brandenburg Ensemble were presented in this series and, in a vocal tour de force, Dame Joan Sutherland, Marilyn Horne, and Luciano Pavarotti performed two concerts in Avery Fisher Hall. Throughout the decade, prominent American and international orchestras were presented as part of the series.

Live from Lincoln Center flourished in the 1980s, led by John Goberman, presenting live performances by the New York Philharmonic, the City Opera, the City Ballet, and a two-hour special featuring The Juilliard School. This series of television broadcasts was a revelation for viewers in the United States and beyond because, unlike in the digital age of the twenty-first century and the access it affords to seemingly infinite sources of content, *Live from Lincoln Center* was often the first and only opportunity for a wide audience to enjoy the highest level of live classical music and dance performances. Therefore, the series became a sensation for aficionados of the arts and garnered many broadcasting awards.

The Mostly Mozart Festival, led by Gerard Schwarz, celebrated its twentieth anniversary in 1986. Even the less traditional Lincoln Center Out of Doors realized considerable success each summer with an eclectic mix featuring everything from *Sister Suzie Cinema: A Doo-Wop Opera* to Jacques d'Amboise's National Dance Institute.

Perhaps the grandest special performance of the decade oc-curred on October 22, 1984, when Lincoln Center celebrated its twenty-fifth anniversary, tracing its "birth" to the groundbreaking ceremony of 1959. Twenty-five Klieg searchlights shot beams of light into the dark sky. The telecast of the event a few days later fea-tured highlights from past *Live from Lincoln Center* and *Live from the Met* excerpts. The broadcast was truly a mélange: Pavarotti singing "E lucevan le stelle" from *Tosca,* Itzhak Perlman playing the final movement of the Tchaikovsky Violin Concerto, *and* a presentation of the "Coda and Apotheosis" from the Balanchine-Stravinsky ballet *Apollo* featuring Peter Martins.

Although some believed that the anniversary celebration could have been curated with a bit more focus, the event did show off the remarkable artistic capacity of the maturing Lincoln Center. The level of artistic excellence on display was a gratifying realization for Lincoln Center leaders who began to understand the adage that, in the arts, you are only as good as your last performance.

CHAPTER NINE

It Will Flourish as Long as a
Civilized Society Survives

WITH THE DIVISIVE QUESTION of the Beaumont settled, Nathan Leventhal, Lincoln Center's new president, was able to address the many issues facing the individual constituents, as well as their collective relationship to Lincoln Center, Inc. The Center's founders believed that the autonomous constituents should not only manage their own artistic, educational, and financial matters, but also work cooperatively to make the Lincoln Center concept come alive. This laudable goal was frustrated by factors which often caused constituents to look inward and ignore the gains that could occur through potential cooperative ventures involving multiple organizations.

Artistically, most of the constituents did, in fact, realize their own destinies, with the obvious exception of the Beaumont Theater and the Music Theater, which failed in 1970. The constituents had been able to weather the financial challenges which came about over the course of the following decades' normal economic cycles. Regrettably, the one area where constituents still experienced friction with Lincoln Center had to do with the production of artistic ventures. The Center's founders never envisioned that the umbrella organization would be an active producer on campus, apart from filling the Center's halls during the summers when the constituents were on break, but William Schuman's entrepreneurial spirit changed that direction.

Leventhal, coming from the challenging environment of City Hall, had a realistic outlook on the tasks ahead: "There's always been both good relations but also a certain amount of tension between Lincoln Center and the constituents . . . because some of them view Lincoln Center as the landlord and . . . nobody likes their landlord. . . . [But] as Lincoln Center . . . developed more and more programming initiatives, and, therefore, the need to raise funds for itself as opposed to the constituents . . . I think that tended to make people uncomfortable."[1]

Leventhal worked with constituents both individually and collectively, through the monthly meetings of the Lincoln Center Council, to bring the recalcitrant institutions together. His efforts to make the Lincoln Center Council a more deliberative body were particularly fruitful. The Council had been envisioned as an organization that would assemble on a regular basis the CEOs of each Lincoln Center constituent to discuss common topics, such as security and scheduling. Under Leventhal's leadership the Council met with a carefully developed agenda, and the president operated with a "light touch" that involved providing useful information while keeping the conversation moving forward with goodwill and humorous comments.

In Leventhal's early years, the Council met monthly for lunch in the Helen Hull Room of Fisher Hall, a small reception space that included a full bar. Lincoln Kirstein, representing the City Ballet, would have no qualms about imbibing three martinis during the luncheon and progressively challenging Leventhal regarding the "real estate operation" that Lincoln Center had become in his view. Other members of the Council at that time included Beverly Sills of the City Opera, Anthony Bliss of the Metropolitan Opera, Albert K. (Nick) Webster of the New York Philharmonic, and Vartan Gregorian of the New York Public Library, all of whom were amused by Kirstein's barbs and Leventhal's equanimity.

Although Leventhal played a critical role in the resolution of the Beaumont problem, he expressed concern that Segal was not pleased with the outcome: "It was a very difficult time for me since my boss thought I might be going too far. . . . He [Segal] told me later, privately, that I may have made a bad mistake, that they [Beaumont] might not do anything."[2] After the Lincoln Center board voted to pass the Beaumont agreement, Segal made "quite an emotional speech that the agreement was essentially fraudulent, that Lincoln Center had been 'snookered' and that the Beaumont would never put on any performances while accepting the Corporate Drive and garage revenues . . . [his opposition] probably having something to do with his exceptionally bad relationship with Linda [Janklow], which never got any better," according to Leventhal.[3] The situation had considerably calmed by the time former mayor John V. Lindsay became chair of the Beaumont in 1985. Soon thereafter Richmond Crinkley resigned as the Beaumont's executive director and would die only four years later, at the age of forty-nine.

Lindsay's tenure as chair resulted in the appointment of Gregory Mosher as artistic director and Bernard Gersten as executive producer of the Lincoln Center Theater Company, leading Gersten to quip that this administration would represent "the fifth ascent on Mt. Beaumont" referring to the failed "expeditions" that had taken place before their arrival.[4] Gersten and Mosher began their work together on July 1, 1985.

Mosher had studied acting and directing at Juilliard and went on to work in Chicago's Goodman Theatre, where he eventually became its director. During his time in Chicago, Mosher focused his producing primarily on new American plays and worked closely with David Mamet.

Gersten came to the Beaumont following an extensive career in theater and film. From 1960 to 1978 he worked with Joseph Papp as his associate producer at the New York Shakespeare Festival and assisted him when the Shakespeare Theater functioned at the Beaumont.

Leventhal had worked in the Lindsay administration for five years and knew and trusted the former mayor. Segal had known Gersten for several years and was pleased he would be leading the Beaumont with Mosher. As Leventhal said, for the first time "Marty started to think maybe there was some hope after all for the theater."[5]

In a significant statement, Mosher and Gersten made the point to Lincoln Center officials that they did not want to create a repertory theater but would rather produce shows on an ad hoc basis.

Neither person wanted to limit what the theater could do. Gersten remarked, "In attempting to reactivate the Beaumont . . . why would we impose limits, when the taste [of the audience] was fairly general? Yes, let's do new plays, let's do old plays, let's do classics, let's do musicals [but] we knew what we weren't going to do. We weren't going to even make a pass at being a repertory theater because how could we do *Anything Goes* and *Serafina* . . . with a repertory company? And how could you then do David Mamet?"[6] Mosher and Gersten also visited Leventhal soon after their appointment and made it clear that "they were no longer interested in having a committee or anyone else consider major renovation of the theater," Leventhal recalled.[7]

Leventhal had a good working relationship with the Mosher-Gersten team, but he still was nervous when several Beaumont-produced shows were transferred to Broadway, often with a commercial investment. Such shows included the South African musical *Serafina* and Mamet's *Speed the Plow* starring the pop star Madonna. Leventhal feared that such productions might endanger the Beaumont's nonprofit status and reflect badly on Lincoln Center. Gersten also provoked Leventhal's (admittedly mild) ire when, for the first time, neon signs advertising currently running plays were put on the glass walls of the Beaumont Theater facing the North Plaza and the Henry Moore sculpture. Gersten had to come to Leventhal for permission to display the signs, to which Leventhal replied, "Gee, this is Lincoln Center Bernie." "Oh, relax a little," Gersten said. "We're in the theater. We can be outrageous."[8]

For a person who reveled in the power of Lincoln Center's chair, it was curious that Martin E. Segal chose to step down after only five years, advising his board in June 1985 that he would resign effective June 1986. At the time of Segal's last board meeting as chair, on June 2, 1986, he distributed a detailed report on the results of his time as chair (1981–86). Although five years is a comparatively brief time in the history of an institution like Lincoln Center, Segal accomplished a great deal. The Center's finances improved significantly during his tenure, with its endowment growing from $32 million in 1981 to $57 million in 1986. In addition, annual fundraising had been successful, doubling the moneys raised for the annual fund and the Corporate Fund. In turn, the operating deficits of the 1960s and 1970s were reversed, resulting in an almost $1 million surplus in 1986.

Segal also oversaw a multimillion-dollar renovation of the New York State Theater and announced plans for the creation of the first new building on campus since 1969, eventually known as the Rose Building, as well as a generous distribution of $48.5 million to participating constituents in the sale of air rights for the construction of the Rose Building to be located directly west of the Juilliard building. Segal made it clear to the constituents, however, that Lincoln Center could have kept all the air rights proceeds if it had chosen to do so.

Segal made mention of a time beyond his tenure as chair by announcing the creation of a "Committee for the Future" which would study the Center's long-term needs. The new Lincoln Center chair would be George Weissman, a familiar member of the community, who would bring an entirely different style and focus to his position. Segal ended his report by stating that Lincoln Center "is one of the great innovations of our age. For centuries, the art of painting and sculpture have been gathered in museums, and the art of the written word in libraries and universities. But the performing arts are so ephemeral—and so alive. Lincoln Center has gathered them together to take strength from one another, not only to preserve but to create, not only to delight today's generation but to inspire and educate tomorrow's. It will flourish as long as a civilized society survives."[9]

As the new chair, George Weissman brought an avuncular persona to the Center that in some ways mirrored the goodwill of Amyas Ames and the trusting nature of JDR 3rd. He was born in the Bronx in 1919 and delivered at home by a physician with the ominous name of Dr. Faustus, which Weissman often amusingly said "really prepared me for my role at Lincoln Center."[10] He attended City College and saw a good deal of action in the navy during World War II, serving in both the European and Pacific theaters. He began working for Philip Morris in 1952 in the marketing department and was one of the developers of the Marlboro cigarette brand.

He first began volunteer work for Lincoln Center in the late 1950s through his association with David Ogilvie, one of the national

(Left to right): *Martin E. Segal, Nathan Leventhal, and George Weissman.*
(Segal photo by Robin Platzer / Filmmagic via Getty Images; Leventhal
photo © Patrick McMullan; Weissman photo by Neal Boenzi /
The New York Times/Redux Pictures)

leaders in PR and marketing and a principal in the well-known firm
of Ogilvie and Mather. Weissman helped with the 1959 Eisenhower
groundbreaking event and eventually joined the Film Society board
in 1967, helping to bring it to constituent status. Weissman always
respected the arts, but he had an epiphany of sorts which enhanced
that appreciation when he happened upon a performance of *La
Traviata* in Palermo, Sicily, soon after its liberation by the Allied
forces in August 1943. Seeing the Verdi masterpiece in person made
him an opera lover for the rest of his life.

Weissman would join the Lincoln Center board in 1972 while
he led Philip Morris's international division. He was an unabashed
proselytizer for the joys of smoking tobacco. At the beginning of his
tenure as chair, guests at Lincoln Center dinners would be greeted
at their individual place settings by a three-cigarette pack of Marl-
boros, and he often commented how pleased he was to see Juilliard
students taking a cigarette break outside the School's entryway.

As Weissman began his tenure as chair in June 1986, he supported the concept of Lincoln Center playing a robust producing
role, which corresponded with Nathan Leventhal's position on the
issue. Weissman's simpatico relationship with his president was di-
ametrically opposite from what Leventhal had experienced with

Segal. Whereas Segal was detail-oriented and hands-on as chair, Weissman took the more traditional position that the president of Lincoln Center functioned, in effect, as the chief executive officer who would run all important decisions by the chair.

Weissman's most significant challenge had to do with the intricacies of developing a building to accommodate various Lincoln Center constituents, but first he had to address the creation of a new member of the Lincoln Center community.

The process of adding new constituents to Lincoln Center had been regularized over time through the creation of "exploratory committees" comprising potential board members for the new entity along with experts in the area of the proposed constituent's discipline. These committees would carefully examine the artistic and financial feasibility of a new constituent. The Chamber Music Society, the Film Society, and the earliest meetings of the founders of Lincoln Center were all organized in this way.

However, the process was different for the School of American Ballet's constituency review. Created by George Balanchine and Lincoln Kirstein in 1934, the School of American Ballet (SAB) was an affiliated entity of Balanchine's ballet company. When asked by Kirstein in 1934 if he would like to start a ballet company in New York, Balanchine famously replied, "But *first* a school."[11]

SAB had functioned for many decades in rented quarters on the Upper West Side of New York at 2291 Broadway, but upon its lease's expiration Kirstein negotiated an arrangement with Peter Mennin, Juilliard's president at the time, to have access to new dance studios, which would be built in the Juilliard building at Lincoln Center. Remarkably, in this arrangement, SAB would also become Juilliard's dance division, replacing the dance department headed by Martha Hill that had existed at Juilliard since William Schuman created it in 1951.

Mennin was never satisfied with the public performance quality of his dance program, although such dance luminaries as José Limón, Anna Sokolow, Agnes de Mille, and even Martha Graham had taught at Juilliard over the years. In Mennin's defense, Martha Hill believed that all dance forms could be taught at one time to the same group of students. Under her leadership, publicly presented dance concerts would include both classical ballets, with women on point, as well as contemporary works. Although the approach was philosophically laudable, in practice it often resulted in dance presentations of uneven quality. Mennin saw the arrival of SAB, with its emphasis on classical ballet as shaped by Balanchine, one of the greatest choreographers in history, as the solution to his problem, allowing him to replace the existing dance program with one of the world's great ballet schools.

True to form, the wily Kirstein negotiated an agreement that considerably benefited SAB's interests. SAB would teach and rehearse in four dance studios on the third floor of the new Juilliard building, occupying seventeen thousand square feet of space, complete with offices and locker rooms for men and women. Unfortunately for Mennin, Hill mobilized intense opposition to the change and was able to save the Juilliard dance division, though it would have access only to two studios and makeshift office and locker space, also on the third floor in the new building.

Ultimately, Kirstein never agreed to have SAB function as Juilliard's dance division. As a result, SAB had access to high-quality dance studios at a below-market rental rate from 1969 when the Juilliard building opened until the Rose Building's construction in 1990. Kirstein was so possessive of the space that he installed a glass wall with an entrance door that bore the SAB logo, which barred Juilliard students, faculty, and administrators from entering "his" rarefied premises.[12]

Lawrence A. Wien, a powerful and generous member and vice chair of the Lincoln Center board, decided, in consultation with Weissman and Leventhal, to propose that SAB become a Lincoln Center constituent. Wien's late wife Mae, who had passed away in 1986, had always been a devotee of the City Ballet and took particular interest in the training of new dancers at SAB. In her honor, and with the support of his two daughters Enid (Dinny) Morse and Isabel Malkin, Wien called various constituent heads and made sure there would be no opposition to the constituent status of SAB, since a new constituent on campus would receive funds from the Consolidated Corporate Fund as well as garage revenues, thus diminishing those distributions to the other organizations.

On May 4, 1987, George Weissman announced that the School of American Ballet had become Lincoln Center's eleventh constituent. At the same time, the Mae L. Wien Awards were inaugurated, presented to members of the SAB faculty and highly promising students. The new SAB studios in the soon-to-be-built Rose Building would be funded by the Irene Diamond Fund and named in honor of Lincoln Kirstein.

The idea of a new Lincoln Center building which would accommodate the growing artistic and administrative constituent forces had surfaced soon after the completion of The Juilliard School building in 1969. As early as 1965, Edgar Young had testified before the Board of Estimate about Lincoln Center's need for more land to expand the Juilliard building and allow the entire Center to grow. The elimination of the proposed Metropolitan Opera office tower, considered in the original design of the Center, also brought the need for more space into focus.

The land under the Brandeis High School Annex, located to the west of the Juilliard building, was eventually released by the Board of Education for a price of approximately $6 million, and Lincoln Center was able to plan a new building for the site, which stretched west to Amsterdam Avenue from mid-block on both Sixty-Fifth and Sixty-Sixth Streets. The process of building the new structure required the creation of a complex legal agreement involving the participating constituents (in fact, the Metropolitan Opera, the New York City Opera, and the Lincoln Center Theater were the only constituents *not* involved with the building).

Each constituent's financial responsibility involved the payment of a proportionate share of the cost of the core and shell of the building. In turn, the constituent would receive the same percentage amount for any common gifts that were donated, though it would take 100 percent of gifts designated exclusively to the constituent.

As is typical of large New York City real estate projects, the process of building the new Lincoln Center building process was complex, namely because of the permission needed from the city to build a residential tower (eventually called Three Lincoln Center Plaza) next to the Lincoln Center constituent building. Lincoln

Center worked with the developers Abbott and Allan Stillman of Mayfair Associates to fashion a deal whereby the air rights owned by Lincoln Center would be sold to the Stillmans for $48.5 million. The Stillmans also offered another option of participating in the profits accrued through the sale of the tower's residences, but a Lincoln Center committee headed by Weissman and including trustees Segal, Fred Rose, Richard Shinn, and Willard Butcher wisely decided that the money be taken up front, "which was a very fortunate decision because we got our $48.5 million and then subsequently [Mayfair Associates] went bankrupt in 1992," Weissman recalled.[13]

Since both Leventhal and Lincoln Center board member Gordon Davis had extensive contacts in city government (Davis had worked in the Lindsay and Koch administrations and was Koch's parks commissioner), the potentially perilous authorization by the Board of Estimate, prefaced by the intricate and complex Unified Land Use Review Process mandated by the city, was realized quite efficiently.

In developing the preliminary program for the building, Segal, Rose, Leventhal, and Davis met with several architects but quickly settled on Lew Davis (no relation to Gordon) of Davis, Brody & Associates. Davis presented a plan in which the entrance to Juilliard would be shifted from its narrow and "rabbit warren–like" opening on West Sixty-Sixth Street (as Peter Jay Sharp, the Juilliard board's vice chair, often referred to the School's entrance) to an elevated entryway one story above Sixty-Fifth Street facing out to Lincoln Center's North Plaza. In addition, Davis's design had the new building's western windows and auxiliary stairs facing out to Amsterdam Avenue, an important symbolic gesture to the community, which had always seen Lincoln Center as having its "back" to the Amsterdam Houses project, Martin Luther King High School, and the Fiorello H. LaGuardia High School of Music & Art and Performing Arts.

The new entry to Juilliard provided easy access to the large bridge which covered the street and provided an elegant walkway from Broadway heading west to the new building's entrance. Leventhal saw this approach as "the single most important design feature of the new building."[14]

Lew Davis had always seen the Sixty-Sixth Street entrance to Juilliard and the underground offices of Lincoln Center, which had replaced a public restaurant called Footlights Cafeteria, as anathema to the openness the Center wished to realize with this new architectural plan. He created a new sense of arrival for both Juilliard and the proposed building that was attractive to all parties. In addition to shifting the Juilliard entryway to Sixty-Fifth Street, he also added a much-needed recital hall below the new Juilliard entrance (eventually named Morse Hall). The promenade from Broadway included the Juilliard Bookstore, a ticket office, pleasant views of the North Plaza, and entrances to both the Film Society Theater and the Rose Building.

The $48.5 million air rights proceeds, of course, came with the construction of a second building to house the private developer's condominiums. Lincoln Center officials knew that the community would object to the much taller condominium tower because it would cast a shadow at certain times of the day and add significantly to the area's population density, further crowding the subway and adjoining streets. In an amusing moment during a tense meeting of Community Board #7, one resident complained that the shadow of the building would fall on her apartment window for a few specific hours every day. Gordon Davis replied, "Madame, for that to happen the sun would have to rise in the west and set in the east," at which point the frustrated resident said, "Please don't bother me with silly details."[15] The board ultimately rejected the building plan, but fortunately the decision was not legally binding.

The Lew Davis–designed structure included in its ten-story, 235,000-square-foot institutional base building residence halls for both Juilliard and the School of American Ballet; offices for Lincoln Center, Inc., and many of the participating constituents; a suite of rehearsal rooms and offices for the Chamber Music Society of Lincoln Center; new studios for the School of American Ballet and City Ballet; a full service cafeteria; a 268-seat theater for the Film Society of Lincoln Center (the Walter Reade Theater, opened on December 3, 1991); archival and office spaces for the New York Philharmonic, the Lincoln Center Archives, the Metropolitan Opera Guild, and the City Center of Music and Drama; a large performance and reception space overseen by Lincoln Center but available to all constituents (the Stanley H. Kaplan Penthouse); a black box theater for the Lincoln Center Institute (named the Clark Studio); and the

Riverside branch of the New York Public Library (accessible to the entire community).

Above the institutional base building would be an eighteen-story, 115,000-square-foot residence hall for 375 Juilliard students and 100 students from SAB, plus student lounges and visiting faculty suites for Juilliard. The privately developed apartment tower would rise next to the Juilliard-SAB residence tower and include apartments ranging from studios to duplexes.

The Lincoln Center building and fundraising project was chaired by Frederick Phineas Rose, a successful New York real estate developer and member of the Lincoln Center board. Rose was a no-nonsense yet elegant person who once described himself by saying, "I don't read trash, watch TV or have an interest in spectator sports. This leaves time for active participation in things I enjoy: music, chess, golf, travel, skiing and friendship."[16] He and his wife, Sandra Priest Rose, gave away over $95 million to various charitable causes during their lifetimes. As chair of Lincoln Center's new building committee, Rose brought a high personal energy and "can-do" attitude to every meeting he attended. In addition to fulfilling all the city authorizations and negotiating with the Stillman group, the committee also needed to undertake a major fundraising effort.

As with any large building project, early estimates of the expenses were well below the final cost. At first, a $75 million campaign was envisioned, which quickly grew to $100 million, a goal that did not include the $48.5 million proceeds from the sale of the air rights. Planners also intended to include a $25 million operating endowment as part of the fundraising goal. The project was aided by a prosperous economic environment at the time, with the significant exception of Black Monday, October 19, 1987, when the stock market dropped by more than 20 percent in a single day, still the largest one-day percentage decrease ever. October 19 was also the opening night of the Beaumont's production of Cole Porter's musical *Anything Goes*, starring Patti LuPone as Reno Sweeney. When she spoke an original line in the show during the performance about the vagaries of the stock market, the audience broke into spontaneous and nervous laughter.

Leventhal commented that "the building would have been dead in the water if we had tried this three or four years later. We just could never have done it."[17] The project ultimately cost about $150 million to complete. The concern of constituents fighting over common donors, in fact, did not come to pass: "Amazingly enough . . . it [fundraising] worked better than anyone would have anticipated. I still cannot believe how well it worked. . . . Almost no fights among the constituents. They would actually sit and discuss the prospects."[18]

The successful fundraising was due in great part to Fred Rose, who participated in numerous solicitations and who also provided the leadership gift of $15 million to name the building after his father, David, and uncle, Samuel. Although it seems clear that Rose did not need much prodding to provide his generous gift, Leventhal recalled that he had told Rose he believed Donald Trump "was an excellent prospect, that I thought he was interested."[19] Rose called Leventhal that night and said that he wanted to provide the exclusive naming gift, obviating any chance that the Trump name would be emblazoned on a Lincoln Center building. The Rose gift was kept secret until very late in the fundraising process, since Rose felt uncomfortable soliciting funds for a building that would bear his own name.

The building was scheduled to open in late August 1990, but delays in acquiring certifications from various city agencies caused Juilliard to house more than three hundred of its students in the West Side YMCA on Sixty-Third Street and another student group farther south at the Sloane House Y on Thirty-Fourth Street. Security and the quality of lodging at the temporary facilities were of great concern to Juilliard officials, but a certificate of occupancy for the new building finally was issued in mid-October, which resulted in a stream of happy Juilliard students moving into their exceptional accommodations on October 22, 1990, which provided extraordinary views of Lincoln Center Plaza and the Hudson River. During the move-in, the ongoing joke was that Juilliard students living in the residence would never be able to afford such views after their graduation.

Critical response to the building's architecture was generally positive. Although there was some concern regarding the presence of a multistory tower in the middle of Manhattan's West Side, for the most part critics saw the Rose Building and its companion condominium tower to have been realized with considerable skill.

The editorial board of the *New York Times* enthusiastically supported the new building: "The expansion proposal provides a shrewd composite solution to the pressures pinching Lincoln Center. As a treasure that ennobles the whole city, it deserves [the City's] support."[20] Even the curmudgeonly Lincoln Kirstein admitted that the project was worthwhile: "Physically [the studios] couldn't be better. I've seen the studios in Moscow, Leningrad and London, and this is much better than anything . . . [but] we'll need a great deal more money now [to support the studios]. So, I'm grateful, but not cheerful."[21]

When the founders of Lincoln Center presented their strategy for bringing so many diverse performing arts organizations together in one place, it was predicated on the belief that they would work together to realize various artistic projects. However, substantive collaboration among the constituents was infrequent. The Juilliard School was a natural institution to welcome members of the other constituents as teachers; however, even with Juilliard, it was primarily through the School's music division that members of the New York Philharmonic and the Metropolitan Opera Orchestra were invited to join the faculty. Rarely did artists in the New York City Ballet or the Lincoln Center Theater ever cross Sixty-Fifth Street to teach as full-time faculty. And certainly there was no collaborative project involving most or all of the constituents until 1991.

It was at that time that the world celebrated the bicentennial of Wolfgang Amadeus Mozart's death on December 5, 1791. Commemorations were planned across the world, and Lincoln Center hoped to do something as well to celebrate Mozart's genius. Leventhal thought it best to test the idea with selected Lincoln Center Council members before presenting the project to the full group. After running it by selected members, Leventhal raised the idea with the full Council, at which point Albert K. Webster, executive vice president and managing director of the New York Philharmonic, suggested that Lincoln Center embrace the idea of doing *all* of Mozart's works in a festival utilizing the considerable resources of the Center's constituents.

The idea had almost immediate traction among Council members, and a small group of administrators funded by Lincoln Center was designated to coordinate the comprehensive project, which aimed to present public performances of all 835 of Mozart's known works listed in the original 626-item catalog compiled by Ludwig von Köchel, plus 209 works discovered after Kochel's catalog was published in 1862. (Mozart's works are traditionally presented in programs with a Köchel number, represented with a K.) Such an endeavor required a considerable level of organization, especially in performing Mozart's lesser-known and incomplete works. University and college conservatories and schools of music were invited to perform in the festival, and local churches agreed to perform Mozart's organ compositions throughout the celebration.

The nineteen-month festival, costing $3 million, involved more than five hundred concerts beginning on Mozart's 235th birthday, January 27, 1991, and concluding on August 29, 1992. Cornell University musicologist Neal Zaslaw was appointed the festival's music adviser, and Fiona Morgan Fein and Johanna Keller provided artistic and administrative assistance.

The opening of the festival on January 27 involved the re-creation of a "benefit concert" originally arranged and conducted by Mozart and performed on March 23, 1783, in Vienna. The three-hour program included the Symphony no. 35 (Haffner) K. 385, Piano Concertos nos. 5 K. 175 and 13 K. 415, plus concert arias and other works. In the concert's early planning, it was hoped that the music directors of the various Lincoln Center orchestras would conduct selected parts of the program. The author chaired a planning meeting that included James Levine of the Metropolitan Opera, Zubin Mehta of the New York Philharmonic, Christopher Keene of the New York City Opera, and Bill Lockwood, representing Gerard Schwarz of the Mostly Mozart Festival, to discuss who would conduct what works. Levine, in particular, expressed great interest in performing as soloist in the piano concerti and conducting the concert arias. The other maestri showed a good level of camaraderie by agreeing that most of the concert should feature Levine. Regrettably, Levine neglected to recall that he was engaged to conduct the Vienna Philharmonic on January 27, 1991. Upon his departure from the concert, the other music directors left the project as well. Eventually, Raymond Leppard stepped in to conduct an orchestra of musicians from the New York Philharmonic and the Juilliard Orchestra.

Plans for the concert on the bicentennial anniversary of Mozart's death, December 5, 1991, went more smoothly, with Erich Leinsdorf conducting the New York Philharmonic in Mozart's *Masonic Funeral Music* K.477, the Piano Concerto No. 27 in B♭ major K. 595 featuring Alicia de Larrocha as soloist, and the *Requiem in D Minor* K.626.

Other notable festival concerts and events included Mitsuko Uchida and de Larrocha performing the complete piano sonatas over eight concerts, several sacred music concerts presented by orchestras and choruses from visiting American conservatories and universities, a festival of films about Mozart presented by the Film Society, and a six-day international musicological symposium at Juilliard, chaired by Zaslaw, exploring the relationship of scholarship to performance in Mozart's works. Leventhal was particularly pleased with the festival "much more because of the cooperation than in doing all the works of Mozart, which for me is just a vehicle for achieving that cooperation."[22]

The public was invited to experience all the music and performances, which were often free when they took place at Juilliard or in the Bruno Walter Auditorium of the New York Public Library at Lincoln Center. The press was not as enthusiastic about the festival as were Lincoln Center officials: articles often referred to a "checklist mentality" on the part of planners to realize performances of all the works.

However, this point of view seemed shortsighted to the organizers. Not only was the cooperative environment developed among the constituents valuable, but the opportunity to hear rarely performed works of Mozart was a unique experience, one that allowed the listener to compare similar works or to be surprised as to how Mozart would adapt portions of certain works for use in later compositions. The Mozart Bicentennial Festival at Lincoln Center to this day remains the largest project in the history of the Center involving all constituents.

The 1980s saw significant changes in the artistic and administrative leadership of several Lincoln Center constituents. Bruce Crawford became the general manager of the Metropolitan Opera in 1985, replacing Anthony Bliss, who had served as executive director and then general manager since 1974. In 1989 the arts administrator Hugh Southern took over for Crawford as general manager, but his tenure in that position was exceedingly short, as he announced his resignation on June 22, 1990, to take effect on July 1 of the same year. He had practically no direct experience in producing opera and little opportunity to maneuver artistically or administratively with James Levine as artistic director and Bruce Crawford continuing on the board as chair of the finance committee.[23] The situation was complicated further by the presence of Joseph Volpe, assistant manager of the Met at the time, who made it clear to the board that he wanted to be general manager—which indeed came to pass in 1990.

Composer Peter Mennin had been president of The Juilliard School since 1962 when he succeeded William Schuman, who became president of Lincoln Center at that time. Mennin served as Juilliard's president for twenty-one years and oversaw the move of the School from 122nd Street and Broadway to Lincoln Center. He was instrumental in starting the drama division and created the American Opera Center at Juilliard. He died in 1983 and was succeeded by the author, who became the sixth president of Juilliard on September 4, 1984.

With the departure of Pierre Boulez in 1977, who had succeeded Leonard Bernstein in 1971, Zubin Mehta was appointed the New York Philharmonic's music director in 1978 after his music directorship of the Los Angeles Philharmonic Orchestra. Mehta's thirteen-year tenure as music director of the New York Philharmonic would be the longest in the ensemble's history. In 1991 Mehta left the orchestra and was replaced by Kurt Masur, who was previously Kapellmeister of the Leipzig Gewandhaus Orchestra. Masur would serve as the Philharmonic's musical head until 2002.

The New York Public Library for the Performing Arts at Lincoln Center also went through a transformative period in the 1980s under the strong leadership of first Vartan Gregorian and then Father Timothy Healy as president of the New York Public Library. Lincoln Center Library's structure was significantly changed by merging the separate units of circulation, research, and the Shelby Cullom Davis Museum into one management unit. Robert Marx, formerly director of the theater programs at both the New York State Council on the Arts and the National Endowment for the Arts, was engaged to take on the new position of executive director of the Lincoln Center Library. The name of the institution was changed as well during Marx's tenure from the Library and Museum of the Performing Arts to the New York Public Library for the Performing Arts. Performances presented by the Library were held in the two-hundred-seat Bruno Walter Auditorium, the only theater at Lincoln Center named after an artist or musician.

Without doubt one of the great losses in the history of the Lincoln Center community was the death of George Balanchine on April 30, 1983. As the cofounder of the New York City Ballet and the School of American Ballet, he was one of the most important choreographers, teachers, and leaders in the history of dance. As Anna Kisselgoff of the *New York Times* wrote, "More than anyone else, [Balanchine] elevated choreography in ballet to an independent art."[24] Balanchine was often grouped with Stravinsky and Picasso as one of the greatest artists of the twentieth century.

The artistry of Balanchine was matched by another great artist who graced the Lincoln Center campus: Leonard Bernstein. Although Bernstein left the music directorship of the New York Philharmonic after a ten-year tenure in 1969, his presence on campus continued until his death on October 14, 1990. He was a frequent conductor at the Philharmonic and the Metropolitan Opera, gave master classes at Juilliard, had his musical theater and opera works produced by the New York City Opera, and composed for Lincoln Center ensembles.

His exuberant podium style and multifaceted skillset added more than a touch of panache to the Philharmonic when he opened Philharmonic Hall in 1962. Through his intelligence, wit, creativity, and artistry, he became one of the key figures in shaping how Lincoln Center was perceived throughout the globe.

The AIDS epidemic ravaged the entire world throughout the 1980s, though the death toll in the arts community was particularly egregious. Many members of Lincoln Center's community succumbed to the disease, including Christopher Keene, general director of the New York City Opera, and Paul Jacobs, solo pianist and harpsichordist for the New York Philharmonic. Keene tried to work until the very end, and even conducted a groundbreaking performance of Hindemith's rarely produced and extraordinarily complex opera *Mathis der Maler*, opening the 1995 New York City Opera season on September 7. Tragically, he would be dead one month later, on October 8. He was forty-eight years old.

Since Lincoln Center constituents worked within tightly knit communities that came together with special intensity when productions or performances were presented, the tragic loss of colleagues was particularly impactful during the AIDS epidemic.[25] The seemingly uncontrollable losses due to the disease cast a pall over Lincoln Center. Renowned artists as well as lesser-known individuals were taken with impunity from the Center's community. The Proustian concept that suffering can trigger creativity is seen in the numerous artistic works created as a result of the AIDS crisis.

New York–based creators developed two prominent AIDS-related works. Future Juilliard professor John Corigliano's Symphony no. 1 was written to commemorate the friends he lost to the AIDS pandemic. The work was premiered by the Chicago Symphony Orchestra, conducted by Daniel Barenboim, in March 1990, and Corigliano won a Grammy Award for the composition the following year.

The artistic work most associated with the AIDS crisis is most likely Tony Kushner's *Angels in America: A Gay Fantasia on National Themes*. This two-part play explored AIDS and homosexuality in America in the 1980s. The work officially premiered in San Francisco in May 1991, though there had been a preliminary Los Angeles production in May 1990. The first New York performances of *Angels*, presented as a workshop, were produced by the Juilliard drama division in 1992, just after Kushner's time in residence at Juilliard as the School's Lila Acheson Wallace Playwright. The play garnered many honors, including the Pulitzer Prize and a Tony Award.

Though the disease would eventually become less pervasive and more manageable, the scars of the AIDS crisis would last forever. The loss of so many artists to the disease had a devastating impact on the arts community throughout the world.

CHAPTER TEN

This Is a Dream Come True

I N THE HISTORY OF LINCOLN CENTER, composer William Schuman had been the only artist to serve in a position of administrative leadership. This changed dramatically in January 1994 when it was announced that Beverly Sills would succeed George Weissman as the Center's chair, effective June 13. In addition to being a world-class performer, Sills was the first woman to chair Lincoln Center's board and the first chief trustee who had previously not been a board member. Sills, of course, had shattered many glass ceilings throughout her illustrious career, and this new responsibility reflected her ambition and capabilities.

Born Belle Silverman on May 25, 1929, in the Crown Heights section of Brooklyn, she was nicknamed "Bubbles" because she had purportedly been born with bubbles in her mouth. The sobriquet remained throughout her life. She began radio work at the tender age of four and by seven was on the widely heard radio show *Major Bowes Capital Family Hour*, where she not only tap-danced but also sang opera arias. She attended Erasmus Hall High School in Brooklyn, where Martin E. Segal had also been a student, and the Professional Children's School. She studied with her only voice teacher, Estelle Liebling.

Sills joined the New York City Opera in 1955 and successfully debuted as Rosalinde in Johann Strauss's *Die Fledermaus*. Soon thereafter she met and eventually married Peter B. Greenough, an independently wealthy associate editor of the *Cleveland Plain Dealer.* In 1959, Sills gave birth to a daughter, Meredith (Muffy), and two years later to a son, Peter (Bucky). Muffy was born deaf and Bucky was eventually diagnosed with severe autism that required his institutionalization.

The medical diagnoses of her two children came within six weeks of each other. Sills would later muse, "When you've already lived the worst day of your life, very little fazes you. . . . You put everything in proportion."[1] Instead of feeling overwhelmed by her children's medical conditions, she transformed her approach to being an artist and moved forward. "I felt if I could survive my grief, I could survive anything. . . . Onstage I was uninhibited, and I began to have a good time," Sills later said.[2]

Her breakthrough success in 1966 as Cleopatra in Handel's *Giulio Cesare* at the New York City Opera launched a career that brought her to the great opera houses of the world and eventually to the Metropolitan Opera in 1975, three years after Rudolf Bing retired as general manager. In 1978, at the height of her popularity, she announced that she would retire from the stage in 1980 at the age of fifty-one. However, Julius Rudel decided to leave the New York City Opera as general director in 1979, which fast-forwarded Sills's timetable: she assumed the post that same year and never sang in a staged opera again.

In her ten years leading the New York City Opera, she reduced ticket prices, was closely involved in the renovation of the New York State Theater, initiated the use of supertitles, and managed the results of a disastrous warehouse fire that destroyed over ten thousand costumes for seventy-four productions.[3] By the end of her tenure, the City Opera budget had grown from $9 million to $26 million and a $3 million deficit became a $3 million surplus.[4] Leaving the New York City Opera in 1989, she joined the Met Opera board in 1991 and subsequently became Lincoln Center's chair in June 1994. Sills always had a sense of when to move on to the next challenge, prompting her husband to give her a ring engraved with the words "I did that already."[5]

In fact, it was her husband who urged her to take on the Lincoln Center chair. Sills recalled, "He thought my life was full of a lot of unfocused work. He preferred I did one or two things and finish them successfully as opposed to running around in so many disparate directions."[6]

Leventhal remembered that the idea of Sills taking on the Lincoln Center chair happened spontaneously when both individuals took part in a conference at the Museum of Television and Radio (now known as the Paley Center for Media) and decided to explore the appointment in a casual conversation. The power of the proposed appointment was palpable for all who learned of it, and the Lincoln Center board agreed to the Sills candidacy with enthusiasm.

In a prescient, if problematic, epiphany, Leventhal thought twice about the Sills chair as it was being officially authorized, fearing that her leadership would be similar to Martin Segal's, which had been a persistent thorn in his side. However, the die had been cast. Ultimately, Leventhal would enthusiastically welcome Sills to the position, saying publicly, "There is no one in the world like Beverly Sills. This is a dream come true."[7]

Her public visibility as a successful artist and her engaging personality were attributes that helped her manage the responsibilities of the Center's chair, although she played down her renown at the time of her appointment: "This is not going to be Miss Celebrity time. . . . It's an interesting and complicated job. . . . And I think that once the novelty of my appointment wears off, it will be just like the directorship of the New York City Opera. I'll be doing a job, and I'll be working hard."[8]

Sills was acutely aware of the Center's problems as she took on the role because, as she said, "I used to be one of the people complaining. But I do not want the relationship between Lincoln Center and its constituents to be adversarial."[9] Tensions on the Center's campus at the time often focused on the projects of Lincoln Center Productions, the Center's presentation arm, which produced more than three hundred events a year in 1994. These presentations continued to be seen as competing with the constituents' offerings for both audiences and donations.

Sills believed that the Lincoln Center leadership would be similar to her duties as general director of the New York City Opera, but such an assumption was flawed. At City Opera, she oversaw the entire operation, managing the daily details involved in the running of a complex organization. At Lincoln Center, her role was not as the institution's CEO (although Martin Segal saw his position that way). By the beginning of Sills's tenure, Leventhal had already been president for ten years and had become accustomed to being the Center's leader in implementing the Center's many projects and processes—and he was not inclined to shift those responsibilities to Sills.

The first six months of her new leadership was a challenging time for both Sills and Leventhal. At the beginning of the new season in September 1994, the Sills-Leventhal problems became common knowledge to the members of the Lincoln Center community, as Sills would complain in public settings, mostly dinner parties, about both Leventhal and Jane Moss, vice president of programming. Sills's indiscreet comments were made to major donors and board members throughout the Lincoln Center campus.[10]

She had clearly expected to be involved in the center's daily operations. Once, in exasperation, she said to Leventhal, "I don't understand what my job is."[11] On another occasion, quipping in typical Sills's fashion—described by one writer as "her schmoozing style and tendency to punctuate her words with frequent gales of laughter"—she said, "I dreamed I took a job, but nobody told me what it was."[12]

For his part, Leventhal felt that the mounting tension with Sills was becoming highly problematic. According to Roy Furman, a member of Lincoln Center's executive committee and a successful Wall Street executive and Broadway producer, "There was great tension between Beverly and Nat early in her chairmanship, and she discussed the possibility of replacing him. I was concerned because Beverly was relatively new to her position and Nat had deep knowledge of the organization and proved himself to be a creative and adaptable leader. I advised Beverly that releasing Leventhal would be both an institutional error and a mistake for her personally."[13] Ultimately, Sills did not act on her inclination to fire Leventhal.

In a telling analysis by an anonymous Lincoln Center official that appeared in a *New York Times* article on Sills, it was stated that "'She's a diva' . . . [said] in an affectionate and even sympathetic tone. 'She wants everybody to love her and everything that is said about her to be positive. Her 'Not being loved,' the official said, 'does more harm to a diva than anything else.'"[14]

In an effort to resolve the tension and to find a path forward, Sills and Leventhal decided to meet with Edgar Vincent, the powerful New York publicist who counted Sills as a client and Leventhal as a friend. In one long session in Vincent's office, the various slights, upsets, and misunderstandings came tumbling out; years later Leventhal would refer to it as "couples' therapy." Leventhal was exhausted by the experience, but he remembers that Sills found it invigorating and cathartic.[15]

After the Vincent session, the Sills-Leventhal contretemps subsided. Leventhal grew to understand that Sills felt a sense of insecurity and isolation in her new job because Leventhal rarely informed her about what was taking place at the Center. From then on, Leventhal was careful to brief Sills almost daily and invite her to take part in meetings. Once both individuals found this new common ground, Sills rarely second-guessed Leventhal's decisions. Over the next five years they developed a close working and personal relationship, which continued after Sills stepped down as chair.

Both Sills and Leventhal were intent on easing the tension between the constituents and Lincoln Center, Inc. The "us versus them" mentality of past Lincoln Center leadership created a "dysfunctional family" dynamic. Regrettably, the next venture developed by the Sills-Leventhal team only further roiled the waters.

The founders of Lincoln Center had always committed to keeping the Center's halls busy during the summer months when almost all the constituents were on break or performing off campus. Therefore, it did not seem a great leap for the Center's leadership to combine its summer productions into a festival that would bring artistic attractions to campus from around the world and present the public with a new array of performing artists and ensembles rarely seen in New York.

Three months into Sills's leadership, Lincoln Center officials announced the creation of a three-week festival which would "include classical music concerts, contemporary music and dance presentations, stage works and non-Western arts. . . . [The festival would] serve as a showcase for the finest guest artists and companies from New York and around the world."[16] The festival would be led by John Rockwell, the long-tenured *New York Times* arts critic, to be assisted by Nigel Redden, who at the time was executive director of the Santa Fe Opera and a well-respected arts consultant, having earlier worked as general manager of the Spoleto Festival USA. Sills supported the Rockwell appointment: "Few people possess John's enormous breadth of and depth of musical knowledge."[17] For Leventhal's part, he knew he was taking a chance with Rockwell because "he had never put on a performance of any type in his life. . . . But I was hiring his brain, not his experience."[18]

By September 1994, William Lockwood had been gone for three years as executive producer for programming at Lincoln Center, replaced by Jane Moss, who held the title of vice president for programming beginning in 1992. Coming from a theater background, Moss had only modest production experience in music before joining the Center. She wished to direct the festival, but Leventhal did not support her—not because of her lack of experience in music production; but rather because he believed the festival required a full-time director, and she was already busy with her responsibilities overseeing Mostly Mozart, Serious Fun!, and the Great Performers series. In the press release announcing the festival, Moss was given credit for its early development, and she was quoted as saying, "After initiating this program over the past year, I am pleased that Lincoln Center can proceed with our new Festival."[19] Nigel Redden was brought on to the team as a consultant, primarily to assist Rockwell not just in choosing the participants, but in implementing the many logistical, scheduling, and budgetary issues that came with such an ambitious artistic undertaking.

Instead of the constituents coming together with enthusiasm for the new festival, the exact opposite occurred. Leventhal recalled, "The constituents were not happy that we were doing a festival. They thought it would compete with them for audiences, for fundraising, etc. We got a joint letter from Bernie [Gersten] and Andre [Bishop] (who had replaced Gregory Mosher as the Beaumont's Artistic Director in 1992), saying, 'We were appalled to learn about your Festival. You're going to have theater in it. We must demand that you have no theater as a component of your Festival.'"[20] The constituents were particularly concerned by the festival's $14 million budget, an amount which would have required extensive fundraising by Lincoln Center that would potentially diminish constituent donations.[21]

Soon after the festival announcement a highly emotional Lincoln Center Council meeting occurred in which Joseph Volpe, general manager of the Metropolitan Opera, became furious with Leventhal for allowing Rockwell to try to import Peter Sellars's Salzburg Festival production of Olivier Messiaen's mammoth, five-hour opera *St. Francis of Assisi.* The chair of the Metropolitan Opera at the time, Bruce Crawford, had seen the production in Austria and urged Volpe to bring it to the Met. As a result, Lincoln Center and the Met were competing for the same work. Leventhal eventually asked Rockwell to cease his Salzburg negotiations—though, in the end, the Met did not pursue the production either due to prohibitive costs.

The first-year festival budget was reduced to $8 million and fundraising capped at $5 million. However, the constituents' fundamental problem was that they had been blindsided by the festival's announcement. In retrospect, Leventhal admitted that he should have better prepared the festival announcement with the constituents.[22]

Leventhal was intent on creating a high-quality international festival that would be a natural outgrowth of the earlier Serious Fun! summer program, which featured an eclectic mix of contemporary and experimental repertory. He believed that the Mostly Mozart concerts were taking up too large a portion of the Center's summer presentations and saw the festival as bringing a fresh approach. At the same time, critics expressed concern regarding the quality of the Mostly Mozart Festival under the direction of Gerard Schwarz, who served as conductor for the festival orchestra since 1982 as part of his role as adviser and then in 1984 as the festival's first music director.

Schwarz had clashed with Jane Moss over various artistic matters, and even Beverly Sills complained about the quality of the music-making in the Mostly Mozart Festival. Once the Lincoln Center Festival started up, the Mostly Mozart schedule was reduced from seven to four weeks. Jane Moss also took greater control of the Mostly Mozart programming and brought in an increased number of guest ensembles and period-instrument orchestras.

In turn, Schwarz was strongly supported by some of the Center's most significant donors and leaders, including Irene Diamond, Jerome L. Greene, and Martin E. Segal. Segal was particularly miffed about the surprise announcement of the new Lincoln Center Festival—not only because he assumed that there should have been a briefing of the full Lincoln Center board beforehand, but also because the new festival would compete with his own International Festival.

Schwarz announced in 1999 that he would relinquish the music directorship of the Mostly Mozart Festival when his contract ended in 2001, in order to devote more time to his leadership of both the Seattle Symphony and the New York Chamber Symphony. Although all parties announced that there was no friction between Schwarz and the Lincoln Center leadership—for example, Leventhal stated that he "was surprised and disappointed"[23] by the news—the artistic tension between Moss and Schwarz was well known in the field.

Public response to the festival's creation reflected the skepticism on campus, as seen in the *New York Times*'s comment in March 1995 that "no one ever said that creating Salzburg on the Hudson would be easy," but the 1996 festival was ultimately a success for Lincoln Center.[24] Leventhal recalled his consternation at the outset: "It was very scary. You're talking about no audience base whatsoever. All single seats. No coupon books, no subscriptions. . . . And the scariest part . . . that it wasn't until the middle of the end of the second week of a three-week festival that we knew that Lincoln Center [would survive the experience.] Ticket sales were not strong the first week . . . [but] it turned out to be perfectly successful."[25]

In terms of content, the first Lincoln Center Festival featured a wide array of well-curated presentations, including esoterica like the Thang Long Water Puppets from Vietnam and a gospel-soul guitarist from Brazil. The substance of the festival included several remarkable presentations that would ordinarily not take place in New York City, including: both versions of Beethoven's only opera, *Fidelio*, with the early version, *Leonore*, performed by John Eliot Gardiner leading his London-based period instrument ensemble, Orchestre Revolutionnaire et Romantique, and the New York Philharmonic under Kurt Masur performing the final version of *Fidelio* in concert form; the music of twentieth-century composer Morton Feldman presented in a three-concert retrospective; Samuel Beckett's complete stage works (nineteen plays) performed by Dublin's Gate Theatre; Robert Wilson directed the Houston Grand Opera's production of the Virgil Thomson–Gertrude Stein opera *Four Saints in Three Acts*, with Dennis Russell Davies conducting the New York City Opera Orchestra; Merce Cunningham Dance Company presented *Ocean*, the choreographer's final collaboration with the late John Cage, including an appearance by Mikhail Baryshnikov which caused the event to sell out; and eighty free performances presented of the Brain Opera, a high-tech audience-participation creation of the MIT Media Lab under the direction of Tod Machover.

The Lincoln Center Festival would continue for another twenty-one years, directed by Nigel Redden beginning in 1998, and achieved great success through unique presentations from around the world that were frequently New York City premieres. As the festival matured, most Lincoln Center constituents participated in one way or another in the summer performances.

By 2017, Jane Moss managed all artistic planning at the Center as its artistic director. In November 2017, during the presidency of Debora L. Spar, a period of serious budget deficits, it was announced that the festival would cease to exist and that the Center's summer programming in 2018 would drop from seven to five weeks. Redden said that with the festival's demise, "I feel New York will be somewhat poorer for not seeing [the non-Western art forms provided by the festival]."[26]

In her future planning, Moss would expand by up to 40 percent the Mostly Mozart Festival's offerings. She was also deeply involved in the development of the White Light Festival, taking place in the fall, which focused on spiritual elements of the performing arts. Moss retired from her position as artistic director in May 2020.

As the Lincoln Center Festival was getting off the ground in the summer of 1996, another artistic force was coming of age with the creation of a Lincoln Center constituent exclusively dedicated to the art of jazz. In its early years, Lincoln Center officials and constituents viewed the nonclassical arts with a level of condescension and disdain. Although popular artists such as Frank Sinatra, Benny Goodman, Ella Fitzgerald, and Duke Ellington performed at Carnegie Hall over the years, Lincoln Center officials had never been active in creating a series for such performers, although they were pleased to rent Philharmonic/Fisher Hall on a fee basis to nonclassical acts. Certainly JDR 3rd and William Schuman showed little interest or genuine respect for jazz as a musical genre, and Lincoln Center's position did not significantly change in this regard during the 1970s and 1980s.

This institutional position shifted dramatically, however, when Wynton Marsalis—a young trumpeter from New Orleans, schooled in both classical and jazz tradition—came to the public's attention. Marsalis hit the scene with a prodigious musical talent and a charismatic personality. Born in 1961 as the second of six sons of Dolores and Ellis Marsalis, himself a respected performer and music educator in his own right, Wynton became highly proficient as a trumpeter at a young age. He entered Juilliard as a student of the great classical trumpet pedagogue William Vacchiano, but he was soon performing in jazz clubs in New York City. Marsalis once explained that he entered Juilliard just as serious jazz programs were beginning to be developed on America's college campuses, but that before that period, jazz-oriented instrumentalists would study their specific instrument with a "classical" player and then learn to play jazz outside of school. Marsalis had a distinguished predecessor in Miles Davis, who also studied trumpet at Juilliard with Vacchiano before revolutionizing the jazz world.

By 1980, Marsalis was already performing and touring with Art Blakey's Jazz Messengers, but he continued to perform as a classical trumpeter, releasing a debut recording of trumpet concerti by Haydn, Hummel and Leopold Mozart and garnering his first Grammy Award for Best Classical Soloist with an Orchestra. He eventually became a genre-breaking composer, writing works that brought together jazz bands and symphony orchestras on the same stage. In 1997, his oratorio *Blood on the Fields* was the first jazz composition to be awarded the Pulitzer Prize.

Perhaps Marsalis's most powerful attribute is his commitment to social renewal and a type of empathy for which the art of jazz is identified. His integration of jazz performance with racial justice is predicated on his core beliefs of promoting "individual creativity (improvisation), collective cooperation (swing), gratitude and good manners (sophistication) and [addressing] adversity with persistent optimism (the blues)."[27] It was clear to anyone who knew Marsalis that he would not be held back by inherited traditions. Therefore, the success of Jazz at Lincoln Center seemed inevitable once Marsalis was behind the effort.

In 1987, Marsalis teamed with Alina Bloomgarden, Lincoln Center's director of visitors services, Stanley Crouch, and Albert Murray to create a three-concert summer series called Classical Jazz, which sought to attract a younger and more diverse audience. Crouch and Murray were well-known Black writers and critics influential in shaping discussions about race in America. Bloomgarden had proposed a jazz constituent to Leventhal in earlier years, but he was initially cool to the idea. Weissman also became an important force in creating the jazz program once Leventhal moved forward with the idea. In 1991, after four summer seasons, Jazz at Lincoln Center became a department of Lincoln Center and reported to Leventhal.

A Lincoln Center board committee, chaired by Gordon Davis, was formed to study the possibility of Jazz at Lincoln Center becoming a constituent. The new jazz organization quickly developed an international reputation and presented concerts in Asia and Europe. Finally, in December 1995, Jazz at Lincoln Center was authorized to become a constituent, beginning on July 1, 1996. The significance of Jazz at Lincoln Center's constituency was not lost on the press, with the creation of the constituent receiving front-page placement in the *New York Times:* "It is the first time that jazz, an American art form, has been fully accepted by one of the nation's premier performing arts centers, where the bulk of programming is still given over to European arts."[28] Rob Gibson, formerly head of the Atlanta Jazz Festival, who had been involved in helping to run the fledgling organization since 1991, was appointed executive producer for the new constituent.

Marsalis's vision was to develop a robust institution dedicated to the art of jazz involving performances in New York City, the rest of the country, and around the world, but also educational programs, especially Essentially Ellington, which would bring high school jazz bands from around the world to a spring season competition, plus publications, digital vehicles, and recordings. This extraordinary effort was crowned in 2004 with the construction of a grand venue for Jazz at Lincoln Center, located at Columbus Circle, just a short walk south of the main Lincoln Center campus.

The $131 million, hundred-thousand-square-foot space for jazz within the Time Warner Center (now Deutsche Bank Center) was designed by Rafael Viñoly and was presented as the world's first performance, education, and broadcast facility devoted exclusively to jazz. It was also the first constituent facility to be located off the main Lincoln Center campus. It included three performance spaces: the Rose Theater, named after principal donor Frederick P. Rose, which sat approximately 1,200 in a concert format; the Appel Room (initially called the Allen Room),[29] named after Robert and Helen Appel, accommodating about 420 audience members, which was built in the shape of a Greek amphitheater overlooking Columbus Circle, including dazzling views of Central Park; and Dizzy's Club Coca-Cola, an intimate jazz club serving food and featuring smaller

(Left to right): *Frank Bennack, Wynton Marsalis, and Reynold Levy, 2007. (Photo by Djamilla Rosa Cochran / Wireimage via Getty Images)*

jazz ensembles. The Irene Diamond Education Center was also created to provide a designated space for JALC's extensive educational programming. Marsalis said of the new complex, "The whole space is dedicated to the feeling of swing, which is a feeling of extreme coordination. . . . Everything is integrated [in] one fluid motion, because that's how our music is."[30]

Jazz at Lincoln Center's success did not come about without considerable negative reactions from the press and portions of America's jazz community to both Marsalis and his artistic aesthetic. Certain critics and jazz musicians expressed concern that Marsalis's programming focused too much on mainstream jazz and largely ignored the avant-garde jazz of the 1960s and '70s. According to one writer, "Mr. Marsalis has been called a nepotist for his assignment of commissions to himself and to young musicians widely seen as his disciples. There has also been criticism of what is seen as a paucity of white players in the program."[31] In response, Marsalis and his allies stated that the criticisms were as old as the art of jazz itself. Marsalis said, "Ellington faced this; Coltrane had to defend himself in writing. . . . There's always some side story that becomes the issue instead of the music. And my whole thing is, what about the music?"[32]

From philosophical and aesthetic points of view, Marsalis was intensely consistent in JALC's early years. He successfully developed performances with the New York Philharmonic and the New York City Ballet, and he also helped to create the degree program in jazz studies at Juilliard, which began as a graduate program in 2001 and added undergraduate and artist diploma programs soon thereafter. Although philosophical and artistic tensions continue, JALC's basic mission of bringing the art of jazz to larger and more diverse audiences succeeded, and its building at Columbus Circle became a major center for jazz performances and education in the United States and beyond.

CHAPTER ELEVEN

An Innovative, Risk-Taking, Adventurous, Artistic Entity

S THE 1990S CAME TO A CLOSE, Sills and Leventhal raised the important issue of the Center's future by commissioning a study titled "Committee for the 21st Century: Report to the Lincoln Center Board of Directors." One aspect of the report involved a poll of each of the constituent's physical plant needs. Sills expected to receive reports on heating and cooling problems in the campus's buildings or the increasing cost of repairing travertine, but instead she received requests from the Philharmonic to have Avery Fisher Hall renovated once again and for City Opera to leave the New York State Theater altogether for a home of its own. As a result, a preliminary plan was proposed to overhaul the entire campus at an approximate cost of $1.5 billion.[1]

Lincoln Center had not undertaken a physical plant project since the construction of the Rose Building in 1990. Although many constituents benefited from that structure, the added space was mostly in the form of offices, rehearsal rooms, and residence hall facilities. Apart from comparatively small venues used by the Chamber Music Society, the Lincoln Center Institute, the Film Society, and the Kaplan Penthouse, no significant performance space—and certainly no space able to accommodate an audience of a thousand or more—had been constructed within the Rose Building.

Leventhal in particular was intent on creating a new theater, which was needed to accommodate the presentations of the Lincoln Center Festival, concerts by Jazz at Lincoln Center, performances by the New York City Opera, and other concerts throughout the year. The Peter J. Sharp Theater in the Juilliard building was always seen as the perfect size and design for certain Lincoln Center presentations, offering a seating capacity of just under one thousand, a large fly space, and an orchestra pit to accommodate about sixty musicians. It was not available for outside users, however, since its performances were only for academic credit–bearing presentations and therefore exempted from the presence of union stagehands belonging to Local 1 of the International Alliance of Theatrical Stage Employees or from regulations set by Local 802 of the American Federation of Musicians.

Leventhal explored ways that a new theater at Lincoln Center, similar in size and function to the Sharp Theater, could be built close to campus. A site for this new venture was considered at the American Red Cross building at Amsterdam Avenue and Sixty-Seventh Street.

In early 1997, Sills and Leventhal tried to move this idea forward, and Leventhal gave presentations about the proposed theater to various Lincoln Center boards. Many of the constituent chairs were unenthusiastic about the venture. This proposal came on the heels of the first Lincoln Center Festival, and several constituents still felt they had not been adequately consulted regarding the summer performances. Also, it was feared that the project's cost, although not definitively established at that time, would negatively affect future constituent fundraising.

In the face of such resistance, Leventhal dropped the idea. However, in January 1997, Rob Gibson of Jazz at Lincoln Center reported at the monthly Lincoln Center Council meeting that his organization was going to develop a new theater of its own. Gibson said that the theater would be created based on Wynton Marsalis's vision. Eventually, this approach would grow into the JALC complex at Columbus Circle.

In the same spirit of change embraced by Jazz at Lincoln Center, Paul Kellogg, general and artistic director of the New York City

Opera, decided to act independently to find a new performance space for his organization. Kellogg had been quite public regarding his negative view of the New York State Theater's acoustics for the presentation of opera. At the beginning of the 1999–2000 season, Kellogg installed a "sound enhancement" system that he had experienced in Denmark, comprising a network of microphones and speakers placed throughout the hall that distributed sound based on acoustical best practices. Kellogg insisted that it was not amplification and did not change the quality of the voices.[2]

The public response to the new sound enhancement system was mixed at best, with most opera aficionados believing that any electronic enhancement of the voice was detrimental to the opera experience. Although Kellogg claimed that the New York City Opera singers and orchestra members were pleased with the results, one singer in particular considered the sound installation anathema to the opera experience: Beverly Sills.

Sills was quite public in her opposition to the system's installation, reminding the opera world that neither she nor her longtime colleague and friend Plácido Domingo had ever had any problems projecting their voices in the theater during their years with City Opera. Her negative position on the issue was based on a deep sense of unease regarding her former opera company, openly expressing her feeling that the company had diminished both artistically and financially since her departure.[3]

Kellogg and his board developed a plan in the fall of 2000 to find a new theater, with the hope that their project could be folded into Lincoln Center's overall redevelopment campaign. Potential sites considered by City Opera included the construction of a new theater on Damrosch Park land just west of the New York State Theater or the construction of a new opera theater integrated into the renovation of the American Red Cross site first identified by Leventhal, with the support of the property's private developer.

Strong opposition to the City Opera project surfaced on campus, and the New York City Ballet expressed no interest in taking on the full cost of running the State Theater if the City Opera departed. Joseph Volpe argued that a new theater for the City Opera would financially destroy the struggling company and therefore negatively affect the other Lincoln Center constituents. He also voiced vociferous opposition to a new house in Damrosch Park, located just south of the Met. As with the issue of the State Theater acoustics, Sills was also publicly negative about a new theater for the company. In hindsight, the installation of the sound enhancement system in the State Theater and the search for a new hall accelerated City Opera's downward slide at Lincoln Center, which had already commenced due to past financial and artistic decisions on the part of its board and management.

By the time Sills and Leventhal announced the creation of the Committee for the 21st Century in March 1998, which had grown out of Martin E. Segal's earlier work with his Committee for the Future, Lincoln Center constituents were poised to undertake a major renovation of campus buildings, with the New York Philharmonic and the City Opera leading the charge.

This new committee was chaired by Roy Furman and included seventeen other board members. The formal report from the committee was issued to the members of the Lincoln Center board on November 30, 1999, and presented an estimated cost for all the redevelopment projects at $1,497,073,000, including a new $150 million New York City Opera house seating 1,500.[4]

An audience development component of the study involved the commissioning of various surveys on the demographics of Lincoln Center audiences. Proposals included cross-constituent marketing and strategies for moving a patron from single ticket purchases to buying a subscription. Of special interest was the creation of a visitors' center to serve as a "welcoming gateway to Lincoln Center's audiences."[5] While certain suggestions in the report regarding audience development were examined by selected constituents, the only element that was ultimately realized was the creation of the visitors' facility, named the David Rubinstein Atrium at Lincoln Center and located on Broadway between Sixty-Second and Sixty-Third Streets.

In May 1999, the planning and architectural firm Beyer Blinder Belle was engaged to develop a "capital needs assessment" and eventually a campus-wide master plan, working closely with the well-known architectural firm Cooper Robertson. According to this new structure, a Project Leadership Committee, chaired by Sills and including all the constituent chairs and chief operating officers, was formed to oversee the entire project, with Furman's Committee for the 21st Century reporting to it.

The Project Leadership Committee went one step further by creating three additional subcommittees to address the plan's actual implementation. The most important of the three was the Redevelopment Committee chaired by Marshall Rose, who immediately built a staff led by Rebecca Robertson as executive director, in what would officially be known as the Lincoln Center Constituent Development Project, Inc. Robertson was a highly respected and experienced urban planner who had previously worked for the Shubert Organization and the 42nd Street Development Project. Committees focusing on fundraising and finance were also created, and constituents were represented on all three subcommittees.

Marshall Rose was a particularly important participant in the new redevelopment effort. Born in Brighton Beach, Brooklyn, in 1937, he attended City College and earned a law degree from New York University. After law school, he joined the law firm of Dewey Ballantine but moved on to become a successful real estate developer, founding the Georgetown Company in 1978, which developed many residential, commercial, and mixed-use properties across the United States. He also became an active philanthropist, chairing the New York Public Library board for most of the 1990s. He was an effective fundraiser comfortable on construction sites, in the board room, and at galas, where he would often escort his new wife, the actress Candice Bergen, whom he married after both had lost their longtime spouses.

Even before the Center's complex committee structure was finalized, Leventhal and Sills were delighted to announce on September 15, 1998, that the financier Julian Robertson had donated $25 million to Lincoln Center for the new campaign. The gift became the largest single contribution to Lincoln Center at the time, exceeding the Avery Fisher gift by $15 million. As a result of the gift, Lincoln Center's central plaza was named after Robertson's wife, Josie.

On December 20, 1999, as the fundraising for the project became more focused, a small group of Lincoln Center officials including Sills, Leventhal, Davis, Linda Janklow, Joseph Volpe, and the author, met with Mayor Rudolph Giuliani in his City Hall office, cluttered with New York Yankee memorabilia, to make a pitch, as it were, for city support of the project. The goal of the meeting was to obtain a grant of at least $160 million over ten years, but the meeting participants also put forward a proposal for support of as much as $240 million, an amount Giuliani ultimately authorized.[6]

This significant fundraising initiative resulted in an item placed in Mayor Giuliani's budget of $24 million provided to Lincoln Center annually for ten years. Although one mayor's budget is not binding on the next, Leventhal and Davis assumed that the money would be authorized in the future based on the rationale presented to Giuliani, as characterized by Leventhal, that "assuming it is a $1.5 billion [Lincoln Center] project, the City, traditionally, has funded 16% of Lincoln Center's capital expenditures, so we would like you to continue to fund 16%. And he [Giuliani] said 'Well, I'm not falling out of my chair.' And 16% of $1.5 billion is $240 million."[7]

Efforts were also initiated to have federal and state funds support the project. Common gifts would be divided in a prearranged formula and constituent-specific gifts would be kept entirely by the constituent (i.e., the same method for allocating gifts first developed during the construction of the Rose Building). The committee report noted that the estimated $1.5 billion cost was realistic since the Center comprised twelve performing arts institutions, working in seven separate buildings, one park, three plazas, and several underground structures housing support facilities and garages.[8]

Center leaders were also quick to mention the benefit that Lincoln Center had brought to the city, state, and nation, no doubt to reinforce the concept that funding for the proposed project from these three governmental entities would be money well spent for the long-term health of the economy. The report trumpeted the fact that "Lincoln Center's economic impact to New York City totals well over $1 billion annually . . . [with] the taxable value of real estate in the Lincoln Square neighborhood expand[ing] 18 times between 1962 (when Lincoln Center's first building opened) and 1999."[9] In this initial stage of the project, the only constituent not participating was the New York Public Library, which was just about to complete a building-wide redesign of its Lincoln Center facility created by the Polshek Partnership. However, this neatly packaged organizational structure did not consider the personalities who would be reacting to these committees' decisions nor the deep-seated resentments still held by certain constituent leaders toward Lincoln Center, Inc.

Within this complex, high-stakes environment, Sills and Leventhal decided to be as aggressive as possible in finding needed financial resources to support the project. So began the unlikely saga of the sale of a work of art that made the troubled authorization of the placement of works by Calder and Moore on Lincoln Center's north plaza in the 1960s seem like child's play.

The work of art in question was a painting by the American painter Jasper Johns titled *Numbers 1964*. Paintings by Johns had been fetching extremely high sale prices, with one work, *False Start* from 1959, selling in 1988 for $17 million. *Numbers 1964* had supposedly elicited offers in excess of $15 million. The painting had been hanging in the lobby of the New York State Theater for thirty-five years in relative obscurity until its potential sale was made known to the public. Art historians saw the piece as important since it represented the largest of Johns's paintings using numerals as a motif. Its materials and manner of construction were also considered unique. It was claimed by Philip Johnson, architect of the New York State Theater, and others that the painting was an integral part of the Lincoln Center complex, although Leventhal strenuously objected to that idea. The New York City Opera was in favor of the sale; the New York City Ballet was opposed.[10]

At the December 1998 Lincoln Center board meeting, its members authorized Sills and Leventhal to explore the sale of the painting based on correspondence with the artist. However, in January the board learned that there were not one, but two letters from Sills and Leventhal to Johns, the first of which, dated October 7, 1998, had not been shared with the board. The first letter stated that although the Center had been approached by "several individuals" about the sale of the painting, the board "had no intention of considering these offers or seeking others. . . . On the contrary, we have every intention of continuing to display this wonderful painting for many generations to come."[11] The second letter from Sills and Leventhal to Johns of early December, however, *was* known to the board and made it clear that a sale of the painting was in the works and that the board had agreed to consider it. Sills admitted that the board had been informed of the second letter to Mr. Johns but not the first, claiming, "We simply forgot."[12]

Such an omission would ordinarily trigger a hostile response from an uninformed board, but Sills's charm and Leventhal's longevity obviated that reaction. Sills in particular was exceedingly thin-skinned about negative publicity, and both she and Leventhal quickly backed away from the sale, especially after the *New York Times* published an editorial chastising Lincoln Center for trying to sell the painting.[13]

One would assume that this contretemps would fade into history, but there was a postlude involving the sale that was never divulged by Lincoln Center officials. It seems that in the summer of 2000, Johns had confidentially contacted Lincoln Center officials and proposed that he make a duplicate of *Numbers 1964* that would hang in place of the original in the State Theater.

In a 2000 oral history interview, Leventhal remembered, "[Johns] recently proposed to us that he make a duplicate of it, hang that in the State Theater, and let us sell the original, to which Beverly and I both said 'We'll let the next people do that. We had our fun being pillaged.'"[14] Ironically, unless a visitor to the State Theater knows of the painting's history, it is often the case that audience members on the way to a performance walk by it with nary a glance.

In addition to the Mozart bicentennial celebration and the inauguration of the Lincoln Center Festival, the individual constituents of the Center continued to provide high-quality events during the 1990s. Kurt Masur took on the musical directorship of the New York Philharmonic in 1991 and held the position until 2002. Masur, a classic Kapellmeister, embraced nineteenth-century German symphonic repertoire and did not bring a new vision to the orchestra, although many listeners and critics agreed that he developed an enhanced musical discipline in the weekly performances that were far superior to those of the Mehta years. He also initiated a comparatively modest renovation of Fisher Hall's stage in an effort to improve the acoustical conditions for the orchestra's musicians. Masur was succeeded by another traditionalist, of sorts, Lorin Maazel, who was the orchestra's music director from 2002 to 2009. Early in his career Maazel had developed a reputation for performing new music, but that waned in his later years. His efforts to control every element of a musical work during a performance was a trademark of his time with the ensemble, which diminished the spontaneity and energy one expected from the Philharmonic.

The 1990s represented the apogee of James Levine's leadership at the Met. His artistic control of the opera was complete, and Joseph Volpe assured that all other elements of the organization ran efficiently. Levine did a great deal to enhance all artistic elements of the house, from engaging world-class vocal soloists to developing a high-quality chorus and audience-pleasing productions. Levine also brought the Met Orchestra to a new level of excellence, not only when they were in the pit but also when they were featured as an ensemble at Carnegie Hall or on tour. The orchestra was consistently ranked as one of the world's best during this period.

The Met also unveiled in the 1995–96 season its Met Titles, a system of computer screens mounted on the backs of seats displaying the libretti of operas in various languages. An earlier iteration of seatback titles had already been presented by the Santa Fe Opera a season or two before, which the Met adapted for its own purposes. Although both Levine and Volpe were not initially enthusiastic about any system that visibly distracted audience members from the stage, the high quality of the experience won over the Met leaders. The Met Titles system literally set the standard for similar experiences around the world.

During the 1990s, the Met also received pledges amounting to $45 million from the financier Alberto Vilar, with the opera dedicating, albeit temporarily, the Vilar Grand Tier in his honor. He was a contributor to many other opera companies, universities, and assorted nonprofits. His firm, Amerindo Investment Advisors, collapsed due to the market downturn in technology funds in 2000. Regrettably, Vilar continued to make pledges he could not honor. In 2010, Vilar was sentenced to nine years in prison on twelve counts of securities fraud. The Grand Tier was ultimately renamed in honor of Met donor Mercedes Bass.

The Lincoln Center Theater found its stride in the 1990s with the presentation of a wide array of dramatic works, from Shakespeare to nineteenth-century dramas to twentieth-century classics such as

The Heiress by Ruth and Augustus Goetz, featuring Cherry Jones; Edward Albee's *A Delicate Balance*, with Elaine Stritch and Rosemary Harris; Lillian Hellman's *The Little Foxes*, featuring Stockard Channing and Frances Conroy; and Tom Stoppard's *Arcadia*. A new musical written specifically for Audra McDonald, with words and music by Michael John LaChiusa, titled *Marie Christine*, also was produced at the end of the decade. In the 1994–95 season a successful revival of Rodgers and Hammerstein's *Carousel* developed the Beaumont's ensuing tradition of producing Broadway musical classics to great artistic and financial success.

Under the artistic direction of Peter Martins, the New York City Ballet continued to celebrate the genius of both George Balanchine and Jerome Robbins as well as developing many new works through the Diamond Project, a choreographic commissioning program funded by the philanthropist Irene Diamond. Martins became a frequent choreographer for the company as part of this project and for other parts of the season as well. Wynton Marsalis also wrote two scores for City Ballet performances in 1999. In 1998, City Ballet celebrated its fiftieth anniversary; around that same time, however, the community mourned the loss of two of its most important artistic and administrative leaders with the death of Lincoln Kirstein in 1996 and Jerome Robbins in 1998.

The New York City Opera underwent a series of transitions during the 1990s. Beverly Sills stepped away from the company and Christopher Keene became general and artistic director in 1989, bringing an austere aesthetic and championing such challenging works as Arnold Schoenberg's *Moses und Aron* and Paul Hindemith's *Mathis der Maler*. Upon Keene's death in 1995, Paul Kellogg assumed leadership of the City Opera and, in selected cases, mounted productions he had developed as head of the Glimmerglass Opera in Cooperstown, New York. Kellogg produced operas by Handel, Gluck, and Monteverdi and championed new or twentieth-century works, including Mark Lamos's *Paul Bunyan*, Tobias Picker's *Emmeline*, Tan Dun's *The Voyage of Marco Polo*, and Jack Beeson's *Lizzie Borden*. Kellogg would significantly increase the City Opera budget during the decade, setting out on a fiscal path that would cause great distress for the company in the new millennium.

Since its inaugural year in 1969, the Chamber Music Society of Lincoln Center had a checkered history. Charles Wadsworth, the founding director who oversaw the Society for twenty years, ended his tenure in 1989. The cellist Fred Sherry succeeded Wadsworth and served until 1993, followed by clarinetist David Shifrin, who directed the Society from 1993 to 2004.

In 1994, CMS celebrated its twenty-fifth anniversary. The review of the anniversary concert by Edward Rothstein of the *New York Times* reflected on the ups and downs of the Society's artistic output during its history. Rothstein commented that the Society "has had a fractious history since Charles Wadsworth left as its artistic director. . . . Audiences have grayed. Reviews have been mixed. Chamber music itself has been eclipsed by the current rage for opera."[15]

In 2004, CMS appointed David Finkel, the cellist of the Emerson String Quartet, and his wife, the pianist Wu Han, as co–artistic directors. Their leadership has been characterized by a higher level of preparation and performance, enhanced touring, and the development of residencies. In 2012, they were both named *Musical America's* "Musicians of the Year."

Within this multifaceted environment, which brought Lincoln Center and its constituents together in a complex choreography of real estate development, fundraising, New York City zoning regulations, and artistic aspirations, Lincoln Center's president announced that he would be leaving his post on December 31, 2000, after seventeen years of service.

Nathan Leventhal telephoned constituent heads on March 27, 2000, to tell them the news that would be announced the next day. Constituent leaders were surprised. He had not signaled any plan to step down from his position, working consistently on Lincoln Center projects and betraying no sense of distraction. His decision was primarily based on his reluctance to lead the redevelopment project that was about to be launched, as well as his personal sense that his time as president had passed: "I don't think I really had it in me to deal with [the redevelopment] project. . . . It's enough."[16]

Leventhal took a good deal of comfort in assuming that Marshall Rose and Rebecca Robertson would oversee the new venture.[17]

He also believed that Rose could be an excellent future Lincoln Center chair when Sills stepped down.

Leventhal's legacy was considerable. During his tenure the Lincoln Center budget always ran a surplus, but he was most proud of the artistic impact he realized during his presidency, commenting "[I helped convert] Lincoln Center, artistically, from an entity known as a solid, classical music presenter loathe to take risks or to be creative or innovative . . . into an innovative, risk-taking, adventurous, artistic entity."[18]

The Mozart Bicentennial Festival, the international festivals, Jazz at Lincoln Center, the American Songbook (a series of concerts celebrating composers and performers of American popular song), Midsummer Night Swing (a social dance "party" on the Lincoln Center Plaza featuring live music and dance lessons), the Rose Building, and the plans for the $1.5 billion redevelopment project— all were created on Leventhal's watch. In a more abstract sense, he was the first president to try to bring the constituents together to realize the goal of the Center's founders that the organization be larger than the sum of its parts. In many ways, he succeeded in that task. He would enjoy a twelve-year tenure as Mayor Michael Bloomberg's chief "talent scout" and would eventually serve as president of the Palm Beach Opera.

It would now be up to Beverly Sills to find a new president to lead Lincoln Center into the twenty-first century.

CHAPTER TWELVE

We're Going to Have to Put
Our Dreams on Hold

S ILLS AND HER LINCOLN CENTER board colleagues set about
quickly to search for Leventhal's replacement. The redevelopment project was picking up momentum, and Sills
often expressed to Leventhal before his departure that she
was "terrified" about what was still to come. In particular, she wondered whether she could manage the challenge without a Lincoln
Center president who would "hit the ground running" and lead the
implementation of the entire venture.

Even before Leventhal stepped away from his presidency, there
were dark clouds on the redevelopment horizon. At a June 20, 2000,
Lincoln Center Council meeting, in a surprisingly matter-of-fact
tone, Sills remarked that Paul Montrone, president of the Metropolitan Opera board, had mentioned to her that the Met was considering an exit from the redevelopment project. Such a departure
would send all the wrong signals to potential donors and to the
press. The redevelopment project was always presented as a unified
Lincoln Center effort that involved nearly all constituents, with the
understanding that the Library and Jazz at Lincoln Center were not
participating due to recently completed or ongoing projects. Losing the largest and perhaps most historically prestigious constituent

would present myriad public relations problems for Sills and weaken the master redevelopment plan's progress.

It was also clear to most Lincoln Center leaders by mid-2000 that Joseph Volpe was hardly a supporter of the project. In fact, several constituent leaders felt that it was Volpe, not Montrone or the Met board, who determined the direction the Met would take on this and other issues. Nevertheless, Sills made it clear to the constituents that the Met board, on which she served, backed Volpe: "I wanted them to understand that Joe is not speaking for himself."[1]

By early November 2000 further problems appeared at a Project Leadership Committee (PLC) meeting chaired by Sills. She approached the meeting in a slapdash and lackadaisical manner, ignoring the agenda and making her usual attempts at humorous side comments. In addition, Gordon Davis, the project's legal counsel, exhibited a disengaged and overly sensitive manner during the meeting, which frustrated many committee members.[2] The situation worsened at another PLC meeting on November 29, 2000, at which the discussions could only be categorized as chaotic. Gordon Davis presented lengthy, unfocused statements concerning legal issues, and Volpe often interrupted the flow of the meeting by requesting points of order and legal opinions.[3] Katherine G. Farley, who would eventually chair the redevelopment committee and become Lincoln Center chair, commented that after attending one particularly rancorous meeting, she sent Sills a pair of red boxing gloves.[4]

Nathan Leventhal chaired his last Lincoln Center Council meeting as president on December 19, 2000. Although there were the usual celebratory toasts, the meeting participants were unsettled by the fact that Rob Gibson, Jazz at Lincoln Center's executive director, had recently resigned and that Franz Xaver Ohnesorg, artistic and executive director of Carnegie Hall, had announced his resignation that same day to become the intendant of the Berlin Philharmonic.

With the departure of both officials, plus Leventhal, there was a pall over the Council meeting—three major arts leaders in the city were leaving their posts at almost the exact same time. The situation was worsened by an unfocused sense of mission as to where the redevelopment program was going. Volpe capped the meeting by announcing that he had learned that Robert Wilson, former chair of the New York City Opera board, had pledged a gift of $50 million for the construction of a new City Opera house in Damrosch Park, a plan which was completely unacceptable to Volpe.[5]

The search for a new Lincoln Center president moved forward expeditiously, and the final choice was clearly up to Sills. She publicly expressed her fears that the redevelopment project would turn out to be unwieldy and unfundable. Therefore, she wanted a new president whom she knew well and whom she could trust to make the correct decisions moving forward.[6] In her view, that person was Gordon J. Davis.

Davis had been intimately involved with the redevelopment project from its earliest days and had choreographed, along with Leventhal, the meeting with Mayor Giuliani in December 1999, which resulted in the $240 million grant from the city over ten years to support the venture. Davis was a well-known figure in New York City politics and society, having served as parks commissioner under Mayor Koch, as a member of the Lindsay administration, and as an adviser to Mayor Dinkins. He was one of the first Black Americans to become a partner in a major New York corporate law firm at Lord Day & Lord in 1983.

Davis did his undergraduate studies at Williams College and received a law degree from Harvard in 1967. He was the founding chair of Jazz at Lincoln Center and for seventeen years practiced law as a partner in the firm LeBoeuf, Lamb, Greene & MacRae. He had an ebullient personality and was an engaging public speaker and advocate for the arts and social causes.

Davis was elected Lincoln Center's seventh president by the Center's board on October 27, 2000, and began his new position on January 1, 2001. He spoke of his appointment "as the culmination of a . . . career in government, philanthropy and the law. 'Lincoln Center has been so much a part of my life and body and soul for so long . . . I cannot tell you how deeply moving this possibility is.'"[7]

Davis's first Lincoln Center Council meeting as president took place on January 16, 2001, the events of which would presage the exceedingly problematic environment Davis had inherited. Volpe raised the issue of a new opera house for the New York City Opera and asked direct questions of Paul Kellogg, City Opera's general and

artistic director, about its cost, location, and size. A quiet and dignified man, Kellogg was elusive in his answers, which caused Volpe
to press his point even further for nearly three-quarters of an hour.

In an effort to move the meeting to other topics, Davis unveiled
Lincoln Center's new $1 million website. Council members sadly
agreed that the presentation was dismal and the prototype semi-
functional, with more attention paid to Lincoln Center than the individual constituents. This triggered another outburst from Volpe:
"Isn't Lincoln Center here to help us [constituents] out? They
are not doing their job. They're just simply promoting their programs."[8] Davis's first Council meeting could hardly be classified as
auspicious, and it foreshadowed his battles with Volpe over the next
nine months.

Soon thereafter, a letter signed by Volpe and Paul M. Montrone
was sent to Beverly Sills, Marshall Rose, and Gordon Davis, with
copies subsequently distributed to all the constituents and to Ralph
Blumenthal of the *New York Times*, which indicated that the Met
was leaving the capital campaign and the redevelopment project.
As anticipated, on the very next day, January 24, a *New York Times*
article appeared telling of the Met's departure. Many of the Lincoln Center constituent chairs were deeply disturbed by the move,
and Marshall Rose was particularly troubled. The letter stated that
the Met had "been consistently excluded from meaningful involvement" in the project.[9]

Rose, who had just been appointed chair of the board of the Lincoln Center Constituent Development Project, was the only Lincoln Center official to comment publicly on the situation: "The Met
Opera's participation in the Lincoln Center redevelopment project
is the subject of ongoing constructive discussions, which we hope
will be resolved in a manner satisfactory to all parties. The occasional
back-and-forth about issues of concern is part of that process."[10]

As time passed, by mid-March Volpe and the Met had begun to make
noises that they would reconsider their position and perhaps return
to the Lincoln Center fold under new rules that would give them a
much larger say in the redevelopment decisions, including weighted
voting, significantly increasing their influence on the project. It was
also envisioned that the costs for any new building constructed on

campus (that is, a City Opera house) would not be borne by other constituents.[11]

At this moment of seeming rapprochement, many constituent trustees and CEOs on campus became concerned that Volpe was trying to remove Marshall Rose from the project. Volpe's strategy began to play out in public at the March Lincoln Center Council meeting. The written agenda made no mention of the redevelopment project. However, the lack of an agenda item did not stop Volpe from expressing great concern about Rose.

In a lengthy diatribe, Volpe claimed that the Met had an agreement with Rose and Lincoln Center to reenter the project, with Rose extending his hand to Volpe at that time and saying, "We're now all partners again," but that Rose had backed out of the agreement a few days later.[12] Volpe explained what was included in the aborted agreement, talking about proportional voting, a new structure for a budget committee, and Lincoln Center Council members working on design and construction issues. Volpe made it clear that the Met could no longer work with Marshall Rose. The tension in the room was palpable, as many board members sensed that Lincoln Center as an institution was coming apart at the seams.[13]

Volpe was preparing for a head-on clash with the Lincoln Center leadership—with one important caveat. In a telephone call with the author after the Lincoln Center Council meeting, Volpe stated that, although he had problems with Rose and Davis, he believed that Beverly Sills completely agreed with him about the issues at hand.[14] And he turned out to be right about that.

As anticipated, Volpe and the Met ultimately decided to rejoin the project in early May 2001, with the understanding that the master plan would be developed by the end of the summer and that if any of the constituents rejected it, the project would be automatically ended and each constituent would be responsible for costs incurred. This new agreement allowed city funding to be released for the project.[15] At the time, Volpe presented a more conciliatory stance: "I can't imagine that this project will not go forward. We have to find a way to make it go forward."[16]

Much of the progress that had been realized since the Met left the project in January was due to the nonconfrontational, diplomatic, and highly effective efforts of Bruce Kovner. Kovner had recently taken on the Juilliard chair in 2001 and was immediately identified by his trustee peers as an important and effective leader.

Kovner was born in Brooklyn and raised in Southern California. He entered Harvard College in 1962 and after graduating stayed on to pursue a PhD in political economy at the Kennedy School of Government, but never completed the degree. He became a successful investor and also developed a focused philanthropic strategy: Kovner involved himself in a charitable organization only after he understood its finances and believed in its mission. He would eventually become one of Juilliard's greatest benefactors, second only to Augustus Juilliard, whose estate provided, in 1919, a testamentary gift to establish the Juilliard Graduate Institute.

As the redevelopment project moved forward, Beverly Sills approached Kovner in April 2001 to see if he would be willing to succeed her as Lincoln Center's chair. Kovner was intrigued but noncommittal, leaving the vacancy unresolved for the moment.

On May 15, 2001, the redevelopment project received what seemed to be a much-needed boost when an elaborate presentation involving a new design concept for the campus took place in the World Gym building at 1926 Broadway, which provided an enormous space for the gathering. The principal presenters were Marshall Rose, Rebecca Robertson, Jaquelin Robertson of Cooper Robertson, and Frank O. Gehry, one of the world's most celebrated architects.

Gehry had been approached by Rose to develop an architectural concept for most of the Lincoln Center campus. His approach, in brief, was to put an enormous transparent roof over the Fountain Plaza, which had on its perimeter the Met, Avery Fisher Hall, and the New York State Theater. Gehry explained that because he was from Southern California, when visiting Lincoln Center during the winter months he saw the need for a covering that would provide much-needed protection from the elements. The concept of the "dome" was thus put forward.

Since Gehry worked in three-dimensional models, not sketches, wooden mock-ups were spread around several connecting rooms in the large space. At one point in the meeting, boisterous laughter rang from one of the rooms, and many meeting participants stood to see that Peter Martins, ballet master in chief of the New York City Ballet, had put domes not only over the Fountain Plaza but also over the North Plaza and Damrosch Park. Everyone nervously applauded, although the result looked as if Lincoln Center had been invaded by a fleet of glass flying saucers. In defense of Gehry's design, Rebecca Robertson said that the word "dome" was inappropriate; rather, "roof" would better describe the glass covering, because what Gehry had created was an undulating span of glass that had various curvatures and angles which Robertson saw as quite artful.[17]

To add further awkwardness to the four-hour meeting, the concept of a new, 2,200-seat house for City Opera located in Damrosch Park was presented. As before, Joseph Volpe made it clear that this would not be allowed by the Met. Paul Kellogg was visibly upset by the contretemps. Also upset was Gehry, offended by the realization that his design had not been embraced with enthusiasm by the group, especially since he believed that his approach—into which he had already put a considerable amount of time—had already been accepted by Rose and Sills, who had visited the architect at his studio in Santa Monica, along with Rebecca Robertson, before the May 15 meeting. Ultimately, the elaborate Gehry design was rejected primarily because it did not conform to the prevailing aesthetic of the Center's main plaza; however, other related mundane questions raised concerns as well, such as how to keep the roof transparent, with Sills commenting "Who's going to clean all that glass?"[18]

Soon after the Gehry presentation, several Lincoln Center executives made it known that Gordon Davis's position as president was in serious jeopardy.[19] With the summer approaching, the Davis situation remained in stasis, but any issues regarding the Center's leadership were instantly pushed to the background on Tuesday, September 11, 2001. The terrorist attack on the World Trade Center paralyzed the city as all air, rail, and automobile access to Manhattan was shut down.

On September 12, a special Lincoln Center Council meeting was held in the Kaplan Penthouse of the Rose Building. Davis began by asking for a moment of silence, but there was a tension in the room that made the acknowledgment brief and ephemeral since all the constituent heads immediately wanted to address questions of security, the installation of metal detectors in the halls, and the schedule for reopening the Center.

In fact, at the urging of Mayor Giuliani, the New York City Opera opened its season on Saturday, September 15, a few days later than originally planned, with performances of *Der fliegende Holländer* (*The Flying Dutchman*) by Wagner in the afternoon and *The Mikado* of Gilbert and Sullivan in the evening. Before the Wagner performance began, Paul Kellogg addressed the audience, surrounded onstage by cast members, stagehands, and staff, saying in a trembling voice that the performing arts have many functions, including "catharsis, consolation, shared experience, reaffirmation of civilized values, distraction. . . . So we are back."[20] Then all assembled stood for a moment of silence and the singing of "The Star-Spangled Banner." Next door to the State Theater, the Metropolitan Opera displayed an enormous American flag from its front portico in a gesture seen throughout the city.

Redevelopment meetings continued soon after the 9/11 attacks, but during a September 19 meeting Marshall Rose seemed distracted in his duties as chair and Davis was uncharacteristically quiet.[21] The reason for this lack of focus became clear on September 25, when it became known that Gordon Davis would resign as president in the next few days. As anticipated, on September 28 at noon, a news release was sent by Lincoln Center stating that Davis was leaving the Center's presidency; he explained that he had visited "the devastation of the World Trade Center [which] played a role in his resolve to step down without delay, sparing Lincoln Center a protracted struggle."[22]

Davis wrote in his resignation letter to Sills that "things are not working in the way either of us hoped or expected." Sills's response was to express regret and say, "I agree your decision is correct."[23] Sills and Davis had experienced numerous public and private disagreements since his appointment, and the Lincoln Center administrative staff members were publicly complaining about Davis's leadership style.[24] Lincoln Center trustees were not surprised that friction had occurred when "two formidable individuals [held the top Lincoln Center posts]: a chairwoman who is [a] powerful and strong-willed former diva who raises millions of dollars for the organization and a president who is a longtime member of the city's informal power structure and who is more given to issuing orders than following them."[25]

On October 1 the Lincoln Center board met to discuss Davis's resignation and to appoint a search committee for a new president led by Frank A. Bennack, Jr., the Hearst Corporation chair. Davis was provided a $1 million severance package, equivalent to about two years' salary.[26]

Janice Price, Lincoln Center's vice president for consumer markets and new technology, was appointed the Center's interim executive director. She would depart in February 2002 to become head of the Kimmel Center for the Performing Arts in Philadelphia. Schuyler Chapin, New York City's commissioner of cultural affairs and a Lincoln Center veteran, commented, "Now, with a war and a major rebuilding effort in lower Manhattan on the horizon, the renovations [of Lincoln Center] will necessarily have to be different projects. . . . There will probably be changes."[27] Linda Janklow, chair of the Lincoln Center Theater, stated what most Lincoln Center insiders assumed: "We're going to have to put our dreams on hold."[28]

At the time of the Davis resignation, Sills was trying to prepare her own exit. She and other Lincoln Center board members had numerous discussions with Bruce Kovner urging him to take on the chair, to no avail.[29] Sills's lack of energy in her role as chair caused further challenges for the redevelopment project. She often sided with Volpe and the Met on critical issues and was hesitant to publicly commit to a transformative venture that would prepare the Center for the twenty-first century.

The tense Lincoln Center environment was reflected in the almost daily conflicts between Volpe and the redevelopment leaders, which centered on both the unacceptability of the Gehry plan and the Met's implacable opposition to a City Opera house in Damrosch Park. Sills attempted to present a positive view of the situation: "There are going to be moments of great frustration. . . . But it's all resolvable. I promise you there will be a day of bricks and mortars, even if I won't be here to see it."[30] Her words turned out to be prescient.

Lincoln Center leadership was facing an existential threat brought on by the redevelopment project, in the process exposing the problematic structure that loosely bound the Center's constituents.

In an insightful *New York Times* article, Robin Pogrebin and Ralph Blumenthal, both of whom had covered the Center extensively, described the organization as "a confederation of Balkanized states, with a host of strong-willed constituents held together by guile, geography and varying degrees of need."[31]

With the resignation of Gordon Davis, the continuing problems with the Met, and the halfhearted support of Sills for the project, the inevitable occurred with the resignation of Marshall Rose as chair of the redevelopment committee on October 22, 2001, months before he had said he would leave. Rose had been a principled and dignified leader who had donated his time as chair, but he was frustrated by the weak and perhaps duplicitous leadership of Sills as well as constant problems raised by Volpe and the Met.

In a formal presentation to the Lincoln Center executive committee on October 12, before his resignation was publicly announced, Rose was candid regarding his feelings about the redevelopment project and his plans for the future. In a telling statement at the beginning of his presentation regarding the numerous leaks to journalists which had recently taken place, Rose said, "I'm sticking to my notes due to the porous nature of confidential meetings at Lincoln Center. . . . So at least I'll know what *I* said."[32] He then went on to summarize his view of the work that needed to be done:

> We were asked to put together a transformative Master Plan; that begins with assembling a world-class team of professionals. . . . Working hand-in-hand with the Constituents, this team delivered all of the essentials of the Master Plan [including] a total renovation plan [for each building]. . . . There is probably an inability to reach consensus on a transformative plan. I believe the consensus process is fundamentally flawed—primarily by the lack of collegiality of the people and perhaps their own institutional agendas. This is unlike most of our businesses, where we have a vertical decision process.[33]

He ended his presentation by presaging his plans for the future: "[Recent events] also reaffirmed my thoughts that I must promptly rethink what role, if any, that I want in the continuing project. I am enormously proud of the work that has been done over the past 15 months, and I've enjoyed working with *most* of the Constituents."[34] Rose said in a later news article that he was stepping down because he had completed his work.[35] However, anyone experiencing the angst on campus knew otherwise. Rose had allegedly said of Sills that she "stabbed me in the back."[36] Although he denied saying that, Rose would publicly express great frustration with the redevelopment process, such as when he stated, "I didn't take this on pro bono or give a year of my life just to fix some plumbing."[37]

Marshall Rose's last meeting as chair of the Redevelopment Corporation took place on November 5. The meeting's goal was to unanimously agree on a plan to be sent to Mayor Giuliani so that Lincoln Center could receive the first tranche of $24 million of the total authorized amount of $240 million over ten years in support of the project. It was not more than a few minutes into the meeting that the proceedings became contentious. Volpe commandeered the discussion, insisting on various changes to the plan. Ultimately, however, the plan was approved by all participating constituents. The meeting was a deflating experience for most participants; Sills expressed consternation that this argumentative process would have to stop and unsettled the proceedings further by saying that she wished to resign as chair as soon as possible.

As 2001 ended, the redevelopment project seemed hobbled at every turn. At the final Lincoln Center Council meeting of the year on December 18, Council members were greeted by Sills and Volpe both sitting at the head of the board table, with the two functioning essentially as cochairs. Volpe brought up the idea of the Lincoln Center Council taking over the primary direction of the redevelopment project, then overseen by the chairs of the various constituents. The proposal was viewed as impractical and quickly dismissed.

The meeting concluded with many constituent heads believing that a paradigm shift would have to take place in the project's organizational structure if the transformative renovation of Lincoln Center, which had excited so many Center officials only a few months earlier, were to occur.

CHAPTER THIRTEEN

I Would Have Preferred
a More Collegial Approach

A T A TIME WHEN AMERICA WAS grappling with the implica-
tions of a presidential election which had to be decided by
the Supreme Court and recovering from the first foreign
attacks on its soil since Pearl Harbor, one could not
blame Lincoln Center's leadership for feeling a bit bruised by all
that had occurred in the earliest years of the new millennium. The
concomitant economic stress caused by 9/11, including a significant
drop in ticket purchases by international patrons, created long-term
problems for the arts center.

By January 2002, the Redevelopment Committee was chaired
on a temporary basis by Martin Oppenheimer, who also served as
chair of City Center, but Bruce Kovner was emerging as the individual who could lead Lincoln Center out of the morass posed by the
redevelopment project. In a series of confidential discussions with
selected board chairs and constituent CEOs, Kovner presented a
strategy whereby the project could move forward and still avoid the
roadblocks presented by the Met and Joseph Volpe *if* the venture
were separated into two phases: the first related to the constituent
organizations on the north side of Sixty-Fifth Street (that is, Juilliard, Tully Hall/Lincoln Center, the Film Society, and the School
of American Ballet, with the Lincoln Center Theater joining that
group, although located on the south side of the street). This first

phase would be appropriately dubbed the Sixty-Fifth Street Project. A second phase would then be realized sometime in the future, focusing on renovations south of Sixty-Fifth Street, involving the New York Philharmonic, the Metropolitan Opera, and the two occupants of the New York State Theater, the City Ballet and the City Opera. Such a strategy would separate Volpe and the Met from the deliberations related to renovations during the "phase 1" work. In fact, when this strategy took hold, it was Volpe who sardonically coined the term "northern and southern alliances," reflecting the dichotomy and also using terminology drawn from the newly initiated war against the Taliban in Afghanistan.

Before the bifurcation strategy was initiated, however, Volpe increased his efforts to move the redevelopment project in his desired direction. On January 17, 2002, the year's first Lincoln Center Constituent Development Project committee meeting took place, preceded by a subcommittee meeting whose members included Kovner, Guenther, Sills, Oppenheimer, Howard Solomon (chair of the New York City Ballet), and Irwin Schneiderman (chair of the New York City Opera), with Paul Montrone on the phone from his home in New Hampshire.

At the subcommittee meeting, Montrone proposed alternative budget authorizations for the project which reflected Volpe's previous demands. Schneiderman and Solomon added fuel to the fire by getting into an intense discussion about the percentage of city money allotted to their two institutions, with Sills stating in exasperated tones, "I'm tired of all this. I'm going to move that the entire project be dissolved."[1] Fortunately, Kovner was able to calm the proceedings and asked to move the prearranged motion, which simply stated, "The committee unanimously accepts all elements of the budget," amounting to about $32 million in support of work for the ensuing seventeen months.[2]

Kovner polled the members of the committee, all of whom voted "yes," until it came to Montrone, who voted "no." Further discussion ensued, and enough information and pressure were put forward so that Montrone changed his vote to "yes," resulting in unanimous acceptance of the budget.

By now, the participants in the larger redevelopment meeting gathered in the Kaplan Penthouse were wondering where the members of the subcommittee were and suspected that something important was taking place. The second meeting finally began when the subcommittee members arrived. The agenda moved quickly until it was time for the budget report, which Montrone presented from the phone. He stated that the committee had unanimously agreed to authorize all elements of the budget. The entire redevelopment committee then voted on the budget, which passed with no objections. There was a pregnant moment of silence after the vote and then Volpe said, "Are we saying it [the budget] is authorized as such, with no changes?" and from the phone Montrone replied, "Yes." Paul Guenther then said in a self-satisfied tone, "Well, Joe, you are ably represented at the subcommittee by your chairman, Paul Montrone."[3]

Volpe shot back, "The only person I trust is myself for making the right decisions for the Metropolitan Opera."[4] Volpe left in a huff while many committee members smirked. The meeting may have provided the "icebreaker" that the project needed, but the sense of forward movement was diverted considerably only a week later when Montrone advised the subcommittee that he wished to rescind his "yes" vote on the budget; not only that, the Met would continue to vote "no" until the budget could be modified further. Even the calm and composed Kovner was outraged by this move.

In early February 2002, a highly detailed and widely read article appeared in *New York* magazine written by Leslie Bennetts which analyzed the redevelopment project's various problems. Titled "The Metropolitan Soap Opera," it was accompanied by a satirical cartoon drawn by Michael Witte depicting the principal players in the drama (Sills, Volpe, Rose, Davis, and Kellogg), all attired in either Roman or medieval costumes, holding swords (except for Rose, who had a sword inserted in his back), and Volpe as the costumed Mephistopheles.

The article set the stage as follows: "Lincoln Center is a community in deep distress, driven by a conflict over a grandiose $1 billion redevelopment plan. . . . Instead of uniting the center's constituent arts organizations behind a common goal, the project has pitted them against one another in open warfare more reminiscent of the shoot-out at the OK Corral then of a night at the opera."[5]

Bennetts summarized the various stages of the project, noting the departure of Davis and Rose, the tabling of the Gehry plan due to the controversy around its design, and the limbo status of a proposed New York City Opera house. Instead of blaming Volpe for those difficulties, she presented a different scenario, which was not surprising to Lincoln Center insiders: "With Lincoln Center buzzing like an angry hive, it has finally dawned on its major players that they underestimated the Machiavellian role played by the reigning grande dame. . . . Because of her glory-filled past . . . even the most astute insiders were remarkably slow to figure out that the former Queen of City Opera had become its most insidious enemy."[6] Throughout the article, Bennetts presented Sills as the principal source of the project's problems.

In turn, Volpe publicly relished his role in the brouhaha, saying, "Who's the bad guy in the Lincoln Center redevelopment? It's me! . . . Who's the bad guy with all the other constituents? It's me! . . .

An illustration by Michael Witte accompanying an article in New York *magazine by Leslie Bennetts titled "The Metropolitan Soap Opera," February 4, 2002. (Left to right):* Marshall Rose, Beverly Sills, Paul Kellogg, Joseph Volpe, and Gordon Davis. (Illustration by Michael Witte)

If you're slightly aggressive about your position, people take it as an affront.... But I find that if you are not slightly aggressive, they don't pay any attention to you."[7]

The article, which Leventhal called a "hatchet job" and was roundly condemned by the entire senior staff of Lincoln Center, concluded by addressing the effectiveness of Sills as the Center's chair; according to a quote from an unidentified board member, "I think it's time for Beverly to move on, because she's become a lightning rod for a lot of positive and negative feelings.... Someone with better vision, and larger vision, and a lot of patience is going to have to come in."[8] Soon thereafter this individual's wish would come true.

Sills had often said that she planned to step down as chair upon the appointment of a new president who would succeed Gordon Davis. The search committee, chaired by Frank Bennack, understood that the president's appointment was not only a fundamental component of having the redevelopment project go forward but also a reinforcement of Lincoln Center's leadership structure.

By late February 2002, it was announced that Reynold Levy, president of the International Rescue Committee (IRC), had been chosen as Lincoln Center's eighth president.[9] Before Levy's work with the IRC, he had been a senior officer at AT&T and president of the AT&T Foundation, earlier serving as executive director of the 92nd Street Y. He earned an undergraduate degree from Hobart College, a law degree from Columbia, and a PhD in government and foreign affairs from the University of Virginia.

Levy's appointment was soon followed by Sills's expected announcement that she would vacate the chair on May 1, 2002. Sills said, "Having been involved with the selection of Reynold Levy ... I feel confident that Lincoln Center is in excellent hands and I feel my departure can finally become a reality."[10] Her plans to leave had been delayed on at least two separate occasions—because of Leventhal's unanticipated departure and then the short tenure of Davis. She candidly remarked that "right now all I can think about is I would like a little of my privacy back. I need a little peaceful time. I'm going to be 73 years old in May, and I want to smell the flowers a little bit."[11]

Sills was credited with raising a considerable amount of money for Lincoln Center during her eight-year run. She also brought twenty new members to the Center's board, many of whom were major corporate leaders. During her leadership, she was particularly proud of the creation of the Lincoln Center Festival and the elevation of Jazz at Lincoln Center to constituent status. The American Songbook series was also inaugurated during her tenure. However, the $1.5 billion redevelopment project was clearly her bête noire, having taken on, in her own words, "a life of its own."[12] In addition, City Opera's desire to build a new opera house, first in Damrosch Park and then off the Lincoln Center campus entirely, put her in direct confrontation with her old opera company.

In retrospect, Sills's leadership had been a mixed blessing for Lincoln Center. Levy commented at the time of her resignation that "there is no question Beverly Sills leaves Lincoln Center and its constituents stronger than when she found them."[13] Such a statement could be honestly debated. Obviously, she was a brilliant fundraiser and a global opera celebrity. Yet, sadly, she lacked the qualities needed in a successful Lincoln Center chair. The problematic issues of the redevelopment project coupled with the tragedy of 9/11—which for Lincoln Center specifically meant a depressed local economy and a drop in ticket sales throughout the campus—required a leader who was serious, disciplined, forthright, and willing to make hard decisions. Sills fell short in those areas. Although she was a superb artist and a charming individual, she had great difficulty making decisions which put her in conflict with colleagues.

The reasons for her alliance with Joseph Volpe and the Met remain a matter of speculation. After she left the City Opera in 1989 as general director, she joined the Met board in 1991 and put her former opera company in the rearview mirror. Volpe, for all his bombastic outbursts at redevelopment meetings, was consistent in one sense: he always put the needs of the Metropolitan Opera first. Sills, on the other hand, never forthrightly protected her own institution—Lincoln Center—often deferring or making decisions which benefited the Met more than the other constituents. As always, she was engaging and funny in her interview with the *New York Times* about her departure, stating that she no longer wanted to talk about conflicts: "Can't I have a nice resignation story?"[14] It would not be long before she was back in the news.

Levy's tenure as Lincoln Center's president began much more aus-
piciously than that of Gordon Davis. In earlier years, Leventhal
developed Lincoln Center Council agendas that were precise and
well-paced, and his personality seemed to adjust to the particular
challenges of each meeting's circumstance. Davis was engaging and
often ebullient when chairing a meeting, but such gatherings tended
to meander. Levy's persona at Council meetings could be described
as lugubrious: clear agendas were rare and a more conversational
environment prevailed. However, Levy's expertise, experience, and
calm demeanor added an important new element to the redevelopment meetings. He once commented that visiting war-torn areas
around the world as president of the IRC made the contentious Lincoln Center meetings seem comparatively benign.

On June 17, 2002, Bruce E. Crawford was elected the new chair
of Lincoln Center. As a former president and general manager of the
Metropolitan Opera, he knew the Lincoln Center community well.
He had left the Met as general manager in 1989 to become chair of
the advertising conglomerate Omnicom Group. He was reelected as
the Met's president in 1991 and served in that capacity until 1999.
In fact, it was Crawford who recommended Volpe to be the Met's
general manager after Hugh Southern relinquished the position.[15]

Crawford was a 1952 graduate of the University of Pennsylva-
nia, where he majored in economics. With a full head of white hair,
oversized glasses, and a Boston accent, Crawford embodied a dignified and experienced persona and brought a needed gravitas to the
Center's chair, a change welcomed by all.

In late September 2002, Peter Lehrer assumed the Lincoln Center Constituent Development Project board chair, replacing Martin
Oppenheimer, who had been serving on an interim basis after Marshall Rose's resignation. Lehrer had founded the construction firm
Lehrer McGovern and eventually partnered with Bovis Ltd. to create one of the largest construction companies in the world. A calm,
quiet, and somewhat dour individual, he was first and foremost a construction expert, not a planner, which would not help him navigate
the complex political and architectural landscape that lay before him.

About four months after Beverly Sills retired from the chairmanship
of Lincoln Center so that she could finally "smell the flowers a little

bit," she said, "I smelled the roses and developed an allergy," thus announcing her decision in October 2002 to become chair of the Metropolitan Opera.[16] Such a humorous line straight out of vaudeville did little to mute the surprise of Lincoln Center constituents, who saw her new role as a reinforcement of Joseph Volpe's negative view of the redevelopment project.

At seventy-three, Sills once again proved that her ability was second to none in achieving the highest levels of power within the complex hierarchy of New York City's arts environment. She would succeed James W. Kinnear, the former president and chief executive of Texaco. Paul M. Montrone would remain as the Met's president. In public announcements Sills's appointment was closely tied to her strong relationship with Volpe, who said to the press that he would welcome "my dear friend and colleague" to the Met.[17] It was evident that her new leadership role put the Met in a very strong position to determine many of the Center's decisions in the time ahead. In a gesture of goodwill, both Paul Kellogg of City Opera and Paul Guenther of the Philharmonic publicly praised the appointment.

Sills explained that she would focus on fundraising, a vital need at that time.[18] According to one report, "a sharp drop in foreign tourists after the terrorist attacks of September 11 set the opera back $7 million in ticket sales last season [2001–2] and the tanking stock market has shrunk its endowment [from $309 million at its peak to $260 million]."[19]

Sills was not overly generous in juxtaposing her new chair with her previous one, saying, "I can't tell you how happy I am to have an office in a theater . . . [instead of worrying about] real estate and fountains."[20] She continued by saying that she never secretly favored the Met during her years at City Opera or Lincoln Center. "Everyone knows what I think," she said. "I don't have the brains to keep my mouth shut. . . . I need new mountains to climb, which is why roses don't appeal to me."[21]

Although Beverly Sills's decision to become the Met chair was a surprise to Lincoln Center leadership, a truly shocking announcement occurred on June 1, 2003, when the New York Philharmonic and Carnegie Hall announced that they would merge as institutions and that the Philharmonic would leave Avery Fisher Hall and cease being a Lincoln Center constituent.

Bruce Crawford and Reynold Levy were blindsided by the move. Both men had heard that low-level discussions might have been taking place in earlier months regarding a merger, but no one expected such a monumental move to happen. In fact, Lincoln Center officials were told that there was no truth to the rumors of a Philharmonic move to Carnegie; according to Crawford, "I had been assured by the Philharmonic this was not a real option. I would have preferred a more collegial approach."[22]

It was announced that the move to Carnegie could occur as soon as 2006. Sanford I. Weill, CEO of Citigroup and chair of Carnegie Hall, said, "There is no reason why it shouldn't be a done deal. . . . I worked on a lot of mergers, and I've never seen a fit as perfect as this." The move was presented as a win-win arrangement for both organizations; for the Philharmonic, it would gain access to an acoustically superior hall and have no need to spend hundreds of millions of dollars to renovate its old performance space. In addition, it would move from a rent-paying tenant to becoming a partner in running its own venue. In turn, the Philharmonic subscription audience would give Carnegie a stable revenue base, and the merged entity would create an endowment valued at close to $350 million. Paul Guenther, chair of the New York Philharmonic and former president of the PaineWebber Group, said, "It was not a question of luring the Philharmonic to Carnegie Hall, but of the Philharmonic doing what is best for its long-term interests." The preliminary plan for the merger's administrative structure had Zarin Mehta, the Philharmonic's president, overseeing the orchestra's activities and Robert J. Harth, Carnegie's executive and artistic director, running the house.[23]

The extraordinary move raised several issues for Lincoln Center leadership. For one, the New York Philharmonic had a long-term lease to occupy Fisher Hall, and the orchestra's departure would breach the agreement. However, both Weill and Guenther saw the lease as a minor issue; Weill said, "Leases never stopped anything good from happening," and Guenther noted that the merger had powerful support, crowing "I bet on it."[24]

Martin E. Segal called the merger a form of "cultural cannibalism," but non–Lincoln Center officials looked on the move in more benign terms. Both Mayor Michael Bloomberg and Kate D. Levin, the city's commissioner of cultural affairs, regarded the merger positively. Carter Brey, the orchestra's principal cellist, was greatly in favor of the move, saying, "[This is] the best news in the world. . . . I don't think there is a musician in the New York Philharmonic who would not love to be affiliated with Carnegie."[25] Adding insult to injury, Mehta called into question the entire Lincoln Center concept: "I think the idea of having all the stuff [the Center's constituents] in the same area is not good from a civic standpoint. To have them dispersed helps the development of [the] city."[26]

The proposed merger also came as the New York City Opera was looking to leave Lincoln Center to pursue a newly proposed opera theater at the Ground Zero site. Such a departure would cause the New York City Ballet to take on full budgetary responsibility for the State Theater's finances.

The precipitous move by the Philharmonic and City Opera's exit strategy raised numerous questions regarding Lincoln Center's continued viability. Although the Center's leadership tried to put the best spin on the Philharmonic departure, saying that Fisher Hall would now be used for more innovative programming, this upbeat tone did not ring true with those in the know. Critics in the press questioned the overall philosophy of Lincoln Center and wondered whether a centralized art center made sense in the twenty-first century.[27] The Center's constituents were stunned by the Philharmonic's action, feeling both betrayed and desperate, since the redevelopment project looked to be irreparably damaged.

Crawford and Levy acknowledged that a new chapter was now beginning for the Center. In a dour tone, Crawford noted, "Times have changed, a half-century has passed, and we have to do business somewhat differently. . . . But we still can be and should be the world's greatest performing arts center."[28]

CHAPTER FOURTEEN

Welcome to the Urbanism
of Lilt and Swoon

W ITH THE ANNOUNCED MOVE of the New York
Philharmonic to Carnegie Hall, both Bruce Crawford and Reynold Levy were intent on determining
whether the Philharmonic-Carnegie merger would
take place. Board members of the merging institutions had already
expressed concern that many details of the venture had yet to be
resolved. The basic question to be addressed was: What would Lincoln Center do about the Philharmonic lease agreement and the
future use of Fisher Hall? Before that could be resolved, however,
an incident occurred at Lincoln Center which distracted its leaders
from the merger.

Peter M. Lehrer, who had only taken on the chair of the Center's Redevelopment Corporation board nine months earlier, resigned and called the project wasteful and badly managed. "A lot
of money has been spent on planning with not enough to show for
it," he said at the time of his resignation on June 12, 2003.[1] Lehrer
indicated that he had been unable to accomplish what he intended
because of a flawed management structure. "I came to the position
with much enthusiasm and interest. . . . Unfortunately, the position
that I was put in did not enable me to have the responsibility for the
management of the project or the staff," he said.[2]

Lehrer had clashed with Rebecca Robertson and demanded her dismissal. For Robertson's part, she recalled that they "stopped talking to each other a month after he [Lehrer] started. . . . He was abusive to the staff, but they kept doing their work."[3] In turn, Crawford spoke to the constituents about Lehrer's demand to let Robertson go, and they strongly supported retaining her.[4] As a result, Lehrer resigned. Lehrer was particularly frustrated by the fact that about $19 million had been spent on project planning, with most of that going to Norman Foster's architectural firm and about $1 million to Frank Gehry for designs which were never used.[5]

The Lincoln Center board faced a full agenda at its meeting of June 16, 2003, but the heart of the gathering dealt with the New York Philharmonic's decision to leave Lincoln Center and the Lehrer resignation. The proceedings began at noon in the Chamber Music Society's large rehearsal room on the tenth floor of the Rose Building. Crawford chaired, and a motion was immediately made to ask any directors of the Philharmonic who were present to leave. The board voted down the motion, but the tension in the room was heightened significantly by such a procedural maneuver.

Crawford reported that in mid-May both he and Guenther had agreed that the latest estimate for the renovation of Fisher Hall, totaling close to $400 million, made the project impossible. Crawford went on to say that he and Levy had met with Guenther and Mehta on May 29, during which Guenther requested that a June 16 meeting, which had been scheduled to discuss other options for the Philharmonic, be postponed because the Philharmonic wanted to explore the idea of moving to Carnegie. Crawford asked that Guenther defer any such exploration until Crawford could confer with Lincoln Center's executive committee. Guenther assured Crawford at that time that a Carnegie merger was not a real option. However, on May 30, Levy received a call from Mehta saying that the press already was aware of the Philharmonic's discussions with Carnegie.

By June 1, the decision-making process had spun out of control, and both the Philharmonic and Carnegie announced a merger after both boards had been convened through conference calls. In a serious but not angry tone, Crawford said that the Philharmonic had breached its lease agreement with Lincoln Center and that "we are not interested in getting mad or being paid back, but we must exercise our rights and have ground rules for the future."[6] However, no substantive decisions about the merger were concluded at the meeting.

Crawford next turned to the topic of the redevelopment project and the resignation of Peter Lehrer as board committee chair. Another motion was made to have Lehrer leave the meeting, but it did not pass. By this time, the tension in the room grew exponentially, causing one attendee to comment that what was taking place with Lehrer was straight out of the pages of Nathaniel Hawthorne's *The Scarlet Letter.*

As anticipated, Crawford explained that Lehrer had demanded that Robertson be fired, and the trustees disagreed. During this public humiliation, Lehrer remained quiet, causing some in attendance to wonder why he decided to attend in the first place. Once again, Lincoln Center had been set back by another challenge, conjuring recollections of the proverbial trials of Job.

As soon as Lincoln Center redevelopment discussions had begun in 1999, the New York City Opera raised the issue of finding a new opera house that would provide better acoustics than its current home at the New York State Theater and allow it to set its own schedule, no longer needing to accommodate to the needs of the New York City Ballet. By 2000, City Opera had put together a board committee to explore a new home for the opera. Paul Kellogg had successfully constructed an admired opera theater in Cooperstown, New York, during his tenure at Glimmerglass Opera, and he was eager to use his past experience to develop a special venue for City Opera, aided by funding from Robert Wilson. Damrosch Park, just west of the State Theater, and the American Red Cross building on Amsterdam Avenue were discussed as construction sites, although building in Damrosch Park was a nonstarter for the Met and Joseph Volpe. The opera's cotenant, the New York City Ballet, also had no interest whatsoever in taking on the full financial responsibilities of running the State Theater if City Opera departed.

By late February 2002, it became known that City Opera wished to participate in a proposed arts complex at Ground Zero.[7] A 2,200-seat opera house was envisioned within the development of other venues to host potential participants such as the Joyce Theater and the Guggenheim Museum. Wilson responded to the opera's proposed move downtown by saying that he would agree to use his $50 million for such a purpose.

Although there was concern on the part of City Opera's leaders that their core audience, which was based on the Upper West Side, might not be interested in traveling so far south to attend opera performances, Kellogg expressed enthusiasm for the idea: "Clearly there are a lot of people who would prefer not to go downtown . . . [but] there will be so much vitality there and such a strong sense of being part of a renaissance of an area where there had been so much despair."[8] The proposed move was discussed at various governmental levels through much of 2002. Although the cost of creating a new opera house was estimated at between $200 and $300 million, the *New York Times* reported that "the concept of a large cultural component on the site is said to have strong support among developers."[9]

The City Opera move had some pundits again questioning the efficacy of Lincoln Center in the new millennium. Many suggestions were made for new approaches for the Center to take in a time of cultural transition, such as bringing a more diverse and younger audience to the Center and the idea that Lincoln Center needed to be more of an innovator in the presentation of the performing arts. Alex Ross of the *New Yorker* wrote a curmudgeonly article about his perceptions of the Lincoln Center experience that used such terms as "a nimbus of corporate blandness . . . [a place with a] 'faintly spiritless air,' [and] 'an airport terminal for the performing arts.'" In this desultory context, Ross urged City Opera to escape the Center's environment and "jump at the chance to leave this rudderless ship."[10]

Although John C. Whitehead, chair of the Lower Manhattan Development Corporation, was enthusiastic about having City Opera at Ground Zero, few, if any, major politicians or community groups were on board. By June 2004 City Opera was advised that it had not been chosen as a participant in the Ground Zero project. Instead, the institutions chosen for the downtown renovation project were the Signature Theater, an innovative drama organization based on Forty-Second Street that specialized in full seasons featuring the work of one, usually American, playwright, and the Joyce Theater, which was known for its presentations of smaller contemporary dance groups. As it turned out, neither the Signature nor the Joyce ever went to Ground Zero. The National September 11 Memorial and Museum opened in 2018 and the Ronald O. Perelman Performing Arts Center was to be built across the plaza from the Museum and scheduled to open in 2023.

After its Ground Zero rejection, City Opera turned back to the original Red Cross site on Amsterdam Avenue, but that location proved unworkable due to an unacceptably small footprint for an opera house. In turn, the finances of City Opera continued to worsen in the first half-decade of the millennium, as fundraising remained flat and ticket sales dropped. Understandably, visionary concepts like a new opera house were pushed to the wayside and, perhaps inevitably, Paul Kellogg announced that he would retire at the end of the 2006–07 season. According to City Opera historian Heidi Waleson, "At sixty-eight, he was exhausted and out of ideas about how to reverse a company in freefall."[11]

As is so often the case with projects announced in early summer in New York City, the Philharmonic-Carnegie merger went quiet for most of July and August, although ongoing discussions between the two institutions continued on the staff level. By September, it became known that the conference calls made on June 1 with board members authorizing the merger had been hastily assembled and both sides still had many questions.

It also became known that the relationship between Robert Harth, Carnegie's executive and artistic director, and Zarin Mehta, the Philharmonic president, had become strained, as each man positioned himself for a controlling role in overseeing the new administrative structure. Carnegie's leadership had quickly come to the realization that with the Philharmonic in residence at the hall, Carnegie could no longer engage visiting orchestras at the rate it had in the past. As of mid-September, no merger papers had been signed.

By the end of September, members of both boards were publicly airing negative comments about the merger. Philharmonic board members expressed discomfort that their organization could lose a good deal of autonomy in pursuing their own artistic objectives. Guenther asked for more time to resolve the prevailing issues. Time, however, could not solve the problems facing the two organizations. On the afternoon of October 7, 2003, it was announced that the

New York Philharmonic and Carnegie Hall had abandoned their merger plans and that the Philharmonic would remain at Lincoln Center.[12]

In retrospect, the word best associated with the proposed merger might be "hubris." The merger failed because Carnegie did not wish to turn over the majority of its schedule to the Philharmonic, and the Philharmonic did not wish to compete with other attractions for access to the hall. Also, Weill left the strong impression that once the merger was completed, he would be the person in charge, a highly unpalatable scenario for Guenther and his board. The lack of any personal chemistry between Harth and Mehta also made the venture that much more untenable.

Guenther, who earlier had announced the merger with great fanfare, saying, "He'd bet on it," finally conceded, "In the end we realized that, due to a variety of reasons, trying to get the two organizations together became insurmountable. . . . We decided to call it a day."[13] The response from Lincoln Center leadership was graciously benign, reminiscent of the biblical return of the prodigal son. Reynold Levy said, "Welcome home. All is forgiven. We have a lot to discuss."[14] Bruce Crawford was both forgiving and realistic: "What we need to have is a partnership based on trust. . . . We need to sit down with . . . the Philharmonic and work out how we can restore a good working environment."[15]

As the Philharmonic returned, one would have thought Guenther and Mehta might make some type of public apology for such an egregious rejection of their long-standing association with Lincoln Center. Such an act of contrition never took place. Sadly, in February 2004, Harth would die of a heart attack at the age of forty-seven.

Remarkably, as various challenges confronted Lincoln Center leadership—with the resignations of two Redevelopment Corporation chairs in the span of one year and the continuous infighting threatening the core values that the Center's founders had established in the mid-1950s—the administrative staffs of the Center and of the Redevelopment Project doggedly continued to move their venture forward. Levy was clearly committed to significant renovations and Robertson had done yeoman's work in maintaining focus despite some very difficult working conditions.

Although a renovation of Fisher Hall was deemed too expensive, which drove the Philharmonic to pursue the Carnegie merger, Lincoln Center and the Philharmonic had earlier engaged Norman Foster's firm to develop a plan for renovation of the hall. Levy was proactive in exploring ways that an eventual renovation of Fisher could happen, and his thinking led him to begin the process of renaming Fisher Hall in return for a substantial gift from a new donor.

Although Levy left his post before negotiations on the hall were completed, for a payment of $15 million to the family of Avery Fisher the naming rights to the hall were released in 2014. Avery had died in 1994 and his wife, Janet, passed away in 2010. The hall had been named for Fisher in 1976. The settlement amount was close to the sum that remained in the Fisher endowment held by Lincoln Center at the time of the name change.

For a gift of $100 million in 2015, the venue name was changed to David Geffen Hall in honor of the Hollywood entertainment mogul. Geffen, in the gift agreement, insisted that his name remain on the hall in perpetuity. Although the Geffen gift was intended to jumpstart a physical renovation of the hall, to begin in 2019, construction work, based on an entirely new architectural plan, was deferred to an undetermined date.

Levy was also innovative in trying to find new sources of financial support for the Center. His most daring effort was to allow the twice-a-year Mercedes-Benz New York Fashion Week to take place on the Lincoln Center campus. The venture was supported by New York City officials, who felt strongly that the Center should host the event. This weeklong gathering was held in February and September of each year, during which new fashion collections by international designers were shown to buyers and the general public alike.

Constituents did not express great enthusiasm for having such an event take place on campus, but their concerns were ameliorated when they were advised that an estimated $17.1 million would be paid over five years for use of the space, which would be proportionally distributed among the various Lincoln Center arts organizations. The first Fashion Week occurred on campus in September 2008.

Levy seemed quite intrigued by the event's many complex elements, including the installation of a large tent on the Damrosch

Park grounds that would house most of the presentations, which were surprisingly brief, averaging about twenty-five minutes each. Peter Gelb, on the other hand, was troubled both by the loud noise from generators used to cool and heat the tent, and by the fact that Levy would not share the Fashion Week contract with the constituents. There were few experiences during Fashion Week which recognized the fact that the festivities were occurring at a major arts center. As the contract for the event lapsed, most Lincoln Center leaders were not displeased with the exit of the world's fashionistas from campus, although the constituents would certainly miss the event's rental revenue.

A master plan for the campus renovation created by Beyer Blinder Belle and Cooper Robertson had been released to the public in 2001, but the design architects were not announced until February 2003. The new architectural team included six firms: Diller + Scofidio, as the design architects, in association with Fox & Fowle Architects. The planner would be Cooper Robertson. L'Observatoire International would serve as the lighting designer and Olin Partnership as the landscape designer. Also joining the team would be 2 × 4 as the graphic designer. Unlike the architects working on the first iteration of Lincoln Center in the late 1950s, this team came together with one aesthetic viewpoint that would be consistent throughout the renovation of Sixty-Fifth Street between Broadway and Amsterdam Avenue. The goal was to provide new street-level entrances and open the Center to neighboring communities.[16]

The choice of Diller + Scofidio as the lead architects for the massive project was a curious one (Charles Renfro would soon join the firm as a partner, thereby changing the organization's name to Diller Scofidio + Renfro, hereafter DS + R), since the husband-and-wife team of Ric Scofidio and Elizabeth Diller had never constructed a habitable building. Most of their work had been done in the theoretical realm, as opposed to the construction of functioning buildings.[17] Scofidio usually deferred to his wife in public settings, so she was the face of the renovation throughout the process. Scofidio was introspective, while Diller was effervescent. She would present architectural ideas in a highly dramatic yet erudite manner, integrating many elements of the existing Lincoln Center design with

(Left to right): *Charles Renfro, Ricardo Scofidio, and Elizabeth Diller ca. 2006, architects of the Lincoln Center renovation completed in 2009. (Photo by Abelardo Morell / Courtesy of Edwynn Hook Gallery)*

innovative new additions that made the campus an engaging open area for the public.

Soon after it was announced that DS + R would lead the Sixty-Fifth Street redevelopment project, an exhibition opened at the Whitney Museum of American Art in late March 2003 titled "Scanning: The Aberrant Architectures of Diller and Scofidio." One critic summed up the Diller + Scofidio aesthetic by writing, "The firm's output over two decades is ingenious, affecting, perceptive and somewhat insidious—Diller + Scofidio do not so much attack the status quo as offer oblique commentary."[18]

Much of the exhibition did not focus on what one would call architecture. Displays included "50 identical Samsonite suitcases . . . ; a sequence of projected corporate logos that morph into one another with ease and fluidity . . . ; [and] 'Bad Press: Dissident Housework Series' pretend[ing] to document a wild, creative rebellion at the ironing board, where shirts were pressed into hilariously dysfunctional shapes."[19] Many Lincoln Center board and staff members were invited to the exhibition, often exiting with a certain level of concern as to why they had engaged DS +R as their lead architects. Although the firm was completing the construction of Boston's Institute of Contemporary Art, the closest DS + R had come to an actual structure was the "Blur Building," a temporary "non-building building" surrounded by thousands of mist-spraying jets, located in the middle of Lake Neuchatel in the town of Yverdon-les-Bains in Switzerland, presented as part of the 2002 Swiss Expo.[20]

Nonetheless, Rebecca Robertson saw something special in Diller Scofidio + Renfro's approach to the project: "Their concept was sensitive to the future needs of Lincoln Center, especially how it could welcome people to the campus in the future."[21] This contemporary view of Lincoln Center as seen through the lens of DS + R was an important element in how the venerated arts center could be revitalized. Not only did a deteriorating physical plant need to be addressed, but the more philosophical question was raised of how to experience the performing arts in a new way.

With the architectural team in place, for the first time there was a sense of optimism that the Center could reenergize itself after earlier setbacks, which were characterized by some critics at the beginning of the twenty-first century as having Lincoln Center caught in "the conflict between elite culture and a democratic society."[22] This observation rang true for many arts leaders and directly conflicted with the precepts of John D. Rockefeller 3rd, first announced in 1956, which saw Lincoln Center using the classical performing arts to uplift American society. Implicit in Rockefeller's concept was that such an embrace of Western classical culture, as provided by Lincoln Center, would effectively raise citizens' levels of education and financial achievement.

However, the place of Lincoln Center in New York City's cultural landscape had been questioned as soon as the Center's plans were made public in the 1950s. The well-known urban theorist and journalist Jane Jacobs, who wrote a highly influential article in *Fortune* in 1958 titled "Downtown Is for People," criticized Robert Moses and the concept of Lincoln Center and predicted that the complex would become a "grim, desolate fortress of the arts."[23]

But Jacobs was ultimately incorrect due to the positive impact Lincoln Center had on its surrounding community, sparking the West Side's revitalization in the 1960s. The DS + R plan aimed to break down further the isolation of the Center from its surrounding neighborhoods and to provide a new face to the city. In some ways, the long-disputed renovation now provided a lifeline for Lincoln Center to address the future with optimism and fresh energy.

The architectural team set about to create a design for a reimagined Sixty-Fifth Street which would be acceptable to its clients—not only Lincoln Center, Inc., but also Juilliard, the Chamber Music Society, the Film Society, the School of American Ballet, and the Lincoln Center Theater. Countless meetings took place from February 2003 to the spring of 2004 in order to build consensus around the design. On March 31, 2004, through a rare unanimous vote, the Sixty-Fifth Street project was approved by the Lincoln Center Constituent Redevelopment Corporation, which enabled the participating constituents to begin fundraising and construction on the estimated $325 million overhaul of the street. It also allowed the city to begin its formal review process.

Bruce Crawford was justifiably thrilled with the authorization: "This is a great step forward. . . . This has been a long and arduous process. I can only say without hesitation that the vote was unanimous, and it was enthusiastic."[24] It was also announced that the second phase of the project would involve the renovation of Josie Robertson Plaza and its iconic fountain as well as small modifications within Damrosch Park, all of which would be overseen by DS + R as well.

The details of the Sixty-Fifth Street redesign were presented to the public during a press conference in the soon-to-be-renovated lobby of Alice Tully Hall on April 13, 2004. The energy in the room

The announcement of the design for the Sixty-Fifth Street project renovation,
April 13, 2004. (From left to right before the architectural model):
Reynold Levy, Mayor Michael Bloomberg, and Bruce Crawford.
(Photo by Bebeto Matthews / AP / Shutterstock)

was high: Lincoln Center officials were delighted that the five
years of planning were ending and construction could finally begin. Mayor Bloomberg was joined by Crawford and Levy in making
preliminary comments. Finally, Rebecca Robertson introduced Liz
Diller to present the project's design elements.

Diller was clear, professional, and slightly dramatic in her presentation, explaining the design's aim to "open" the campus to the
surrounding community. What she presented resulted in a true and
real transformation of Sixty-Fifth Street, Lincoln Center's main
thoroughfare, including new entryways, LED display "blades," and
pedestrian-friendly elements at the street level, as well as substantive
changes to the interiors of Alice Tully Hall, The Juilliard School,
and other constituent venues on the street. Overall, the sidewalks
would be widened and the street itself would be narrowed for easier
pedestrian crossing.

The enormous bridge or deck over Sixty-Fifth Street, which
made its underside a dark and forbidding walkway, would be

removed. Its ten-thousand-square-foot surface would then be replaced by a similarly sized grass roof on the south side of the street
that would slope to the Henry Moore sculpture and the reflecting
pool, functioning as the top of a grand restaurant, eventually called
Lincoln Ristorante. To the bemusement of some of the attendees at
the press conference, Diller described the shape of the roof as a "hy-
perbolic paraboloid," though one architecture critic felt it looked
more like "a tilted potato chip."[25]

The dominant stone facades of the Center's buildings, clad with
travertine marble, would be replaced by glass, giving a sense of
openness to the street's buildings. There would also be significantly
more greenery, not only on the restaurant roof but in a dense grove
of trees directly to the south of the reflecting pool, which would
allow visitors to relax in the natural shade, sitting either on movable
chairs or on a permanent stone bench. Diller attempted to be as
sensitive as possible to the previous design that had been developed
by the great landscape architect Dan Kiley.

Alice Tully Hall would be gutted and its acoustics improved by
the acoustical firm Jaffe Holden. The hall would include new wood
on the walls, which would be installed with backlights that pene-
trated the wood and created a warm red color. In addition, the new
Tully lobby would reach out to Broadway, creating a graceful, trian-
gulated glass atrium.

The Juilliard building would experience extensive renovations,
bringing down its entryway to street level and creating a remarkable two-story atrium for its lobby, named after its chair emerita,
June Noble Larkin. Also included would be new rehearsal halls, a
student lounge, a new black box theater, a dance studio overlooking Broadway, and a specially climatized room to house a collection
of 141 rare musical manuscripts and first editions contributed by
Bruce Kovner.

A new venue for the Film Society of Lincoln Center (renamed
Film at Lincoln Center in 2019) on the south side of Sixty-Fifth
Street, the Elinor Bunin Munroe Film Center, with interior space
designed by David Rockwell, would have two theaters seating 140
and 85 respectively, as well as an amphitheater and a cafe. The Center would open in June 2011. A narrow glass footbridge would tra-

verse the street at mid-block close to the street-level entrance to the Lincoln Center Theater.

The Lincoln Center Theater would engage the well-known architect Hugh Hardy to create a black box theater on the roof of the Beaumont, designed to harmonize with the original Saarinen architecture. The new space would be called the Claire Tow Theater, named after the wife of longtime Lincoln Center Theater board member Leonard Tow, and feature the programs of LCT 3, a program that focused on the work of emerging playwrights, directors, and designers. Its intimate setting would seat 131, and a second level would feature a green roof and a terrace looking over the Center's North Plaza. The theater would open in June 2012.

Lincoln Center officials were clearly proud of what had been presented. Robertson said of Sixty-Fifth Street, "We want to create a street of the arts . . . to take what is now a neglected alley and make it a famous street."²⁶ In emphasizing the design's intent to make the campus more user-friendly, Levy stated, "It's really important to us, to present a new and welcoming face to our neighbors to the west," referring to the Amsterdam Houses, a New York City housing project, and the LaGuardia and Martin Luther King High Schools on the west side of Amsterdam Avenue.²⁷

In an evaluation of the design, Herbert Muschamp of the *New York Times* wrote that the entire North Plaza had become more inviting: "The reflecting pool has been rethought. . . . The pool's edges will be shaped to make it look as if the water were doing weird antigravitational things. They are a pleasingly off-balance ensemble, the roof, the pool, the grove: three characters in search of waltzing in the rain. . . . Welcome to the urbanism of lilt and swoon."²⁸

Through several changes in Lincoln Center executive leadership, two redevelopment chairs, and countless hours of meetings and negotiations involving hundreds of staff members and volunteers, Lincoln Center had persevered in arriving at a rational design plan that would achieve the transformative goal leadership had set out to realize. Now it was time to raise money and start the building process that, it was hoped, would not overly disrupt the artistic and educational programs that needed to continue through the construction dust and noise to come.

CHAPTER FIFTEEN

She Had Bet the Ranch

A S A RESULT OF THE COMING construction tumult, The Juilliard School requested a delay in beginning the work, citing its impending centennial celebration during the 2005–6 academic year. The ensuing construction schedule for the entire project was predicated on this arrangement, and demolition began on Sixty-Fifth Street in June 2006. The Juilliard centennial warranted such a schedule consideration since the School had envisioned a celebration that included the commissioning of new works in drama, dance, and music, special events, a *Live from Lincoln Center* gala performance, and, for the first time in its history, an American tour of Juilliard dancers, actors, and musicians as well as a previously planned international tour of the Juilliard Orchestra.

The centennial celebration began in May 2005 when the Rolling Stones kicked off their world tour from the balcony outside the Juilliard president's office. The crowd of hundreds watching the event stretched across the Sixty-Fifth Street bridge and south to the Fountain Plaza. The juxtaposition of the "staid" Juilliard School and the presence of the rock band generated widespread press coverage.

Juilliard commissioned thirty-four works in drama, dance, and music for the centennial year. The first to be presented was Eliot Feld's "ramp dance" titled *Sir Isaac's Apples*, which involved over sixty

Juilliard student dancers moving up and down a forty-five-degree ramp in excess of twenty feet in height made of smooth wood, accompanied by the music of Steve Reich's hour-long work *Drumming*.

A wide array of distinguished international composers, choreographers, and playwrights created new work for the celebration. The extraordinarily full year of events and concerts showed Juilliard's diverse artistic capabilities. The celebration segued into a groundbreaking ceremony on June 12, 2006, and the demolition of the Sixty-Fifth Street bridge was completed by late August. The balcony that once held the Rolling Stones disappeared at the same time.

As the excitement of the Lincoln Center Redevelopment project washed over campus, Beverly Sills was settling in as the new chair of the Metropolitan Opera board. Unlike other leadership changes at the Center, Sills's new position was closely watched by constituent heads because of the important role the Met played within the Lincoln Center community. Moreover, there was pervasive curiosity about how Sills and Joseph Volpe would work together.

Sills was clear in October 2002, at the beginning of her new tenure, that Volpe would be running the house, and she would raise funds and seek out new audiences. Sills was comfortable returning to the Met and enjoyed greeting stagehands and other workers who had known her over the years. She inherited a challenging fiscal environment caused by the negative impact of the 9/11 attacks, which resulted in foreign operagoers returning to Met performances in low numbers. As usual, she was optimistic about the future, saying, "I always said art is the center of civilization. This is a rough patch, and we will get over it."[1]

Soon into Sills's Met leadership it became known that the supposedly positive relationship between herself and Volpe was moving in a negative direction. Such an astute political operator as Volpe certainly knew that his relationship with Sills would not always be placid, but he assured his former chair, Bruce Crawford, that he "could handle her."[2] According to Crawford, Sills "didn't like Joe and Joe knew it."[3] She hoped to find a new general manager early in her time as chair. "I want Joe out as soon as possible," she said, according to Crawford, reminiscent of her earlier struggles with Nathan Leventhal.[4]

*Beverly Sills and Joseph Volpe, ca. 2004–6. (Photo by Beth Venesky /
courtesy of the Metropolitan Opera)*

In 2004, Volpe unexpectedly announced that he would be stepping down as the Met's general manager in 2006. The announcement was met with mixed reactions. Many staff, artists, and trustees
of the Met credited Volpe with keeping the largest performing arts
organization in America on a steady course, although financial and
artistic challenges inevitably surfaced. Others welcomed the anticipated tranquillity that would theoretically come with his departure.

Sills was deeply involved in the search for Volpe's successor and
would have the final say. Bruce Crawford reported that three can-
didates were seriously considered for the post: Deborah Borda, the
highly successful president of the Los Angeles Philharmonic; the
great tenor/baritone Plácido Domingo, who had administrative experience as head of both the Washington Opera and the Los Angeles Opera; and Peter Gelb, a well-known media producer working
for Sony. Sills settled on Gelb.

Although Peter Gelb had never run an opera company, which
critics saw as his fatal flaw, his experience in the arts and especially
in contemporary media initiatives stood him in good stead to lead
the Met into a new era. He commented soon after his appointment,

"I think what I'm doing is exactly what the Met engaged me to do, which is build bridges to a broader public. This is not about dumbing down the Met, it's just making it accessible."[5]

Gelb proudly recounted that he had been a Met usher in his teens. He left Yale College after one semester of study and worked for Sol Hurok; he eventually managed Vladimir Horowitz and touring artists and ensembles around the world. He founded and led CAMI Video and, in the 1980s, was executive producer of the PBS series *The Met Opera Presents*. He also worked with artists such as Julie Taymor and Seiji Ozawa in producing stage and film versions of operas. He was president of Sony Classical Records from 1995 to the time of his Met appointment. Therefore, he had a good deal of experience in developing and presenting new musical works and had honed his own personal aesthetic, which would soon affect future Met productions. He became the Met's sixteenth general manager on August 1, 2006.

Beverly Sills's trademark effervescence seemed to dim during her tenure leading the Met. As early as 2003, indications that Sills's health was failing were evident to those who worked closely with her. Her personal assistant at the Met, Danielle Collura, wrote numerous memos to Sills attempting to buoy her spirits with such messages as "Get well soon. . . . We want you to get well," accompanied by sketches of flowers and smiling faces.[6]

Gelb dedicated the entire 2005–6 season to shadowing Volpe and learning the many intricacies of the "house." He was assigned a tiny office near the company's media department offices on the building's top floor. However, Sills announced on January 25, 2005, after the Gelb appointment was completed, that she would be leaving her post in the spring. This time it seemed clear that she would no longer be allergic to "smelling the flowers," as she said, "I am stepping down for good. I had already decided that I was not really serving any of the masters well."[7] Sills went on to explain that a recent knee fracture and the placing of her husband, Peter Greenough, in a care facility brought her to the decision. Although she was not yet aware in 2005 that she was suffering from cancer, the disease would take her life on July 2, 2007.

In an appreciation written by Verlyn Klinkenborg, which appeared in the *New York Times* two days after her death, Sills's life was celebrated through all her artistic and administrative accomplishments: "She represented her art as though she had been elected to the task, and she took the job of representing it seriously. . . . In some sense, nearly the entire history of Lincoln Center has been entwined with Ms. Sills. It will be hard to imagine the place without her."[8] Lincoln Center would now have to address the completion of the redevelopment project and the future of the New York City Opera as a constituent without Sills's outsized personality and influence.

Many constituent leaders felt that the City Opera would not have decided to leave the New York State Theater and Lincoln Center had Sills not passed away when she did. Although Sills kept a considerable distance from her former opera company during her years leading Lincoln Center and the Met, she often expressed a certain tenderness toward the organization that had launched her operatic stardom, once stating, "The Company [New York City Opera] means a great deal to me. I love it. I always will."[9]

Yet her opposition to City Opera's efforts to build a new opera house in Damrosch Park when Sills was Lincoln Center chair negated an opportunity that might have allowed the company to flourish in the future. As Robert Wilson said of Sills, "Her bitterness and hostility towards a new house is baffling."[10] However, the problematic path that City Opera followed since it triumphantly reopened the Lincoln Center performance calendar after the 9/11 attacks was paved with incompetent board leadership, unrealistic artistic planning, and poor fundraising.

In the first decade of the twenty-first century, City Opera experienced long-term financial gaps between income and expenses. The company faced a situation where City Opera's budget grew by nearly 30 percent, to $46 million, between 2000 and 2008, while its revenues remained stagnant.[11] In addition, although City Opera productions generally garnered critical praise, in 2011 performances averaged less than 50 percent attendance; overall, since 2004, the value of its net assets had dropped by more than 80 percent.[12] The company's deficits rose each year, and by 2008 the company received permission from the New York attorney general to invade its endowment to pay for operating expenses, a desperate and imprudent act for any nonprofit organization.[13]

When Paul Kellogg departed as general manager and artistic director in May 2007, the City Opera board sought a replacement who could offset the opera's failure to find a new home after the proposed deal with the Red Cross building developers on Amsterdam Avenue fell through. The new City Opera leader also needed to counter the energy coming from the Met with the appointment of Peter Gelb, who was developing new productions led by innovative directors as well as new media initiatives aimed at younger audience members. Such a deus ex machina appeared when the New York City Opera chair, Susan Baker, attended a dinner at the French consulate in New York City and was seated next to Gerard Mortier.[14] According to City Opera board and search committee member Emilie Corey, "Susan met Mortier and fell in love."[15]

Gerard Mortier was once described as "an iconoclastic impresario and one of the world's premier provocateurs."[16] Born in Belgium, he had held principal leadership positions at the Théâtre de la Monnaie in Brussels, the Salzburg Festival, and the Paris Opera, where he was general director. He championed contemporary composers like Kaija Saariaho, commissioning her successful opera *L'Amour de loin*, and supported the American choreographer Mark Morris when he was at La Monnaie. In addition, he produced projects by the American director Peter Sellars and was instrumental in bringing his Mozart–Da Ponte cycle of operas (*Don Giovanni*, *The Marriage of Figaro*, and *Così fan tutte*) to Europe.

Mortier's rigorous contemporary sensibility, reminiscent of that of Pierre Boulez, was manifested in his comments upon accepting the City Opera appointment: "The most dangerous thing for opera is to make it something in a museum. . . . Even an odd piece by Mozart has to tell us something about today. To be modern is to be sensitive to everything that happens around you."[17] Never one to avoid controversy, his final production as head of the Salzburg Festival was the frothy *Die Fledermaus*, transformed to include Nazi hooligans and illicit drug use in a clear swipe at the conservative Austrian public and its government.

Mortier's appointment was considered a coup by some observers, who saw the arrival of this enfant terrible as a "shot across the bow" of the Met Opera and Peter Gelb. However, professional insiders and opera leaders understood that Mortier would come at a steep price, which would challenge the company's thin resources. Having worked in exclusively state-supported organizations for most of his career, for Mortier, the process of fundraising to support an arts organization was a new concept.

Mortier's plans for City Opera were, indeed, transformative. He proposed having significantly fewer productions per season, pushed for exploring City Opera presentations at various venues around the city, and, perhaps most important, said he was more or less satisfied with the New York State Theater. He would still request, however, a renovation that would involve an enlargement of the pit, the installation of new stage lighting, and the provision of a modern media system, all of which required closing down the City Opera season for a full year. This would require accommodating the City Ballet so that it could continue its performances when construction was not taking place.

Owing to his prior contractual arrangement with the Paris Opera, Mortier planned to begin his full-time duties at City Opera only in September 2009. In the two-year hiatus this arrangement created, Baker assumed greater administrative responsibilities in running the opera. Unfortunately, at this point in its history, the last thing the company needed was Baker operating in such a powerful role. Nonetheless, she and the City Opera board agreed to pay the cost of the New York State Theater renovation and to cease performances for a full season, losing ticket revenue for the year while still paying the orchestra, chorus, and stage staff due to prevailing labor contracts.

For the 2009–10 season, the board agreed to increase the City Opera's annual budget to approximately $60 million, a figure close to double that of the 2008–9 performance year. Mortier's projected first season would present a mix of works light on the bread-and-butter operas of Giuseppe Verdi and Giacomo Puccini in favor of such new productions as Olivier Messiaen's *Saint François d'Assise*, Philip Glass's *Einstein on the Beach*, Leoš Janáček's *The Makropulos Affair*, and Claude Debussy's *Pelléas et Mélisande*.

By the summer of 2008, cracks appeared in the relationship between Mortier and the City Opera board when he announced that he wished to codirect the Bayreuth Festival in Germany. Although he was not invited to take that position, he openly said he had been motivated by a desire to send a "signal" to City Opera trustees who were not showing the appropriate level of enthusiasm for his new ventures.[18] The situation was worsened considerably by the Great Recession of 2008. The coup de grâce came when the City Opera board told Mortier he would have a budget of only $36 million for his first season in New York, about which Mortier said, "I told them with the best will, I can't do that. . . . I cannot go to run a company that has less than the smallest company in France."[19] Robert Marx had warned Baker that Mortier would not stay without the resources that she and the board had promised him. According to Marx, Baker said to him, "He would never do that to us."[20] Nevertheless, he resigned.

Although Baker was gracious in her response to the resignation, saying only that "the board was enormously discouraged and disappointed," the results for City Opera were catastrophic: an entire season was canceled, a major physical renovation of the New York State Theater was in progress, the organization's endowment had been ransacked, and there was no artistic leadership in place.[21] Mortier would land on his feet by becoming the general manager of Madrid's Teatro Real, where he would stage commissioned operas he had initiated while in New York, including works by Philip Glass and Charles Wuorinen. The Madrid position was his last, as he died of pancreatic cancer on March 8, 2014.

Susan Baker's miscalculations and flawed decisions sadly showed that she was not up to the task of chairing City Opera. Essentially, the New York City Opera board threw fiscal caution to the wind in the hope of closing a financial and artistic chasm by engaging a highly talented but controversial general director. The board ignored their fiduciary responsibilities and put the company on a path toward oblivion.

As Heidi Waleson wrote in her history of the New York City Opera, "During her time at Goldman Sachs, Susan Baker had specialized in collateralized debt obligations [the financial vehicle which triggered the subprime mortgage crisis of 2007–9], and she was adopting a similar high-risk, high-reward strategy with City Opera. . . . [She] had bet the ranch."[22] Baker would make one final effort to move the company in a positive direction, but most observers felt it was too little, too late.

During the period when most in the Lincoln Center community were focused on City Opera, important personnel changes were occurring elsewhere. In January 2005, Bruce Crawford announced that he would step down as Lincoln Center chair after a tenure of three years. He had assumed the role at a difficult time for Lincoln Center, characterized by intense infighting concerning the redevelopment project, the administrative disarray caused in part by Sills's Lincoln Center leadership, and the debacle of the Philharmonic-Carnegie merger.[23] Fortunately, Crawford could step down knowing that a strong Lincoln Center president would be in place in the person of Reynold Levy.

During his time as chair, Crawford helped expand the board, revitalize the Mostly Mozart Festival, extend the American Songbook series, and open Frederick P. Rose Hall, the new home of Jazz at Lincoln Center.[24] But perhaps Crawford's greatest accomplishment as chair was more intangible. As Robin Pogrebin of the *New York Times* wrote, "With an elder statesman's gravitas and a businessman's no-nonsense manner, he has been, by many accounts, a welcome antidote to the bickering and occasional backstabbing among the center's various arts groups."[25]

Crawford would be succeeded as Lincoln Center chair on June 21, 2005, by Frank A. Bennack, Jr., a member of the Lincoln Center board since 1994. Bennack was an iconic figure in the publishing profession during his long tenure from 1979 to 2002 as president and CEO of the Hearst Corporation. He initiated a broad range of publishing, broadcasting, and diversified communications ventures which reshaped how a publishing company did business in the digital world. A native Texan with a discernible Southern twang, he began to work for the local paper, the *San Antonio Light*, at the age of seventeen. At the age of thirty-four, he became publisher and editor of that same paper. He was both a hard-nosed business executive as well as an affable and approachable individual. It would be his task to work with Levy and the Center's constituents to raise the money to complete the extensive first stage of the redevelopment project.

As change comes to all things, so it was with Joseph Volpe and the Met. After an extensive career in the opera house, Volpe bid the Metropolitan Opera community adieu in a Wagnerian-length five-and-a-half-hour gala on May 20, 2006. The event involved thirty solo artists, the Metropolitan Opera orchestra and chorus, and various conductors, including Valery Gergiev and James Conlon, substituting for James Levine, who was recuperating from shoulder surgery.

The gala was a successful fundraiser, bringing in over $13 million. Volpe would move on to the consulting firm of Giuliani Partners, joining his old friend and former mayor Rudolph Giuliani, who had been Volpe's ally in making sure a new City Opera house was not built in Damrosch Park. When Peter Gelb walked into his first Lincoln Center Council meeting on April 12, 2006, just before Volpe's departure, a sense of a new beginning was in the air.

Lorin Maazel created an international event of his own in late February 2008 with a forty-eight-hour visit by the New York Philharmonic to the Democratic People's Republic of Korea. The visit would be the first time an American cultural institution would appear in North Korea.[26] Many members of the orchestra were concerned about their personal safety during the short tour given North Korea's history of imprisoning visiting foreigners, but that sentiment passed, for the most part, when they were warmly welcomed to the country. Maestro Maazel conducted a program that included the national anthems of both countries, the prelude to act 3 of Richard Wagner's *Lohengrin*, Antonín Dvořák's Symphony no. 9 ("From the New World"), and George Gershwin's *An American in Paris*. The announced encore was the overture to Leonard Bernstein's musical *Candide*, but the emotional high point of the evening was an unexpected performance of a beloved Korean folk song, "Arirang," known in both North and South Korea. According to Daniel J. Wakin of the *Times*, "Tears began forming in the eyes of the staid audience."[27]

A lively debate took place after the orchestra left Pyongyang as to whether the visit created better relations between the United States and North Korea. Yet, several Philharmonic musicians felt they had made a connection, if only distant, with the crowd. Memories of experiences can last for decades and resurface in unpredictable ways. So it may be with this historic visit by the Philharmonic to North Korea.

Before the Philharmonic's trip, in July 2007, Alan Gilbert was named music director, beginning in September 2009. Gilbert was the first native New Yorker to be appointed to the position. The appointment of Gilbert, at only forty years of age, represented a generational change. He was decades younger than his predecessors, Kurt Masur and Lorin Maazel, and his youth and commitment to new orchestral repertoire augured well for the ensemble's future.

Gilbert would go on to develop inventive programs that involved unorthodox staging, such as György Ligeti's *Le Grand Macabre* with Doug Fitch providing the scenic design and stage direction. He also would create a contemporary music series titled CONTACT! Gilbert would step down from the New York Philharmonic music directorship at the end of the 2016–17 season, soon to become chief conductor of the NDR Elbphilharmonie Orchestra in Hamburg, Germany, beginning in the 2019–20 season, inheriting a brand-new and architecturally stunning concert hall.

The official groundbreaking for the Sixty-Fifth Street renovation took place on June 12, 2006. For this ceremony, instead of lifting a shovel full of soil, various Lincoln Center officials grabbed sledgehammers and broke a slab of the type of stone that would be used for the buildings' facade. By this time, Rebecca Robertson had already left the project staff and was soon to become president and CEO of the Park Avenue Armory, turning it into a major performing arts presenter in the city. By August, the demolition of the Sixty-Fifth Street bridge was complete, though the disruptive construction noise and pervasive dust made working in the affected buildings a distinct challenge. And, as is often the case, construction costs were much higher than anticipated.

Although most design questions were resolved by late 2006, internal debates continued about myriad issues that affected each constituent's project. One concern that involved all the participating constituents focused on a comparatively tiny element of the plan: the construction of a footbridge traversing Sixty-Fifth Street, with one side located close to the entrance to the Rose Building on the north end of the bridge and the south side located next to the street-level entrance to the Beaumont and Newhouse Theaters.

The bridge cost $6.2 million. Several constituent leaders joked that rather than build the bridge, they would prefer to hire, at a considerable savings, a retired four-star general as a crossing guard. The School of American Ballet insisted that the bridge was needed for the safety of younger SAB students who would cross Sixty-Fifth Street often when they performed during the annual *Nutcracker* season. Peter Martins also argued that the bridge would facilitate the short walk from the State Theater to the Rose Building studios for rehearsing City Ballet dancers. The bridge was named in honor of Reynold Levy.

The completion of certain elements of the project occurred as early as 2007 when, on January 23, the DS + R–designed Lincoln Kirstein Wing of the School of American Ballet was dedicated. The most visually stunning part of the renovation involved dance studios which seemed suspended in air. The major gift for this renovation came from Irene Diamond, but she said that she did not want yet another New York space named after her and suggested that the wing be named after Kirstein. Diamond was one of the most generous donors at the time to not only SAB but also Juilliard, Jazz at Lincoln Center, City Opera, and City Ballet. Certainly, it was appropriate to associate Kirstein's name with the SAB, but Irene Diamond's generosity of spirit was still quite remarkable.

In late 2008, after earlier plans were modified to have a Juilliard bookstore located on the corner of Sixty-Sixth Street and Broadway, Lincoln Center and WNET, New York City's public television station, agreed to use that space for a new studio overlooking Broadway. It was an attractive location that added greater life to an already busy corner; the new Juilliard bookstore moved farther west on Sixty-Sixth Street.

By early 2009, corresponding with the fiftieth anniversary of Lincoln Center, Alice Tully Hall reopened on February 23 with a concert featuring Jordi Savall, Leon Fleisher, artists from the Chamber Music Society of Lincoln Center, and the Juilliard Orchestra conducted by David Robertson. Lincoln Center officials considered the Alice Tully Hall renovation the centerpiece of the Sixty-Fifth Street project. Before the renovation, Tully Hall was thought to be a "B plus" hall, owing to its lackluster acoustics and sight lines. The Diller Scofidio + Renfro renovation, with Mark Holden as acoustician, considerably improved the hall's sound isolation. Aesthetically, the hall was enhanced significantly, complete with cherry-toned walls and muted lighting, which created a more engaging environment for the audience. The dramatic new lobby, which faced out to Broadway and included ample space for a convenient dining facility, was one of the highlights of the entire renovation project.

In turn, Juilliard's Glorya Kaufman Dance Studio was inaugurated on March 25. The studio was entirely clad in glass, so pedestrians could peek in and, in turn, dancers could peek out. Juilliard community members saw the space as a type of "jewel box" that took in natural light during the day and glowed in the evening as dancers rehearsed. The studio would humanize the entryway to Juilliard, Tully Hall, and all of Sixty-Fifth Street. The commemoration of the newly renovated Juilliard building as a whole, named after Irene Diamond, took place on September 14.

Upon the Sixty-Fifth Street project's completion, the architecture critic Ada Louise Huxtable, who had never been a fan of Lincoln Center's design, wrote, "Lincoln Center is the product of a lot of obsolete ideas. . . . This was a moment [in the initial construction of Lincoln Center] when the destructive misjudgments of urban renewal, the anti-urbanism of a car-centric culture and a deadening kind of modernist monumentality came together in a disastrous environmental triple play."[28] She was persuaded by the DS + R design, however, which softened the complex's Brutalist gigantism: "The tentatively monumental is being joined by the convincingly contemporary. What was exclusive, forbidding and opaque will become inclusive, inviting and open."[29]

The development of Sixty-Fifth Street would cost approximately $1.2 billion overall, paid for by Lincoln Center and the constituents through the acquisition of many generous gifts and financing vehicles. DS + R's high-quality design raised the firm's profile considerably, and they subsequently received commissions from around the world. As the construction ended, all the project's ups and downs were left in the past, though not entirely forgotten.

CHAPTER SIXTEEN

We Don't Have a
Playbook for This

A S RECOUNTED IN HEIDI WALESON'S history of the New York City Opera, November 4, 2008, was "a day of extreme emotions. There was joy—Barack Obama was elected president of the United States. And there was grief—Gerard Mortier would not be coming to City Opera."[1] With the monumental setback of Mortier's departure, Susan Baker and her board once again attempted to find a new artistic leader for the company.

The board's search committee consulted with City Opera staff, who enthusiastically recommended Francesca Zambello. Zambello had a reputation as a distinguished opera director who had worked at some of the most respected opera houses in the world and with the City Opera on multiple productions. According to Zambello, she met with Baker and board member Mark Neuhaus in late December 2008 and was offered the position of general manager and artistic director. Zambello, seen as a natural choice for the job, hit the ground running and began visiting the company in the first days of 2009 to discuss plans for a new management team. Baker, however, claimed that the offer never took place.[2]

It seems that in early January 2009, Mary Sharp Cronson, a member of the City Opera board, vehemently opposed the Zambello appointment; instead, she wanted George Steel, at the time the Dallas Opera's new general manager. In retrospect, it seems strange that Cronson's voice would carry so much weight regarding the appointment. Never known as a major donor, she did have close ties to the Peter J. Sharp Foundation, named after her late brother, who was a successful hotelier and real estate developer.

The Sharp Foundation held considerable financial resources, though it was in the process of spending down its assets and going out of business. Perhaps Baker thought that a supportive Cronson could deliver a seven- or eight-figure gift to the needy opera company. As it turned out, City Opera received only six-figure annual grants from the Sharp Foundation, but Steel was still hired as the company's new head.

Steel started his new job on February 2, 2009, even though he had only begun as the general manager of the Dallas Opera in October 2008. For eleven years before the Dallas appointment, Steel had overseen the Miller Theater of Columbia University, where he presented an innovative array of contemporary music ensembles and early music groups in the small house. He had worked with Cronson on several projects, such as coproducing events for her Works and Process series at the Guggenheim Museum. Aside from his short stint in Dallas, he had never run an organization the size of City Opera.

The professional jump for Steel was significant, since his producing experience involved a 688-seat, nonunion, university-subsidized concert hall. At City Opera, he inherited a theater of nearly 2,800 seats and a fully unionized repertory opera company, involving hundreds of full-time employees. Baker was upbeat about the appointment: "George is actually the perfect person for City Opera in this chapter of its institutional life. . . . He is scrappy, flexible, adaptable, charming and innovative."[3] Explaining his quick exit from Dallas for New York, Steel said, "It's an opportunity of a lifetime."[4]

Steel's aesthetic was in some ways not far from Mortier's, though with a hint of an American accent. In his first two seasons, he presented a selection of traditional and eclectic operatic fare, including, in the latter category, Leonard Bernstein's dour *A Quiet Place*, Richard Strauss's *Intermezzo*, Arnold Schoenberg's *Erwartung*, and a new opera by the veteran Broadway composer Stephen Schwartz, best known for his blockbuster hits *Godspell*, *Pippin*, and *Wicked*.

Schwartz's opera was based on and named for the 1964 British film *Séance on a Wet Afternoon*. Regrettably, the season choices were not popular with the City Opera audience. *A Quiet Place* played at only 43 percent capacity, and *Intermezzo* had even lower ticket sales.[5] The hope that the Schwartz opera would attract a new audience due to his hits on Broadway also did not materialize.

Although there was a prevailing sense at City Opera that Lincoln Center was not interested in helping the wounded company—for example, one board member, Emilie Corey, said, "Nobody at Lincoln Center gave a shit"—that was not the case.[6] Reynold Levy proactively reached out to Steel in the summer of 2009 to ask whether Steel would meet with him, Adrian Ellis, the executive director of Jazz at Lincoln Center, and the author to develop a plan for the future.

Steel agreed to the meeting and sent the advisory group the company's financial statements for 2007 and 2008. On July 20, Levy sent Steel an analysis of City Opera's current problems. The paper addressed numerous institutional issues and concluded with a section titled "How Lincoln Center Can Help," whose suggestions included the recruitment of new board members and oversight of the David H. Koch Theater, thereby releasing the City Center of Music and Drama from that responsibility.

A meeting to discuss the report took place in early August, attended by Baker, Steel, Levy, and Frank Bennack. To Levy's surprise, Baker said she had no knowledge of the report; Levy recalled that "it quickly became clear that Steel had not shared the paper with Susan at all. It even seemed that Steel himself had never read it."[7] At that point, Levy felt he and his colleagues had done all they could to help a wounded constituent and bowed out of the rescue process.

Although Steel and City Opera tried to continue the company's residency at Lincoln Center over the next two years, it was to no avail. In January 2011, Baker finally stepped down as City Opera chair, to be replaced by Charles Wall, a retired lawyer and a former vice chair of Philip Morris International. Baker remained as a member of the board. In May 2011, the New York City Opera announced that it would be leaving Lincoln Center because it could no longer afford to operate there. Steel contended that the company would perform following a scaled-down model, functioning as a type of touring company within New York City.[8] He announced that the City Opera's annual operating budget would contract from \$31 million to \$13 million.

The New York City Opera's endgame began with its declaration of bankruptcy on October 1, 2013. The company's last performances in its original state involved a production of the American premier of Mark-Anthony Turnage's *Anna Nicole* at the Brooklyn Academy of Music, opening on September 17, 2013. Although the opera production garnered more positive reviews than expected, all company members knew that the New York City Opera would no longer exist as they had known it.

Steel had earlier announced that although all seven performances of *Anna Nicole* would take place, the company needed to raise \$7 million by the end of the month or it could not present three future productions. In turn, if an additional \$13 million were not raised, it was doubtful that there could be a 2014–15 season. Neither fundraising goal was realized. Other individuals would attempt to revive the company, without success. Disastrous decisions and poor board oversight killed a legacy New York arts institution.

During City Opera's slide to oblivion, the Metropolitan Opera began to explore new artistic initiatives under the direction of Peter Gelb. Gelb's first production as general manager was Puccini's *Madama Butterfly*, directed by Anthony Minghella, for the opening of the 2006–7 season. Minghella was an Oscar-winning film director and his production of *Butterfly* had been previously produced at the English National Opera. It was a sensitive depiction of the tragic tale, including some unorthodox twists, with some wags sarcastically wondering aloud when Cio-Cio-San would realize that her son was a puppet.

Gelb's efforts to make the Met a more dramatically compelling opera house had its downside as well. The Swiss-born director Luc Bondy's production of Puccini's *Tosca* garnered loud boos when the production team took its curtain call. *Tosca* is certainly one of the most dramatically powerful operas in the repertoire, but Bondy's direction presented it as a showcase for Scarpia's sadistic persona, with some scenes bordering on the pornographic.

The ultimate test of any opera general director, however, is a production of Wagner's *Der Ring des Nibelungen:* four operas stretching over at least eighteen hours of music that have been brought to life in numerous productions since the 1876 premiere of the complete cycle in Bayreuth, Germany, presenting "allegories of rampant capitalism, enslavement of working people, and the malfeasance of the nobility and the bourgeoisie," as one scholar described it.[9] Gelb pulled out all the stops on his *Ring,* engaging the Canadian director Robert Lepage, who created one of the largest and most expensive opera productions in history by building "the machine," a forty-four-ton set composed of twenty-four rotating planks (which initially made a great deal of noise when the wood slats moved) at a price of about $16 million. The Met's stage was reinforced with additional steel beams to accommodate the weight, which added $10 million to the company's budget.

Each of the *Ring's* four operas—*Das Rheingold, Die Walküre, Siegfried,* and *Götterdämmerung*—was separately performed during the 2010–11 and 2011–12 seasons, with complete cycles presented in 2012 and 2013. Critical response to the gargantuan production was generally negative. Alex Ross of the *New Yorker* provided perhaps the most severe view when he wrote, "Pound for pound, ton for ton, the most witless and wasteful production in modern operatic history."[10] Gelb's hopes for a box office smash were also not realized, but the *Ring* was brought back in 2019 after a six-year hiatus, with less creaking of the machine and a smoother flow in the overall production.

A second exceptional event, this time presented by Lincoln Center in 2014, could not have been more different in its conception or its impact on the audience. As part of Jane Moss's White Light Festival, and coproduced with the Park Avenue Armory and Carnegie Hall, two performances of Johann Sebastian Bach's monumental *St. Matthew Passion* were presented in the Park Avenue Armory's Wade Thompson Drill Hall. The unique event featured the Berlin Philharmonic, conducted by Simon Rattle, and was directed by the provocative and imaginative Peter Sellars. Those who attended a performance of the work agreed the experience was nothing short of transcendent.

A scene from the Robert Lepage–designed Das Rheingold
by Richard Wagner at the Metropolitan Opera, ca. 2012.
(Photo © Ken Howard / Metropolitan Opera)

The three-and-a-half-hour composition for double orchestra, double chorus, and soloists was never intended by Bach to be staged, but Sellars's subtle direction and interactive concept had soloists, choristers, and even principal players from the Berlin Philharmonic moving around the stage in meaningful ways that considerably enhanced the music's intensity. The physical design of the performance stood in marked contrast to the mammoth machine used for the Met's *Ring Cycle*. The Armory's Drill Hall was reconfigured to present a close replica of the Philharmonie, the orchestra's concert hall in Berlin, featuring a wraparound audience seating arrangement. The scenic motif was plain, with white blocks used to represent various elements of the Passion's story. All performers wore simple black outfits.

The *St. Matthew Passion* production could hardly be viewed as inexpensive, however, sporting a price tag of close to $4 million. Jane Moss credited Reynold Levy with supporting the production, which, considering that only two performances occurred in the two-thousand-seat configuration, could never generate the ticket

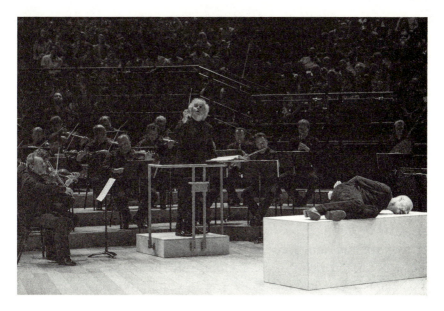

A staged performance of J. S. Bach's St. Matthew Passion *at
the Park Avenue Armory in 2014, with Simon Rattle conducting
the Berlin Philharmonic and Mark Padmore as the Evangelist*
(reclining on block). *(Photo © Stephanie Berger)*

revenue needed to offset costs. However, the *St. Matthew Passion*
performances marked a culmination of productions sponsored by
Lincoln Center and muted, to some degree, those who had said the
Center should not be in the production business.

After five years as Lincoln Center chair, having led the complex
redevelopment venture and helping to find the funds to realize it,
Frank A. Bennack, Jr., announced he would leave in June 2010. His
professionalism and empathetic manner did a great deal to resolve
controversies that occurred during the venture's realization. Bennack was succeeded by Katherine G. Farley, a former board member
of both the New York Philharmonic and Lincoln Center Theater,
who had joined the Lincoln Center board in 2003, become vice
chair in 2005, and chaired the Redevelopment Committee beginning in 2006 after the precipitous exit of Peter Lehrer. In a wise
transitional approach, Farley became chair-designate and worked in
tandem with Bennack during the 2009–10 season.

Farley earned her bachelor's in 1971 from Brown University and her master's in architecture from Harvard's School of Design in 1976. She worked for thirty-two years for the real estate development firm Tishman Speyer, expanding the company's international business and heading divisions in China, Brazil, Germany, Argentina, and India.

Two years into Farley's tenure as chair, Reynold Levy announced in September 2012 that he would step down as Lincoln Center president. He explained that he felt his work was now complete. Levy, known as a diligent worker and a dogged fundraiser, contributed mightily to Lincoln Center during his ten-year presidency. He had inherited a divisive construction project and resolved various issues with grace and calm. In honor of his successful presidency, on October 1, 2012, the much-discussed footbridge across Sixty-Fifth Street was named "The President's Bridge: In Honor of Reynold Levy."

Given Levy's calm and dignified exit, much of the Lincoln Center community was shocked to learn in 2015 that he was publishing a book titled *They Told Me Not to Take That Job: Tumult, Betrayal, Heroics, and the Transformation of Lincoln Center.* In addition to venting about the problems with City Opera and the New York Philharmonic during his tenure, Levy seemed to want to settle scores with certain individuals, especially Peter Gelb. Gelb had many public confrontations with Levy, particularly complaining that Levy was making decisions that affected all constituents without conferring with the other organizations on campus. Although Levy did not exactly become persona non grata on campus after the book's publication, his President's Bridge had been symbolically burned in the minds of some readers.

By May 2013, Katherine Farley and the Lincoln Center board found a new president in the person of Jed Bernstein, a Broadway producer who headed the Broadway League, a national trade association. Farley was positive about Bernstein, saying that he "really understands the arts."[11] However, that was not the opinion of many leaders in the field, who questioned Bernstein's involvement and understanding of orchestral music, opera, chamber music, and ballet, the Center's core performing genres. It was reported that Mayor Bloomberg strongly supported Bernstein's appointment.

Bernstein's tenure would last for just over two years, ending in April 2016. It was announced at the time of his departure that he resigned due to an inappropriate relationship with a female staff member, which violated Lincoln Center guidelines, but those who experienced his leadership felt that the position of president did not suit him. His progress in moving forward the renovation of David Geffen Hall was uneven at best, and he spent a considerable amount of time attempting to develop a Lincoln Center Hall of Fame, eventually called Lincoln Center Legends, in hopes of creating an annual ceremony to rival the visibility of the Kennedy Center Honors in Washington, DC. After one class of artists was inducted as Legends, including Leontyne Price and Hal Prince, the initiative faded.

With Bernstein's departure, Farley needed to move quickly to find new Lincoln Center leadership, and did so in November 2016 with the appointment of Debora L. Spar as the Center's tenth president and first female CEO. Spar would begin her tenure in March 2017 after leaving the presidency of Barnard College, located sixty blocks north of Lincoln Center, which she had successfully led for nine years. She was a respected author and former professor at the Harvard Business School. Although, like Bernstein, she had little working knowledge of the performing arts, her strong track record as a fundraiser and manager of a large organization indicated that she would take to her Lincoln Center responsibilities with alacrity. However, this was not the case.

In April 2018, only one year into the job, Spar resigned. In her official departure statement she said, "Moving from academia to the performing arts world pushed me to think, learn and lead in new ways. While we have achieved a lot together over the past year, I have also questioned whether the role is right for me."[12] In interactions with Spar, one encountered a highly accomplished and intelligent person who seemed insecure when discussing the performing arts.

During Spar's twelve-month presidency, she continued to develop renovation plans for Geffen Hall, ended the Lincoln Center Festival, and faced a budgetary deficit. Spar also enacted a series of faux pas that alienated her staff and certain constituent heads. She engaged a strategic planning firm whose personnel showed little understanding of the performing arts or Lincoln Center, and the effort fell flat. She also hired a former Barnard colleague as her second-in-command, which alienated senior Lincoln Center staff members, who would no longer be reporting directly to the Center's president. There was also clear friction between Spar and Farley. Spar's understanding of her role in budget management and fund-raising was contrary to the direction Farley and the board's executive committee wished her to take. Ultimately, the Lincoln Center board accepted Spar's resignation.

The quick departure of yet another Lincoln Center president was an awkward problem for Farley. However, this was not the first time a Lincoln Center president served a short tenure: Maxwell Taylor was called to Washington to address the Bay of Pigs debacle after only a few months on the job. Glenn Ferguson and Gordon Davis both left after one year of service due to conflict with their chairs, and Bernstein and Spar both had issues with either their chair, in the case of Spar, or lack of support from staff, in the case of both presidents. Russell Granet, Lincoln Center's executive vice president of education and community engagement, was named acting president until a new president was appointed.

Independent of the problematic personnel issues Farley had to address, her leadership began to shape a novel approach to how Lincoln Center responded to its neighbors and how it presented the performing arts. As chair of the Redevelopment Corporation, she brought the Sixty-Fifth Street renovation to fruition, focusing on Diller Scofidio + Renfro's goal of opening the campus to the surrounding neighborhood. Her work in obtaining the $100 million grant from David Geffen for the renovation of the former Avery Fisher Hall also centered on developing a plan that would provide new amenities for the public when visiting Lincoln Center, including an education center and other attractions in the renovated hall available to non-concertgoers.

During Farley's time as chair, the David Rubenstein Atrium on Broadway between Sixty-Second and Sixty-Third Streets became a heavily used venue for free concerts featuring a variety of performing arts genres. Moreover, discounted tickets for Lincoln Center events and campus tours originated from the Atrium. As time would progress, social and political events would cause Farley to address

further Lincoln Center's changing role in supporting and presenting the performing arts.

Throughout its history, Lincoln Center was generally not an institution affected by political or social movements, but that changed
when the #MeToo movement became a prominent societal force
in 2017. The term "Me Too" was first brought to public attention
by Tarana Burke, a social activist from the Bronx, who coined the
phrase to encourage women to publicly decry the sexual abuse and
harassment they had experienced.

In turn, the viral hashtag #MeToo was popularized by the actor Alyssa Milano during early public disclosures of the allegations
of sexual assault against movie producer Harvey Weinstein. Unlike
other periods in history when accusations of criminal activity would
fade after a rush of initial attention, the #MeToo movement had a
staying power that touched all sectors of American society. According to one federal criminal defense attorney, the #MeToo movement
"clearly shattered cultural norms and radically altered our collective
understanding of acceptable behavior. . . . [The Weinstein guilty]
verdict has solidified #MeToo not just as a social and political movement but as a legal movement too."[13]

The impact of #MeToo toppled some of Lincoln Center's most
powerful leaders. James Levine, who artistically defined the Met for
over four decades, was accused in 2017 of sexual abuse. The circum-
stances involved Levine purportedly sexually abusing several men
when they were students of his, some of them teenagers. Levine was
first suspended by the Met and then fired in March 2018, with the
Met stating that it had "uncovered credible evidence that Mr. Levine
engaged in sexually abusive and harassing conduct toward vulnerable artists in the early stages of their careers, over whom Mr. Levine
had authority."[14]

Levine denied any wrongdoing. Suits and countersuits ensued,
and the Met and its insurance company ultimately paid Levine
$3.5 million to settle the matter. Levine, a giant of the opera world,
would never conduct at the Met again. Already managing various
health problems that required him to use a motorized wheelchair,
he would pass away on March 9, 2021, in Palm Springs, California,
from a combination of Parkinson's disease and coronary problems.

Peter Gelb (left) *and Yannick Nézet-Séguin on the set of the
Metropolitan Opera's production of Alban Berg's* Wozzeck,
2019. (Photo: Jonathan Tichler / Met Opera)

His replacement was the French Canadian conductor Yannick
Nézet-Séguin, who was also music director of the Philadelphia
Orchestra. Nézet-Séguin had already been chosen to be the Met's
next music director before Levine's troubles were made public. As
the crisis worsened, Nézet-Séguin upped his starting date by two
years and became the Met's music director in the 2018–19 season.
A superb conductor with particular sensitivity to and knowledge of

operatic and vocal repertoire, he would quickly fill the artistic gap at the Met occasioned by Levine's departure.

The Met was also rocked by accusations from several women that they had been sexually harassed by superstar tenor/baritone Plácido Domingo, who had sung for fifty-one consecutive seasons at the Met. After these accusations surfaced, Domingo withdrew from a production of Verdi's *Macbeth* in September 2019 and announced that he would not return to the Met in the future.

The New York City Ballet was affected through the forced retirement of Peter Martins, a former star of the company who had led the City Ballet since 1983. In late 2017, an anonymous accusation of sexual harassment and physical abuse of dancers surfaced against him. Both the City Ballet and the School of American Ballet, where he was artistic director and chairman of the School's faculty, began an investigation. The company never "corroborated the allegations against him but called for new policies to keep dancers safe."[15] Martins announced his retirement on New Year's Day 2018. He was succeeded in 2019 as artistic director by Jonathan Stafford and associate artistic director Wendy Whelan. Both Stafford and Whelan were former principal dancers of the City Ballet. Stafford would also take on the position of SAB's artistic director and faculty chair.

The City Ballet subsequently removed three male principal dancers who had been accused in a lawsuit of sharing sexually explicit photos of women.[16] Chase Finlay resigned and two other dancers, Zachary Catazaro and Amar Ramasar, were first suspended without pay and then fired. In April 2019, an arbitrator ruled that Catazaro and Ramasar had to be reinstated. Catazaro decided not to return, but Ramasar did rejoin the company after mandatory counseling.

In September 2018, the New York Philharmonic fired two wind players: Liang Wang, the principal oboe, and Matthew Muckey, the associate principal trumpet. Such terminations were highly unusual for the orchestra. Both players were dismissed after an investigation concluded that allegations of sexual misconduct were credible. The men denied wrongdoing and their union, Local 802, filed a grievance to contest the terminations. In April 2020, an independent arbitrator, Richard Bloch, restored the two performers' employment status.[17]

Two well-known conductors who had appeared as guests on several occasions with the Philharmonic, Charles Dutoit and Daniele Gatti, were also accused of inappropriate conduct over a period of many years. Although their appearances with the Philharmonic were canceled, both continued to conduct in Europe and Asia.

Not all personnel matters at Lincoln Center involved litigation. The New York Philharmonic saw changes in the positions of both music director and president. In 2018, Jaap van Zweden, the respected and exacting Dutch conductor, began his first season as music director. He was previously music director of the Dallas Symphony Orchestra for ten years and continued as music director of the Hong Kong Philharmonic, a post he had held since 2012. An accomplished violinist who had studied at Juilliard, van Zweden, at the age of nineteen, had been appointed the youngest-ever concertmaster of the Royal Concertgebouw Orchestra.

The new Philharmonic music director took over while Matthew VanBesien, who succeeded Zarin Mehta, was still president of the orchestra. That would change when VanBesien announced in January 2017 that he would be leaving the presidency after a tenure of about five years to become president of the University of Michigan Musical Society, a college presenter known as one of the largest and artistically most diverse in the nation. VanBesien's departure caused considerable concern for Lincoln Center leaders since he had been deeply involved in planning the renovation of Geffen Hall. However, his successor, known well to the orchestra and Lincoln Center, was quite experienced at building new concert halls.

Deborah Borda returned to the New York Philharmonic as president and chief executive officer in 2017 after serving as head of the Los Angeles Philharmonic for seventeen years. She had previously served as administrative chief of the New York Philharmonic from 1991 to 2000, while Kurt Masur was the music director. Borda accomplished much as the head of the Los Angeles Philharmonic, completing the Frank Gehry–designed Walt Disney Hall, significantly increasing the orchestra's endowment, balancing its budget, and engaging a very talented young Venezuelan, Gustavo Dudamel, to succeed the orchestra's music director, Esa-Pekka Salonen, in October 2009. Borda's arrival in New York reinvigorated the Phil-

Jaap van Zweden and Deborah Borda, ca. 2019.
(Photo by Chris Lee / © 2021 Chris Lee)

harmonic board, supported the artistic vision of van Zweden, and paved the way for a successful hall renovation.

David Geffen Hall had been dedicated on September 23, 2015, with a leadership gift of $100 million to be used to renovate the venue. In 2008, David Koch, a libertarian political activist who with his brother, Charles, was well known in conservative circles, had given the same amount to rename the New York State Theater. Therefore, two major Lincoln Center venues faced each other across the Josie Robertson Plaza bearing names of the politically liberal Mr. Geffen and, in turn, the conservative Mr. Koch. One observer looked at both marquees and uttered with a quizzical sigh, "Only in America."

After thirty-four years as Juilliard's president, the author stepped down in June 2018 and was succeeded by the distinguished former principal dancer of the New York City Ballet Damian Woetzel. After retiring from the Ballet, Woetzel pursued a varied career, earning a master's degree in public administration from the John F. Kennedy School of Government at Harvard, leading the Vail Dance Festival as artistic director, directing the Aspen Institute Arts Program, and participating in President Barack Obama's Committee on the Arts and Humanities. An individual of vision and empathy, Woetzel has exhibited great dedication to the values of equity, diversity, and inclusion, setting new standards for an American performing arts conservatory and influencing other Lincoln Center constituents in this area.

After seeing two presidents come and go within the span of about three years, Katherine Farley and the Lincoln Center board were intent on finding a new CEO who would have the gravitas and experience to oversee the Geffen Hall renovation, develop a strong working relationship with the constituents, and set a clear strategic path for the future. In February 2019, Henry Timms, previously the head of the 92nd Street Y, was appointed Lincoln Center's eleventh president. Born in Exeter, England, he helped create #GivingTuesday, which asked individuals to donate to charities of their choice the Tuesday after Thanksgiving, and developed it into a national movement. He also wrote, with Jeremy Heimans, a book titled *New Power*, which analyzed leadership issues in today's complex world.

Timms's appointment was supported by the various constituent heads. Peter Gelb, for one, stated that Timms was a "great choice."[18] And Deborah Borda, who would be Timms's partner on Geffen Hall, said, "I think it is an exceptional appointment, and I really felt an immediate click of a true partnership with him."[19]

That partnership would be activated only ten months later when, in December 2019, a new plan for the renovation of Geffen Hall was announced that showed signs of finally realizing a dream

Henry Timms and Katherine Farley, 2020. (Photo by Bennett Raglin / Getty Images Entertainment via Getty Images)

that had been put forward many years earlier. Timms and Borda jointly presented a project design that would truly transform the concert hall, developed by Diamond Schmitt Architects, led by Gary McCluskie, with Tod Williams Billie Tsien Architects crafting the public spaces, Paul Scarbrough of Akustiks addressing the acoustics, and Joshua Dachs of Fisher Dachs Associates focusing on theater planning and design.

The new plan involved eliminating the proscenium, moving the stage forward by twenty-five feet, and wrapping audience seating around it. Audience capacity would be reduced by 500 seats to

*Rendering of the new design for the interior of David Geffen Hall by
the architects Diamond Schmitt and Tod Williams Billie Tsien, 2019.
(Photo: Diamond Schmitt Architects.jpg)*

2,200, and a steeper incline would be added to the orchestra level,
in the hopes of improving acoustics and sight lines.[20] Other innovative elements of the design included a media streaming wall in the
lobby; "The Sidewalk Studio" on the corner of Sixty-Fifth Street
and Broadway, which would house educational, artistic, and community activities; and "The Light Wall," which would wrap around
three sides of the interior top of the building, creating space for
dynamic architectural lighting reminiscent of Shanghai's skyline.
It was announced that $360 million—two-thirds of the construc-
tion budget—had already been raised. The project was scheduled
for completion by March 2024, but world events would conspire to
make an earlier completion date possible.

Lessons learned from great works of art can be prophetic. A compelling truth comes forward when, in Wagner's opera *Die Walküre*,
the god Wotan looks to his wife, Fricka, and says, "Today you have
witnessed it. . . . Learn that a thing can suddenly happen that's never
happened before."[21] Of all the world events that transpired since

President Eisenhower put a commemorative shovel in the ground to celebrate Lincoln Center's inauguration in May 1959, nothing could have prepared America and the world for the pandemic of 2020.

The existence of a highly contagious and deadly coronavirus, eventually known as SARS-CoV-2, came to the world's attention when Chinese leaders announced in late January 2020 that they had detected a human-transmissible disease which had pneumonia-like characteristics in the city of Wuhan, a massive urban area of about eleven million people.

The first case of COVID-19 (the disease caused by SARS-CoV-2) in the United States was discovered on January 21, 2020. The first death due to the virus was reported on February 29, involving a patient living near Seattle, Washington. New York's governor, Andrew M. Cuomo, declared an emergency for his state on March 7. A national emergency was declared by President Donald Trump on March 13. Two days later, the Centers for Disease Control recommended that no gatherings of fifty people or more take place for the next eight weeks. And thus began the closing of Lincoln Center as well as the cancellation of performances at Carnegie Hall, on Broadway, and in countless performance halls and other cultural gathering places around the nation.

In rapid succession, on March 19, the Metropolitan Opera announced the cancellation of its entire spring season, followed by similar cancellation notices from the New York Philharmonic on March 23 and the City Ballet on March 26. Live performances ceased to exist for the first time in anyone's memory. At the same time, all restaurants, bars, schools, gyms, and professional sports leagues closed. Colleges and universities sent their students home, and educators at every level scrambled to implement distance-learning protocols to complete the spring semester's work.

Financial losses created by the pandemic were catastrophic for Lincoln Center constituents. The Met estimated that it would be exposed to a net budgetary shortfall of between $50 million and $60 million for the 2020 fiscal year. Deborah Borda summed up the situation for the Philharmonic when she said, "The human toll and the possible economic ramifications are simply stunning, and they're simply not known yet. We don't have a play book for this. We're inventing it as we go along."[22] The Metropolitan Opera stopped paying its orchestra, chorus, and stagehands at the end of March, although health benefits were kept in place. The Philharmonic created a plan for reduced compensation of the orchestra members while also maintaining health benefits. The New York City Ballet saw an $8 million drop in revenue for fiscal year 2020.[23] Most performing artists on campus and throughout the city simply lost their livelihood and had nowhere to turn except limited and dwindling federal unemployment benefits.

By late September, the Met dropped its original plan to open on New Year's Eve 2020 and announced that the entire 2020–21 season would be cancelled, resulting in a projected loss of about $150 million. Soon thereafter, all other performing constituents on campus also canceled the remainder of the 2020–21 season. Even when the COVID-19 pandemic subsided, artistic administrators could not predict whether audiences would be willing to attend live performances, even when a vaccine was available. Although highly effective vaccines were made available to the public early in 2021, regrettably, a new variant of the disease, dubbed Delta, surfaced in the spring and set back plans to escape from the pandemic's social distancing and masking protocols. In addition, a significant percentage of the American population refused to be vaccinated by the summer of 2021, which allowed the Delta variant to spread further. As Peter Gelb said, "It's transparently obvious that social distancing and grand opera cannot go together. . . . It's not just the audience; it's the health of the company."[24] Simply put, the pandemic presented an unprecedented, existential threat to Lincoln Center and its constituents.

During this frightening pandemic, the joined voices of the Black Lives Matter movement came to the fore after the death of George Floyd while in police custody in Minneapolis on May 25, 2020. The Minneapolis police officer who caused his death, Derek Chauvin, was found guilty of second- and third-degree murder, as well as of second-degree manslaughter, on April 20, 2021. Floyd's murder was sadly only one in a long series of Black American deaths at the hands of law enforcement, including Michael Brown and

Breonna Taylor, to name only two high-profile cases over the last few years. As one university publication aptly put it, "America is in the vortex of a 'perfect storm' of crises—police brutality towards Black communities, COVID-19 and the searing number of related deaths, historically high unemployment rates and divisive federal governance and leadership—and each of these is connected to systemic racism."[25]

A sense of responsibility for racial injustices resonated with Lincoln Center's leaders as Black Lives Matter demonstrations occurred throughout the world, amplified by the tense and vulnerable environment created by COVID-19. It was as if the virus had exposed society's weaknesses as well as its humanity, pushing individuals to no longer settle for the status quo. Lincoln Center and its constituents faced a reckoning. The organization had been created by white men of power and influence who viewed the arts as an effective way to enhance the quality of life for all Americans. Although their goals were commendable, they thought little about displacing thousands of economically disadvantaged, mostly Black and Latinx families in order to construct the Center. In addition, the core repertoire presented at Lincoln Center since its inception has been overwhelmingly white, with the obvious exception of the work of Jazz at Lincoln Center.

This climate of social change created a sense of discomfort for some artists who began to realize that the artistic legacy they had embraced was tainted with racist or discriminatory practices. Rather than feel guilt for such a legacy, which would put into question the true genius of many of the works presented each year on Lincoln Center stages, the time was ripe to examine the future landscape of the arts in America and explore new strategies that would present the performing arts to the American public in different and more diverse ways. Such an approach would necessitate the rethinking of traditions and practices that had been the foundation of the Lincoln Center experience.

Such new directions were already being mapped by Lincoln Center constituents. Under the presidency of Damian Woetzel, Juilliard began a major initiative in the areas of equity, diversity, inclusion, and belonging, addressing the complex question of how young artists in dance, drama, and music view artistic tradition as a foundation on which to base their growth as performers and communicators of human values. How do artists of color, in particular, bring established works to life without compromising their own personal values or beliefs? In this process, the role of works by Shakespeare, Balanchine, or Beethoven in shaping the young artist, for example, was put into question by some as a vestige of a bygone colonial or Western-centric era. However, there was also an understanding that great works of art form the foundation of Western culture and should not be discarded. Following such a draconian course of action would uproot the many historical and cultural traditions which are crucial parts of twenty-first-century global society. The quest for a suitable compromise continues.

Katherine Farley and her new president, Henry Timms, announced in early June 2020 that Lincoln Center would, in the future, look "to present artists and points of view that better reflect the City of New York, [doing this in part] by establishing commissioning funds specifically to center the voices of artists that have been underrepresented on our campus. [The Center would also dismantle] structures across Lincoln Center . . . that foster inequity and replacing them with practices that promote true inclusivity."[26] This pronouncement was followed in the fall of 2020 by a publicly announced plan that, for the first time, showed Lincoln Center becoming a proactive force in developing programs on campus that would address the issues of racial and cultural inequality that have haunted American society for centuries.

Earlier in 2014, the Center began a successful program, called Audition Bootcamp at Lincoln Center, to prepare economically disadvantaged middle schoolers in New York City for auditions to enter the city's arts-focused high schools. By 2018, 239 students took part in the two-week summer program, and a remarkable 95 percent of participating students were accepted to their preferred school.

Beginning in 2015, the School of American Ballet dedicated itself to enrolling dancers of color in its program, which resulted in a significant increase in Black and Latinx dancers in the student body; an action that was in contradistinction to the formative policies of Balanchine and Kirstein, where dancers of color, especially females, were rarely hired by the company. SAB also announced in 2020 that Aesha Ash would become the first Black female member of the School's permanent faculty. Although some critics saw Ash's appointment as too little, too late, her appointment did represent a rejection of practices previously embraced by City Ballet and its affiliated school.

Never before had constituents been so focused on developing programs which emphasized the role of the arts in realizing social change. Appointments of specific individuals to oversee newly created equity programs were made by most Lincoln Center organizations during the second half of 2020, in the hope that their work will bear fruit once the pandemic subsides.

Many suggestions for substantive change of established practices at Lincoln Center and beyond have been advanced by individuals in the performing arts profession. Anthony Tommasini's suggestion perhaps generated the most debate when he wrote that professional orchestras in America should stop the "well-intentioned but restrictive practice" of blind auditions for gaining employment with a professional orchestra.[27] Orchestral administrators and conductors agreed that the use of a screen was transformative in American orchestras for gender representation but not for racial diversity.[28] Tommasini's proposal was seen by some as reflecting earlier affirmative action efforts relating to nonartistic elements of America's workplace. Practitioners in the field, however, doubted that America's professional orchestras could operate under a system of racial quotas since entry to a professional orchestra had always been based purely on the quality of the performance of the candidate at the time of the audition. Other suggested initiatives included shortening concerts and omitting intermissions, in order to attract a younger and more diverse audience, and fully embracing the music of composers of color, such as by committing "fifteen percent of subscription series repertoire to Black and Latinx composers for the next decade."[29]

As the third decade of the twenty-first century begins, with artists and artistic organizations grappling with a new reality and an alternative consciousness caused by an international pandemic and domestic social upheaval, thought leaders at Lincoln Center and beyond have begun the process of reconceiving their current reality. As the theater critic Eric Bentley wrote, "Experimentalism in the arts always reflects historical conditions, always reflects profound dissatisfaction with established modes, always is groping towards a new age."[30]

It will take many years and much thought to find authentic avenues through which the great works of the past, which established the traditions associated with Lincoln Center, can be meshed with a new aesthetic, a new way of interpreting and presenting the performing arts that continues to permit the human spirit to be fulfilled and challenged through the power of an artistic experience. With the proposition that traditional artistic repertoire embodies problematic values and prejudices of the past, the philosophical foundation on which Lincoln Center was created has been called into question.

In turn, the arts can be a powerful vehicle through which community members may reconnect with each other as the isolation of the pandemic passes; moreover, it may help to ameliorate the racial and political divisions that characterized 2020. With such a path before us, our global society may be able to find a new sense of humanity and equity through the experience of appreciating great works of art.

The art critic Holland Cotter wrote of a unique exhibition of selected pieces by the sixteenth-century painter Titian that toured Europe and America in 2021 by stating that such works of art "are invaluable for the lessons they teach: We can love art for its beauties and call it out for its blindness. We can exalt it to the skies, and still wrestle it to the ground. Old or new, art is us at our best and our worst, and it really *is* us, with everything that means, and useful beyond fashion and price."[31]

Lincoln Center and its kindred institutions around the United States will need to decide how to respond to a modern environment that requires respect for the past as well as real change for the future. In the emotional and tension-filled year of 2020, it is challenging to find the correct path, one that permits the free interchange of ideas involving multiple viewpoints. This approach has been made that much more difficult by a toxic political climate created by former

President Trump and his supporters that has put into question the basic issue of what truth is. This continuing exchange of ideas will require vigilance and equanimity, since, as one writer noted, "No society can long flourish when contrarians are treated as heretics."[32] With rational thought and intelligent leadership, Lincoln Center for the Performing Arts must address the transformative task of re-imagining itself and finding its place in a fundamentally changed global society.

Epilogue

THE DAWN OF 2021 COULD hardly have been less conducive to support of the arts. In the early afternoon of Wednesday, January 6, 2021, a mob of pro-Trump insurrectionists broke through police barriers and occupied the U.S. Capitol while a formal tally of the 2020 electoral vote was being certified by the House and Senate. Vice President Mike Pence and legislators from both bodies were rushed to safety while angry Trump loyalists ransacked both legislative chambers and adjacent offices. Many accused President Trump of inciting a violent riot and violating America's democratic principles by giving an angry speech before the mob moved to the Houses of Congress at his urging. A week later, the House of Representatives voted to impeach Trump a second time for inciting the attack on the Capitol. On February 6, the Senate acquitted him on the single charge of "incitement of insurrection."

In this new year, the confluence of a pandemic, the continuing calls for racial justice manifested in the Black Lives Matter movement, and the actions of a renegade U.S. president contesting an election he lost to Joseph R. Biden, Jr., shook the bedrock of American society. To Darren Walker, president of the Ford Foundation, writing in the summer of 2020 (and therefore before the Trump election drama), the upheaval felt "like 1918, 1932 and 1968 all at once."[1]

Within this chaotic environment, the arts and its practitioners were once again pushed to a place of secondary importance within

American society, making artists feel abandoned. With concert venues, theaters, and museums shut down, the arts, more than most other professions, experienced a catastrophic economic disruption that went well beyond the recent crises of 9/11 or the Great Recession. Nevertheless, there was also hope that the arts could restore to the world a sense of compassion and empathy—that the arts might become a powerful force for the revival of American citizenry's social and psychological well-being.

The return of live artistic performances throughout the country remained in question in 2021. There was hope that a large percentage of the population could be vaccinated in time for the new performance season in September, based on the assumption that audience members would be comfortable congregating in packed halls if all members were vaccinated. The situation was exacerbated by a new paradigm for experiencing the arts, involving a mix of in-person and online performances, all of which might significantly decrease audience size. Moreover, there was a widespread conviction that the pandemic had reshaped the ecosystem of New York City and beyond, creating a particularly difficult economic burden for the arts community as organizations large and small reevaluated their missions and tried to find ways to attract new audiences.

As with so many other world crises, the 2020 pandemic had unexpected ramifications. Since the New York Philharmonic canceled its entire 2020–21 season, Lincoln Center and Philharmonic leadership came together to move the renovation of Geffen Hall forward. By January 2021, the orchestra and Lincoln Center had jointly raised $500 million, with another $50 million needed to complete the project's fundraising. Construction began in December 2020, and the new hall's opening was scheduled for October 2022, two years earlier than previously announced, sparing the orchestra a multiyear peripatetic existence while construction was taking place.

As I write this, the Philharmonic's new season is scheduled to open tomorrow, on September 17, in Alice Tully Hall, followed by a different program in Rose Hall at Jazz at Lincoln Center on September 23. Both venues were chosen because of the renovation of Geffen Hall. The programs included works which did not require large orchestral forces, responding to the smaller audience capacity of the two halls in comparison to Geffen Hall. All concerts will be conducted by the Philharmonic's music director Jaap van Zweden and presented without intermission. However, van Zweden has just announced that he plans to leave his post as the Philharmonic's music director at the end of the 2023–24 season, explaining that the pandemic has made him reconsider his life priorities. New York City Ballet is due to have its opening night on September 21, featuring works of Balanchine and Christopher Wheeldon.

Some Lincoln Center constituents will need to realize a significant economic resurgence to rebound from the disaster of 2020. The New York Philharmonic faced a $21 million loss in earned income and reduced its staff by 50 percent. Deborah Borda was able to negotiate a four-year contract with the orchestra's musicians that temporarily reduced wages by 25 percent until the organization's finances returned to pre-pandemic levels.

Labor concessions were harder to come by at the Metropolitan Opera, where deep hostility between employees and management had been developing for several years. Negotiations with perhaps the most powerful of the Met's unions, Local 1 of the International Alliance of Theatrical Stage Employees, which represents about three hundred stagehands, ended in failure in early December 2020, and the Met announced that it planned to lock out the union's workers. Peter Gelb's draconian decision, driven by a $150 million revenue loss due to the pandemic, caused significant upset for all Met employees. However, the labor negotiations with Local 1 leaders were resolved in the early summer, with the Met orchestra agreeing to a new contract in late August, ensuring that the Met's artistic forces would be in place for the opening-night performance on September 27 of Terrence Blanchard's opera *Fire Shut Up in My Bones*, the first opera production by a Black composer in the Met's history, based on a personal memoir by Charles M. Blow, a *New York Times* opinion columnist, and conducted by Yannick Nézet-Séguin. Opening night was preceded by a free Met outdoor concert in Damrosch Park of Mahler's Second (Resurrection) Symphony on September 4, and a commemoration of the twentieth anniversary of 9/11 on September 11 with a presentation of the Verdi Requiem, all conducted by Nézet-Séguin. The Verdi performance was the first indoor event by the Met since March 2020, and the enthusiastic audience completely filled the hall.

Other Lincoln Center constituents weathered the storm with various levels of success, due to less dependence on ticket revenue or serendipitous production schedules in which costs decreased during the cessation of performances. Federal loans and emergency grants also helped sustain the payrolls of many arts organizations, though at diminished levels. Still, the New York State Office of the Comptroller reported that New York City's employment in the arts, entertainment, and recreation sector plummeted by 66 percent from December 2019 to December 2020.[2]

The 2021–22 season will represent a turnaround year, focused on returning to some level of "normalcy," if that still can be defined, as well as attempting to realize a type of catharsis, as one writer has suggested, through encountering works of art that incite a personal "cleansing, a clarity, a feeling of relief and understanding that you carry with you out of the theater or the concert hall."[3] Others have expressed the belief that the artistic and managerial practices of the past must be modified or restructured completely, making the post-pandemic period one in which new directions for the arts are charted.

Lincoln Center president Henry Timms viewed the post-pandemic period as a time of optimism for the Center. He did not see the COVID-19 siege as an existential threat to the constituents; rather, he saw opportunities for Lincoln Center to address "how the constituents transformatively present their art, engaging new audiences with increased relevance. It will be a time to re-address, to re-imagine the structure of how we do business."[4] In late February 2021, Timms announced the creation of ten outdoor performance and rehearsal spaces on the Lincoln Center campus in the spring and summer to bring artists back to work.

Timms and Katherine Farley had led a successful effort with the Lincoln Center board in the fall of 2020 to authorize a new strategic direction that considerably repositioned the Center's role in constituents' lives. In a letter to the trustees, Timms openly admitted that "Lincoln Center for the Performing Arts is too often seen as acting in its own interests, rather than serving the constituents. This is compounded by a lack of strategic clarity around the choices we [Lincoln Center] have often made."[5]

The letter sets three priorities for the Center which, if enacted, would change the course of how the arts complex functions in the future. The first priority aims to serve and connect the constituents and champion the decades-old "Lincoln Center concept" of creating a whole larger than the sum of its parts. A second, new element supports programs of equity and inclusion that would increase audience and artistic diversity. Timms foresaw Lincoln Center programming becoming "more diverse and strategic, including such genres as contemporary popular music and other disciplines."[6] Finally, it was proposed that a concerted effort begin to "reimagine and strengthen the performing arts for the 21st century" by creating an online research and development lab addressing the future of the performing arts called "The Collider," which would bring together art, social justice, and new technology.[7]

The letter ends by projecting a Lincoln Center four years in the future—the Center's sixty-fifth anniversary—when these and other innovations could serve "as a case study and transformation. . . . We have never been more impactful. . . . We have reset our relationship with the constituents. . . . From professional development opportunities to shared digital platforms, to joint programming, collaboration is constant. The reputation and voice of Lincoln Center have become more powerful and compelling—tides that lift all ships."[8]

The Center reinforced its determination to realize this strategy through its search for a new chief artistic officer. The job prospectus stated that Lincoln Center had "not done enough to ensure that the scope of [the Center's achievements] includes the vast diversity of artistic voices, cultures, disciplines, and traditions found in our New York Community, let alone around the world. . . . This appointment offers . . . a rare opportunity to reimagine what art we present; what voices we amplify; and what stories we tell. . . . [This new vision] brings together and lifts up our constituent organizations, explicitly champions inclusion, and embodies the spirit of innovation."[9]

In early August 2021, the appointment of Shanta Thake as the Center's new chief artistic officer was announced, with the *New York Times* stating that Lincoln Center would work "to broaden its appeal beyond classical music and ballet into genres such as hip-hop, poetry and songwriting." Thake had spent a decade overseeing productions in the cabaret-style Joe's Pub at the Public Theater, and stated that her new position would focus on new directions for the Center. "The goal is expansive reach. . . . What's missing? What have we left out? What stories aren't we telling that feel like they're demanding to be told in this moment?" she asked.[10]

In addition, in July the Center announced the appointment of Mahogany L. Browne as its inaugural poet in residence to develop programs in the summer months involving poetry readings, film screenings, discussions, and performances that would focus on social justice issues.

A heightened sense of responsibility and urgency in developing programs of equity and inclusion in the arts emerged in mid-2020, raising the consciousness of many Americans and energizing efforts to support pro-diversity values and initiatives. If the arts community can actively and consistently implement such an agenda, elements of inequity within America's arts institutions might be ameliorated.

Assuming Lincoln Center's new strategy is realized, it will put the arts center on a distinctly different path, one characterized by better constituent relations, a revitalized artistic aesthetic, and the development of varied performances on campus. This new direction rediscovers some of the values represented in the original Lincoln Center philosophy, but it also responds directly to the issues of equity and diversity in today's world of the performing arts in America.

Although it is long past the time when Lincoln Center can provide realistic "reparations" for the societal harm it spawned in its nascent years through forced evictions of Black and Latinx families, history has conspired to create an environment in which the Center can meaningfully engage with communities of color in an effort to bring the healing and empathetic power of the performing arts to these disenfranchised populations. This transformative initiative will be obliged to balance Western classical performing arts traditions with a new world landscape driven by technology and social awareness.

The year 2021 has also been characterized by the emergence of a new form of "culture war" dating back to earlier iterations in the late

1980s. Its philosophical thrust was epitomized in the pronouncements of a music theorist writing, perhaps in consciously inflammatory terms, that "it would be academically irresponsible to call [Beethoven] more than an 'above average' composer . . . [who has been] 'propped up by whiteness and maleness for 200 years.'"[11]

Questioning the social or intellectual worth of artistic works of another time within the context of a human history littered with discrimination, barbarism, and endless wars should not negate the reality that such works continue to move, inspire, provoke, and console. It seems most productive to join the great artistic works of another era with a new paradigm—a reinvention—that blends an understanding of the past with a positive effort to promote the best values of our humanity, creating a broader perspective for our society and its artists in the time ahead.

Although classic works of an earlier time may be dismissed or denigrated due to their connection with eras whose practices and values should be soundly rejected today, history has shown that the arts are never static. Great art will always be admired and experienced in new ways. Our current concerns and attitudes about the arts will invariably evolve in the future to some other form, unknown to us today.

Lincoln Center stands as an institution that can accommodate these changes and new directions, but it will have to justify its existence every day through its commitment to bringing creativity, new initiatives, excellence in execution, and beauty to a world in need of solace. With this approach, Lincoln Center can rededicate itself to the infinite capacity of the arts to renew the human spirit.

September 16, 2021

Notes

Abbreviations

JDR 3rd: John D. Rockefeller 3rd
JDR, Jr.: John D. Rockefeller, Jr.
JSA: Juilliard School Archives, New York City
LCPA: Lincoln Center for the Performing Arts, New York City
MOA: Metropolitan Opera Archives, New York City
NYPh: New York Philharmonic Leon Levy Digital Archives, New York City
NYPL: New York Public Library for the Performing Arts, New York City
RAC: Rockefeller Archive Center, Sleepy Hollow, New York

Prologue

1. Edgar B. Young, *Lincoln Center: The Building of an Institution* (New York: New York University Press, 1980), 301.
2. JDR 3rd, "The Arts and American Business," *Musical Journal*, February 1959, Archives of LCPA, vol. 1, 97.
3. "Lincoln Center Begins," *New York Times*, May 14, 1959.
4. Ada Louise Huxtable, "Lincoln Center Rejoins the City," *Wall Street Journal*, July 1, 2009.

Chapter One. The Expansion of an Idea

1. Eric W. Sanderson, *Mannahatta: A Natural History of New York City* (New York: Harry N. Abrams, 2009), 71.
2. Ibid., 1.
3. Washington Irving, *Knickerbocker's History of New York* (1809), as quoted in "Final Report," Braislin, Porter & Wheelock, Philip Schorr, Site Manager, November 30, 1959, F-428, B-43, RG-III 2E, RAC (hereafter Braislin).

4. Braislin, 2.

5. Ibid., 2.

6. Kenneth T. Jackson, ed., *The Encyclopedia of New York City* (New Haven: Yale University Press, 1995), 119.

7. Ibid., 1218.

8. Braislin, 2.

9. Glenn Collins, "50 Years In, Lincoln Center's Name Is Still a Mystery," *New York Times*, May 11, 2009.

10. Ibid.

11. *New York Daily News*, March 3, 1959, in Braislin, 1.

12. Robert A. Caro, *Working* (New York: Alfred A. Knopf, 2019), 35.

13. Ibid., 34.

14. Ibid., 52.

15. Ibid.

16. William B. Scott and Peter M. Rutkoff, *New York Modern* (Baltimore: Johns Hopkins University Press, 1999), 356.

17. *New York Times Magazine*, May 10, 1959, Scrapbook, vol. 1, 108, Archives of LCPA.

18. Scott and Rutkoff, *New York Modern*, 357.

19. Letter from Dean Rusk to Chauncey Belknap, August 28, 1956, F-390, B-38, RG-III, 2E, RAC.

20. "Text of Statement by Lincoln Center for the Arts," *New York Times*, September 12, 1957, cited in Kenneth H. Roberts, "The Lincoln Center Repertory Theatre, 1958–1965" (PhD diss., The Ohio State University, 1966), University Microfilms (hereafter Roberts).

21. Samuel Zipp, *Manhattan Projects: The Rise and Fall of Urban Renewal in Cold War New York* (New York: Oxford University Press, 2010), 166.

22. Ibid., 179.

23. Prospectus on Music, F-397, B-39, RG III 2E, app. 1, RAC.

24. Edgar B. Young, *Lincoln Center: The Building of an Institution* (New York: New York University Press, 1980), 15.

25. Rockefeller Archive Center, accessed July 23, 2019, https://rockarch.org/.

26. Young, *Lincoln Center*, 18.

27. Memo to the Committee, June 15, 1956, F-419, B-42, RG III 2E, RAC.

28. JDR 3rd, "The Arts and American Business," *Musical Journal*, February 1959, Archives of LCPA, vol. 1, 97.

29. Ibid.

30. Conference on Proposed Musical Arts Center, February 17–18, 1956, Savoy Plaza Hotel, New York City, F-390, B-38, RG-III, 2E, 31, RAC (hereafter Conference on Proposed Musical Arts Center).

31. Scott and Rutkoff, *New York Modern*, 351.

32. JDR 3rd, "Diary Notes on Lincoln Center, 1955–1959," F-532, B-59, RG 5, 4-LC, RAC.

33. Conference on Proposed Musical Arts Center, 3.

34. Braislin, 20.

35. Letter from Basil Fellrath to JRD 3rd, August 27, 1958, F-428, B-43, RG III 2E, RAC.

36. Letter from O. L. Nelson to Basil Fellrath, September 8, 1958, F-428, B-43, RG-III 2E, RAC.

37. Scott and Rutkoff, *New York Modern*, 357.

38. Minutes, Exploratory Committee, March 19, 1956, F-417A, B-41, RG-III 2E, 2, RAC.

39. Ibid., 3.

40. Exploratory Committee Minutes, April 2, 1956, F-390, B-38, RG III 2E, 1, RAC.

41. Memo from Otto L. Nelson to JDR 3rd, September 30, 1957, F-519, B-58, RG-5, 4-LC, 1, RAC.

42. Letter from JDR 3rd to George E. Spargo, Assistant to Robert Moses, May 14, 1957, F-519, B-58, RG-5, 4-LC, RAC.

43. Annual Report of LCPA, January 1963, as cited in Roberts, 43.

44. "Suggested Use of Auditoria," Day & Zimmermann, May 29, 1956, F-397, B-39, RG III 2E, 3, RAC.

45. "Suggested Events and Attendance Potentials," October 17, 1956, Draft Report to JDR 3rd from H. D. Johnson, Jr., of Day & Zimmermann, F-400, B-39, RG-III, 2E, 14, RAC.

46. Ibid., 16.

47. Ibid., 17.

48. See "Sanitary and Topographical Map of the City and Island of New York," David Rumsey Historical Map Collection, accessed December 14, 2019, https://www.davidrumsey.com/maps6128.html.

49. Letter from Eugene Ormandy to JRD 3rd, January 7, 1960, F-613, B-70, RG-5, 4-LC, RAC.

50. "What's Wrong at Lincoln Center?" *New York Herald Tribune*, January 17, 1960, F-613, B-70, RG-5, 4-LC, RAC.

51. Letter from Sol Hurok to JDR 3rd, December 8, 1955, F-421, B-42, RG-III, 2E, RAC.

Chapter Two. A Mighty Influence for Peace and Understanding

1. Day & Zimmermann report "Education in the New Center," April 30, 1956, F-425, B-42, RG-III, 2E, 1, RAC.

2. Ibid., 1.

3. "Summary of a Conference on Music Education, October 9, 1956, F-425, B-42, RG-III, 2E, 1, RAC.

4. Ibid., 1.

5. Ibid., 2.

6. Ibid., 3.

7. Charles Dollard interview with Howard Taubman, July 11, 1956, New York Times Building, F-615, B-70, RG-5, 4-LC, 1, RAC.

8. Charles Dollard interview with Max Rudolf, July 12, 1956, Metropolitan Opera House, F-615, B-70, RG-5, 4-LC, 1, RAC.

9. Interview involving Charles Dollard, Edgar Young, and Lincoln Kirstein, Gotham Hotel, July 17, 1956, F-615, B-70, RG-5, 4-LC, 2, RAC.

10. Ibid., 1–2.

11. "Prospectus for an Institute of Advanced Training in the Performing Arts," November 8, 1956, F-425, B-42, RG-III, 2E, 1, RAC.

12. Ibid., 5.

13. Minutes of Executive Committee Meeting of December 17, 1956, F-417, B-41, RG-III, 2E, 3, RAC.

14. Letter from Reginald Allen to José Limón, July 8, 1960, F-421a, B-42, RG-III, 2E, RAC.

15. "Notes for a Public Statement on the Lincoln Center," F-419, B-39, RG-III, 2E, RAC.

16. Letter from JDR 3rd to JDR, Jr., November 7, 1956, F-396, B-39, RG-III, 2E, RAC.

17. *New York Herald Tribune*, May 28, 1956, F-393, B-39, RG III, 2E, RAC.

18. Peter D. Franklin, "John D. Rockefeller Jr. Gives Lincoln Center $5 million," *New York Times*, June 30, 1958, F-396, B-39, RG-III, 2E, RAC.

19. Letter from JRD 3rd to JDR, Jr., December 12, 1956, F-369, B-39, RG-III, 2E, RAC.

20. "Final Report," Braislin, Porter & Wheelock, Philip Schorr, Site Manager, November 30, 1959, F-428, B-43, RG-III 2E, RAC, 9.

21. "Lincoln Square: A Slum Clearance Project That Endangers Religious Freedom," F-392, B-39, RG-III, 2E, RAC.

22. Letter from Robert Moses to JDR 3rd, September 17, 1957, F-392, B-39, RG-III, 2E, RAC.

23. *New York Times*, November 14, 1956, F-393, B-39, RG-III, 2E, RAC.

24. *New York Times*, September 13, 1957, F-393, B-39, RG-III, 2E, RAC.

25. Paul Crowell, "Lincoln Square Rivals Clash at Hearing before Planners," September 12, 1957, *New York Times*, F-393, B-39, RG-III, 2E, RAC.

26. Ibid.

27. Ibid.

28. General Otto L. Nelson memo of September 27, 1957, F-392, B-39, RG-III, 2E, 2, RAC.

29. *New York Times*, September 13, 1957.

30. Ralph G. Martin, *Lincoln Center for the Performing Arts* (Englewood Cliffs, NJ: Prentice-Hall, 1971), 13.

31. Harold C. Schonberg, "Six Architects in Search of a Center," *New York Times Magazine*, February 6, 1959, vol. 1, pt. 1, Archives of LCPA, 98.

32. Transcript of interviews by Sharon Zane with Max Abramovitz, June 20, 1990–September 11, 1990, New York City, LCPA Oral History Project (1990), Archives of LCPA, 107.
33. Transcript of interviews by Sharon Zane with Philip Johnson, August 14, 1990–October 4, 1990, New York City (hereafter Zane/Johnson), LCPA Oral History Project (1990), Archives of LCPA, 65.
34. William B. Scott and Peter M. Rutkoff, *New York Modern* (Baltimore: Johns Hopkins University Press, 1999), 359.
35. Zane/Johnson, 66–67.
36. Anna M. Rosenberg, "Organizing a Labor Advisory Committee for Lincoln Center," September 18, 1958, F-619, B-71, RG 5, 4-LC, 2, RAC.
37. Letter from Edgar B. Young to Harry Van Arsdale, Jr., April 24, 1963, F-622, B-71, RG 5, 4-LC, 2, RAC.
38. Memorandum from Edgar B. Young to Reginald Allen and Colonel Powers, September 14, 1961, F-610, B-70, RG 5, 4-LC, RAC.
39. Letter from Lincoln Kirstein to JDR 3rd, May 6, 1959, F-618, B-71, RG-5, 4-LC, RAC.
40. Ibid.
41. Letter from JDR 3rd to Lincoln Kirstein, May 18, 1959, F-618, B-71, RG-5, 4-LC, RAC.
42. Letter from Lincoln Kirstein to Edgar Young, June 18, 1959, F-618, B-71, RG-5, 4-LC, RAC.
43. Letter from JDR 3rd to Lincoln Kirstein, July 1, 1959, F-618, B-71, RG-5, 4-LC, 2, RAC.
44. Letter from Lincoln Kirstein to JDR 3rd, December 12, 1960, F-618, B-71, RG-5, 4-LC, 3, RAC.
45. Letter from Lincoln Kirstein to JDR 3rd, January 31, 1961, F-618, B-71, RG, 5, 4-LC, RAC.
46. Letter from Robert Moses to JDR 3rd, May 4, 1959, F-406, B-40, RG-III, 2E, RAC.
47. Letter from JDR 3rd to Robert Moses, May 6, 1959, F-406, B-40, RG-III, 2E, RAC.
48. Letter from Robert Moses to JDR 3rd, May 7, 1959, F-406, B-40, RG-III, 2E, RAC.
49. "Remarks of Robert Moses . . . at the Performing Arts Groundbreaking at Lincoln Square," May 14, 1959, F-406, B-40, RG-III, 2E, 2, RAC.
50. Personal recollection of the author's many conversations on the topic with William Schuman.
51. Peter D. Franklin, "President Launches Lincoln Square Project," *New York Herald Tribune*, May 15, 1959, Archives of LCPA, vol. 1, 155.
52. Letter from JDR 3rd to President Dwight D. Eisenhower, May 14, 1959, F-406, B-40, RG-III, 2E, RAC.
53. Letter from President Dwight D. Eisenhower to JDR 3rd, May 18, 1959, F-406, B-40, RG-III, 2E, RAC.

54. Letter from Robert Moses to JDR 3rd, May 21, 1959, F-406, B-40, RG-III, 2E, RAC.

55. "Man in the News: Inspired by Vision—John Davison Rockefeller 3rd," *New York Times*, May 14, 1959.

56. Ibid.

Chapter Three. No Longer a Dream but a Reality

1. "Minutes of the Exploratory Committee for a Musical Arts Center," May 14, 1956, F-390, B-38, RG-III, 2E, RAC.

2. Day & Zimmermann Report, F-400, B-39, RG-III, 2E, RAC.

3. "Maxwell Davenport Taylor," U.S. Joint Chiefs of Staff, accessed July 13, 2019, https://www.jcs.mil./About/The-Joint-Staff/Chairman/General-Maxwell-Davenport-Taylor/.

4. LCPA News Release, October 31, 1960, Archives of LCPA.

5. "Minutes of April 24, 1961, Meeting of the LCPA Board," F-417A, B-41, RG-III, 2E, RAC.

6. LCPA News Release, June 26, 1961, Archives of LCPA.

7. William Schuman, letter to Juilliard faculty and staff, September 12, 1961, B-21, F-9, Archives of NYPL.

8. Transcript of interviews by Sharon Zane with Schuyler Chapin, January 7, 1991–January 22, 1992, New York City (hereafter Zane/Chapin), LCPA Oral History Project (1992), Archives of LCPA, 38.

9. Joseph W. Polisi, *American Muse: The Life and Times of William Schuman* (New York: Amadeus Press, 2008), 209.

10. Heidi Waleson, "William Schuman's Memoirs, 1990–92" (unpublished manuscript in author's possession), chapter 10, 18, Schuman Family Archives.

11. Arthur Gelb, "A Deeper Significance," *New York Times*, September 24, 1962.

12. "The Welcoming Address," *New York Times*, September 24, 1962.

13. Alan Rich, "First Lady Pays Bernstein a Visit," *New York Times*, September 24, 1962.

14. Opening Week Program Book (in the author's possession).

15. Transcript of interview by Sharon Zane with Dr. Leo L. Beranek, October 4, 2001, Cambridge, Massachusetts (hereafter Zane/Beranek), LCPA Oral History Project (2001), Archives of LCPA, 65.

16. Ibid., 84.

17. Letter from JDR 3rd to Pablo Casals, August 28, 1961, F-634, B-73, RG 5, 4-LC, RAC.

18. Letter from Pablo Casals to JDR 3rd, September 30, 1961, F-634, B-73, RG 5, 4-LC, RAC.

19. Harold C. Schonberg, "Music: The Occasion," *New York Times*, September 24, 1962.

20. Lincoln Center for the Performing Arts, Minutes of Meeting of the Board of Directors and Members, June 11, 1962, Archives of LCPA, 4.

21. Polisi, *American Muse*, 222.

22. Zane/Beranek, 31.

23. Memorandum from Reginald Allen to JDR 3rd, April 4, 1960, F-517, B-58, RG 5, 4-LC, 1–2, RAC.

24. Polisi, *American Muse*, 224.

25. Letter from numerous modern dance leaders to JDR 3rd, May 25, 1960, F-421a, B-42, RG III, 2E, RAC.

26. Letter from Martha Graham to JDR 3rd, May 19, 1960, F-421a, B-42, RG-III, 2E, RAC.

27. Transcript of interviews by Sharon Zane with Edgar B. Young, June 11, 1990–November 13, 1990, New York City, LCPA Oral History Project (1990), Archives of LCPA, 52.

28. Zane/Chapin, 48.

29. "About the Theater," New York City Ballet, http://www.nycballet.com/About/David-H-Koch-Theater/Fun-Facts.aspx, accessed September 2, 2018.

30. LCPA Press Release, December 31, 1964, F-524, B-59, RG 5-4LC, RAC.

31. Murray Schumach, "Lincoln Center: Hub of Arts: Lincoln Center, 5 Years Old Today, Wields a Major Influence in Nation's Arts," *New York Times*, September 23, 1967.

Chapter Four. You Have Made Something That Will Last

1. Transcript of interview by Sharon Zane with Robert Whitehead, March 21, 1991, New York City (hereafter Zane/Whitehead), LCPA Oral History Project (1991), Archives of LCPA, 17, 18.

2. Howard Taubman, "A New Beginning," *New York Times*, November 26, 1961.

3. Kenneth Tynan, *The Observer* (London), March 1, 1959, cited in Kenneth H. Roberts, "The Lincoln Center Repertory Theatre, 1958–1965" (PhD diss., The Ohio State University, 1966), University Microfilms (hereafter Roberts), 41.

4. Edgar B. Young, *Lincoln Center: The Building of an Institution* (New York: New York University Press, 1980), 243.

5. Zane/Whitehead, 26.

6. Ibid., 29.

7. Milton Esterow, "Lincoln Center Board Planning Talk with Whitehead in Dispute," *New York Times*, December 9, 1964, cited in Roberts, 74.

8. Zane/Whitehead, 35

9. Roberts, 78–79.

10. Robert Brustein, "Subsidized Rubbish," *New Republic*, April 11. 1964, cited in Roberts, 121.

11. Robert Brustein, *Seasons of Discontent* (New York: Simon and Schuster, 1965), 253–55, cited in Roberts, 136.

12. Elia Kazan, *Elia Kazan: A Life* (New York: Alfred A. Knopf, 1988), 694.

13. Interviews of William Schuman by Vivian Perlis, February 2, 1977–November 16, 1977, New York City and Greenwich, Connecticut, Yale University American Music Series, 356.

14. Transcript of interviews by Sharon Zane with Schuyler Chapin, January 7, 1991–January 22, 1992, New York City (hereafter Zane/Chapin), LCPA Oral History Project (1992), Archives of LCPA, 61.

15. Milton Esterow, "Bing Attack Airs Dispute on Theater of Lincoln Center," *New York Times*, December 5, 1964.

16. Transcript of interviews by Sharon Zane with Edgar B. Young, June 11, 1990–November 13, 1990, New York City (hereafter Zane/Young), LCPA Oral History Project (1990), Archives of LCPA, 246.

17. Zane/Chapin, 61.

18. New York State Theater Official Announcement, LCPA, March 13, 1964, F-627, B-72, RG-5, 4-LC, 1–2, RAC.

19. Balanchine's comment can be found at the George Balanchine Trust website: https://www.balanchine.com/Ballet/Allegro-Brillante (accessed September 11, 2021).

20. Letter from Lincoln Kirstein to JDR 3rd, April 22, 1964, F-618, B-71, RG-5, 4-LC, RAC.

21. Letter from JDR 3rd to Lincoln Kirstein, April 27, 1964, F-618, B-71, RG-5, 4-LC, RAC.

22. Zane/Young, 117.

23. Louis Calta, "Acoustics Scored at State Theater," *New York Times*, May 20, 1964, F-627, B-72, RG-5, 4-LC, RAC.

24. Music Theater of Lincoln Center Brochure, September 9, 1963, F-618, B-71, RG-5, 4-LC, 1, RAC.

25. Ibid., 3.

26. Ibid., 6.

27. "Walter Kerr reviews 'The Merry Widow,'" *New York Herald Tribune*, August 18, 1964, F-623, B-71, RG-5, 4-LC, RAC.

28. Sam Zolotow, "Lincoln Center 'King and I' Earns a Princely $438,866 in 5 Weeks," *New York Times*, August 10, 1964, F-623, B-71, RG-5, 4-LC, RAC.

29. Transcript of interviews by Sharon Zane with John W. Mazzola, December 15, 1991–January 29, 1992, New York City, LCPA Oral History Project (1992), Archives of LCPA, 157.

30. Music Theater of Lincoln Center Brochure, 4.

31. "Opening of the Third Lincoln Center Building," LCPA News Release, September 27, 1965, F-621, B-71, RG-5, 4-LC, 4, RAC.

32. New York Public Library News Release, Anna L. Glantz, Chief, Public Relations Office, June 30, 1959, F-620, B-71, RG-5, 4-LC, 1, RAC.

33. Ibid., 2–3.
34. Ibid., 4.
35. Meeting of Architect's Advisory Panel, January 19, 1961, F-514, B-57, RG-5, 4-LC, 2, RAC.
36. Remarks by Edgar B. Young to the New York City Board of Estimate, June 11, 1965, F-614, B-70, RG-5, 4-LC, 4, RAC.
37. Zane/Young, 147–48.
38. JDR 3rd Confidential Schedule Memo, April 21, 1959, F-514, B-57, RG-5, 4-LC, RAC.
39. Ibid.
40. Memorandum from G. S. Eyssell to JDR 3rd, December 29, 1960, F-514, B-57, RG-5, 4-LC, 1, RAC.
41. Memorandum from JDR 3rd to Mark Schubart, July 9, 1964, F-631, B-57, RG-5, 4-LC, 1, RAC.

Chapter Five. It Was Not a Matter of Friendship but Principle

1. Introduction by JDR 3rd at dinner to honor President Ferdinand Marcos, September 20, 1966, F-747, B-92, RG-5, 4-LC, 5, RAC.
2. Ralph G. Martin, *Lincoln Center for the Performing Arts* (Englewood Cliffs, NJ: Prentice-Hall, 1971), 127.
3. Charlotte Curtis, "First Lady Adds to Glitter; Musicians' Strike Is Settled," *New York Times*, September 17, 1966.
4. Harold C. Schonberg, "Onstage, It Was *Antony and Cleopatra*," *New York Times*, September 17, 1966.
5. Ada Louise Huxtable, "Sweet and Sour Notes on the Met," *New York Times*, September 18, 1966.
6. Letter from Robert Moses to Wallace K. Harrison, July 16, 1965, F-631, B-73, RG-5, 4-LC, RAC.
7. References to "Mrs. August Belmont" and, below, "Miss Tully" conform with the way these women were always identified and with how they themselves wished to be addressed.
8. Erika Stark, "The NYC Met Opera's 50th Anniversary and Murals of Marc Chagall: Art Imitating Life," *Untapped Cities*, June 13, 2017, accessed August 17, 2019, https://untappedcities.com/2017/06/13/the-nyc-met-operas-50th-anniversary-and-murals-of-marc-chagall-art-imitating-life/.
9. Ibid.
10. Letter from JDR 3rd to Frank Stanton, March 19, 1965, F-631, B-73, RG-5, 4-LC, RAC.
11. Letter from Howard W. Lipman to JDR 3rd, June 9, 1964, F-608, B-70, RG 5, 4-LC, RAC.
12. Letter from Newbold Morris to Edgar B. Young, March 24, 1965, F-608, F-70, RG 5, 4-LC, RAC.

13. Lincoln Center for the Performing Arts News Release, September 22, 1965, 1965, F-Facilities-Art, B-270076, Archives of LCPA, 2.

14. "Arts Commission Overrides Morris," *New York Times*, July 13, 1965, F-608, B-70, RG 5, 4-LC, RAC.

15. Interviews of William Schuman by Vivian Perlis, February 2, 1977–November 16, 1977, New York City and Greenwich, Connecticut (hereafter Perlis), Yale University American Music Series, 376.

16. "Background of Lincoln Center Film Financial Situation," March 5, 1968, F-5, B-35, RG-3, Rockefeller Family Files, General, 1, RAC, 2.

17. Lincoln Center Film Committee Press Release, August 31, 1967, F-5, B-35, RG-3, Rockefeller Family Files, General, RAC.

18. Henry Raymont, "New Lincoln Center Plan Offers Buildings Rather Than a Mall," *New York Times*, December 12, 1966, F-Facilities-Mall (Proposed), 1966–67, B-270076, Archives of LCPA.

19. Ibid.

20. Ada Louise Huxtable, "A Planning Happening," *New York Times*, December 18, 1966, F-Facilities-Mall (Proposed), 1966–67, B-270076, Archives of LCPA.

21. Ibid.

22. Transcript of interviews by Sharon Zane with Philip Johnson, August 14, 1990–October 4, 1990, New York City (hereafter Zane/Johnson), LCPA Oral History Project (1990), Archives of LCPA, 40–41.

23. Perlis, 349–50.

24. Letter from William Schuman to JDR 3rd, June 6, 1967, F-1, B-27, RG-3, Rockefeller Family Files, General, RAC. 2

25. Memorandum from John W. McNulty to the Files, January 3, 1966, F-608, B-70, RG 5, 4-LC, RAC.

26. Ibid.

27. Letter from JDR 3rd to William Schuman, December 30, 1966, Schuman Family Archives.

28. Ibid.

29. William Schuman "The New Establishment," speech delivered at the Princeton University Conference on the Performing Arts: Their Economic Problems, December 8–9, 1966, Archives of NYPL, F-1, B-79, 2–3.

30. Letter from JDR 3rd to William Schuman, February 22, 1967, Schuman Family Archives.

31. Letter from William Schuman to JDR 3rd, March 2, 1967, Schuman Family Archives.

32. Letter from JDR 3rd to William Schuman, October 28, 1965, F-7, B-51, Archives of NYPL.

33. Letter from William Schuman to Alice Tully, December 6, 1965, F-7, B-51, Archives of NYPL (emphasis mine).

34. Letter from Alice Tully to William Schuman, February 2, 1966, F-7, B-51, Archives of NYPL.

35. Perlis, 378.
36. Confidential Memorandum from Edgar B. Young to JDR 3rd, November 19, 1968, F-3, B-41, RG-3, Rockefeller Family Files, General, 1, RAC.
37. Ibid., 2–4.
38. Letter from JDR 3rd to Alice Tully, December 11, 1968, F-3, B-41, RG-3, Rockefeller Family Files, General, RAC.
39. Ibid.
40. Memorandum (marked "URGENT") from Edgar B. Young to JDR 3rd, December 16, 1968, F-3, B-41, RG-3, Rockefeller Family Files, General, RAC.
41. Memorandum of JDR 3rd to the Files, December 19, 1968, F-3, B-41, RG-3, Rockefeller Family Files, General, RAC.
42. Memorandum re: Meeting of Chamber Music Society, December 20, 1968, F-3, B-41, RG-3, Rockefeller Family Files, General, 1, RAC.
43. Ibid., 2.
44. Transcript of interviews by Sharon Zane with Edgar B. Young, June 11, 1990–November 13, 1990, New York City (hereafter Zane/Young), LCPA Oral History Project (1990), Archives of LCPA, 186.
45. Edgar B. Young, *Lincoln Center: The Building of an Institution* (New York: New York University Press, 1980), 296.
46. Zane/Young, 187.
47. Transcript of interviews by Sharon Zane with John W. Mazzola, December 15, 1991–January 29, 1992, New York City, LCPA Oral History Project (1992), Archives of LCPA, 102.
48. "Some Thoughts on the Second Letter to John D. Rockefeller 3rd," in "Letters I Never Sent," 10–11, Schuman Family Archives.
49. Ibid., 11.
50. Ibid., 15.
51. Memorandum from Edgar B. Young to JDR 3rd and William Schuman, September 12, 1963, F-617, B-71, RG 5, 4-LC, RAC.
52. "Juilliard Comes to Lincoln Center: A Dedication Concert," CBS Broadcast, October 26, 1969, Juilliard Library Audio-Visual Collection.
53. Memorandum from William Schuman to L.K. and M.B. (initials not identified), January 19, 1970, 9, Schuman Family Archives.
54. Perlis, 366.
55. Transcript of interviews by Sharon Zane with Schuyler Chapin, January 7, 1991–January 22, 1992, New York City, LCPA Oral History Project (1992), Archives of LCPA, 92.

Chapter Six. Opening Night and Amateur Night at the Same Time

1. Edgar B. Young, *Lincoln Center: The Building of an Institution* (New York: New York University Press, 1980), 281.

2. Anthony Tommasini, "Amyas Ames Is Dead at 93, a Champion of Lincoln Center," *New York Times*, January 26, 2000.

3. Transcript of interview by Sharon Zane with Amyas Ames, October 17, 1990, New York City (hereafter Zane/Ames), LCPA Oral History Project (1990), Archives of LCPA, 32.

4. Ibid., 37.

5. Ibid., 38.

6. Ibid., 38.

7. Ibid., 40–41.

8. Ibid., 41–42.

9. Transcript of interviews by Sharon Zane with John W. Mazzola, December 15, 1991–January 29, 1992, New York City (hereafter Zane/Mazzola), LCPA Oral History Project (1992), Archives of LCPA, 127.

10. Zane/Ames, 55.

11. Memorandum from Amyas Ames to the Board of Directors, Lincoln Center (draft), January 4, 1972, F-3103, B-513, RG-3.1, Rockefeller Brothers Fund, RAC, 2.

12. Ibid., 3.

13. Ibid., 6.

14. "The Great Inflation: 1965–1982," Federal Reserve History, accessed October 23, 2019, https://www.federalreservehistory.org/essays/great_inflation.

15. Zane/Ames, 45.

16. Ibid., 45.

17. "Lincoln Center Ends Its Capital Fund Drive," by Howard Taubman, *New York Times*, July 2, 1969, F-3101, B-513, RG-3.1, Rockefeller Brothers Fund, RFA.

18. Zane/Mazzola, 201.

19. Zane/Ames, 69–70.

20. Donal Henahan, "Philharmonic Hall Gets a Gift of $ 8 Million," *New York Times*, September 21, 1973, F-19, B-032–02, RG-Managing Director, NYPh.

21. Zane/Ames, 70.

22. Harold C. Schonberg, "New Philharmonic Sound Glows," *New York Times*, September 24, 1969.

23. Harold C. Schonberg, "Philharmonic Hall, and the Listening Is Easy," *New York Times*, October 12, 1969.

24. Harold C. Schonberg, "An 'Era' Ending for Fisher Hall," *New York Times*, May 17, 1976.

25. Donal Henahan, "Why Philharmonic Strike Drags On," *New York Times*, October 24, 1973, F-8, B-1, RG-Fisher Papers, JSA.

26. Zane/Ames, 70.

27. Ibid., 71.

28. Ibid., 72.

29. Transcript of interviews by Sharon Zane with Max Abramovitz, June 20–September 11, 1990, New York City, LCPA Oral History Project (1990), Archives of LCPA, 150.

30. Bruce Bliven, Jr., "Annals of Architecture: A Better Sound," *New Yorker*, November 8, 1976.

31. Letter from Pierre Boulez to Avery Fisher, October 27, 1976, F-1, B-6, RG-Fisher Papers. JSA.

32. Letter from Ranier C. DeIntinis to Avery Fisher, January 4, 1977, F-1, B-6, RG-Fisher Papers, JSA.

33. Letter from Philip Johnson to Avery Fisher, n.d., F-1, B-6, RG-Fisher Papers, JSA.

34. Donal Henahan, "At 'Rug Concert' a Standing Ovation," *New York Times*, June 14, 1973, F-1, B-7, RG-Fisher Papers, JSA .

35. Walter Kerr, *Thirty Plays Hath November: Pain and Pleasure in the Contemporary Theater* (New York: Simon & Schuster, 1969), cited in Saraleigh Carney, "The Repertory Theater of Lincoln Center: Aesthetics and Economics, 1960–1973" (PhD diss., City University of New York, 1976), 410, University Microfilms (hereafter Carney).

36. Carney, 289.

37. "Repertory Theater," Amyas Ames draft, February 21, 1971 (hereafter Ames draft), F-3685, B-090468, RG-02, Office of the Chairman, Archives of LCPA, 1.

38. Ibid., 2.

39. "City Planning Commission News Release," August 2, 1971, F-3685, B-090468, RG-02, Office of the Chairman, Archives of LCPA.

40. Ames draft, 3–4.

41. Ibid., 5.

42. "City Planning News Release," August 11, 1971, F-3685, B-090468, RG-02, Office of the Chairman, Archives of LCPA.

43. *New York Daily News*, August 30, 1971, F-3685, B-090468, RG-02, Office of the Chairman, Archives of LCPA.

44. "Designer Cries 'Rape at Lincoln Center,'" *New York Daily News*, August 24, 1971, F-3685, B-090468, RG-02, Office of the Chairman, Archives of LCPA.

45. *New York Daily News*, August 30, 1971, F-3685, B-090468, RG-02, Office of the Chairman, Archives of LCPA.

46. Carney, 410.

47. Ibid., 414.

48. Ibid., 414.

49. Draft Memorandum from John Mazzola to Amyas Ames, January 25, 1972, F-3685, B-090468, RG-02, Office of the Chairman, Archives of LCPA, 3.

50. Carney, 415.

Chapter Seven. The Cursed Inheritance

1. Transcript of interview by Sharon Zane with Amyas Ames, October 17, 1990, New York City (hereafter Zane/Ames), LCPA Oral History Project (1990), Archives of LCPA, 58.
2. Ibid., 60.
3. Mel Gussow, "Repertory Theater Battles Deficit Woes," *New York Times*, November 22, 1972, F-3685, B-090468, RG-02, Office of the Chairman, Archives of LCPA.
4. Transcript of interview by Sharon Zane with Bernard Gersten, April 7, 1992, New York City (hereafter Zane/Gersten), LCPA Oral History Project (1993), Archives of LCPA, 15–16.
5. Letter from Joseph Papp to LuEsther Mertz, April 10, 1973, F-3685, B-090468, RG-02, Office of the Chairman, Archive of LCPA.
6. Ibid.
7. Email from Robert Marx to the author, December 23, 2019.
8. Zane/Gersten, 18.
9. Mel Gussow, "A Playwright's Invention Named Papp," *New York Times*, November 19, 1975, in Saraleigh Carney, "The Repertory Theater of Lincoln Center: Aesthetics and Economics, 1960–1973" (PhD diss., City University of New York, 1976), 436, University Microfilms.
10. Ibid., 438.
11. Ibid., 443–44.
12. Ibid., 453.
13. "Status of the Vivian Beaumont Theater," memorandum from John W. Mazzola to the Board of Directors of Lincoln Center, July 13, 1977 (hereafter Mazzola memorandum), F-3686, B-090468, RG-02, Office of the Chairman, Archives of LCPA.
14. New York Shakespeare Festival News Release, June 9, 1977, F-3686, B-090468, RG-02, Office of the Chairman, Archives of LCPA, 1.
15. Email from Robert Marx to the author, December 23, 2019.
16. New York Shakespeare Festival News Release, 3.
17. Statement by Amyas Ames, June 9, 1977, F-3686, B-090468, RG-02, Office of the Chairman, Archives of LCPA.
18. "Conversation with Robert Brustein at His Home in Martha's Vineyard, Massachusetts, by Amyas Ames," Confidential Memo for the Files, August 11, 1977, F-3686, B-090468, RG-02, Office of the Chairman, Archives of LCPA, 1.
19. Ibid., 1.
20. Ibid., 3.
21. Mazzola memorandum, 2–3.
22. Zane/Ames, 66.
23. Heidi Waleson, *Mad Scenes and Exit Arias* (New York: Metropolitan Books / Henry Holt, 2018), 30.

24. Ibid., 30.

25. Fred Ferreti, "Endowment Points Up Fiscal Crisis at All Components of Lincoln Center," *New York Times*, September 21, 1973, F-3104, B-513, RG-3.1, Rockefeller Brothers Fund, RAC.

26. Confidential Memorandum from Amyas Ames to the Chairmen of the Constituents of Lincoln Center, June 26, 1973, F-3104, B-513, RG-3.1, Rockefeller Brothers Fund, RFA, 3.

27. Memorandum from Dana S. Creel to Rockefeller Brothers Fund, June 24, 1976, F-3104, B-513, RG-3.1, Rockefeller Brothers Fund, RFA.

28. Ibid.

29. Memorandum from Amyas Ames to William Rockefeller, May 12, 1976, F-3104, B-513, RG-3.1, Rockefeller Brothers Fund, RFA, 2.

30. Working Memorandum from Amyas Ames to the Board of Directors, April 30, 1977, F-3105, B-513, RG-3.1, Rockefeller Brothers Fund, RFA, 2.

31. Damrosch Park and the Guggenheim Band Shell were officially opened on May 22, 1969. The 2.3-acre area, a New York City park used for various outdoor artistic events, is located on Sixty-Second Street between Amsterdam and Columbus Avenues, just to the south of the Metropolitan Opera House. During the Center's earliest years, the Metropolitan Opera hoped to build a chamber theater on part of the site, but Robert Moses would not allow even a small portion of city park land to be sacrificed for any other purpose.

32. James R. Oestreich, "Rudolf Bing, Titan of the Met, Dies at 95," *New York Times*, September 3, 1997.

33. Ibid.

34. Memorandum from Mark Schubart to Stephen Benedict, April 8, 1973, F-3104, B-513, RG-3.1, Rockefeller Brothers Fund, RFA, 2.

35. Richard. F. Shephard, "New Plan for Young at Lincoln Center," *New York Times*, January 12, 1975, F-3105, B-513, RG-3.1, Rockefeller Brothers Fund, RFA.

36. Lincoln Kirstein, *Thirty Years: Lincoln Kirstein's New York City Ballet* (New York: Alfred A. Knopf, 1978), 214–15.

37. Nancy Goldner, *The Stravinsky Festival of the New York City Ballet* (New York: Eakins Press, 1973), 49.

38. Ibid., 222–23.

39. Richard F. Shepard, "Lincoln Center: The First 20 Years," *New York Times*, May 20, 1979, F-3684. B-090468, RG-2, RAC.

40. "Words of Commemoration, Governor John D. Rockefeller IV," John D. Rockefeller 3rd Memorial Service, Riverside Church, July 13, 1978, F-3677, B-090468, RG-02, Office of the Chairman, Archives of LCPA.

41. Letter from Amyas Ames to J. Richardson Dilworth and Donal C. O'Brien, Jr., March 29, 1979, F-3677, B-090468, RG-02, Office of the Chairman, Archives of LCPA.

Chapter Eight. It's Called Accountability

1. Transcript of interviews by Sharon Zane with John W. Mazzola, December 15, 1991–January 29, 1992, New York City (hereafter Zane/Mazzola), LCPA Oral History Project (1992), Archives of LCPA, 303.

2. John Rockwell, "Segal to Succeed Ames as Lincoln Center Chairman," *New York Times*, March 3, 1981, F-Clippings, Lincoln Center-General, 1980–1981, B-270085, Archives of LCPA.

3. Personal recollection of the author.

4. Rockwell, "Segal to Succeed Ames."

5. Personal recollection of the author.

6. Transcript of interviews by Sharon Zane with Martin E. Segal, May 2, 1991–July 1, 1991, New York City (hereafter Zane/Segal), LCPA Oral History Project (1991), Archives of LCPA, 95.

7. Ibid., 95.

8. Ibid.

9. Paul Vitello, "John W. Mazzola, Former President of Lincoln Center, Dies at 86," *New York Times*, July 29, 2014.

10. Ibid.

11. Zane/Mazzola, 300.

12. Ibid., 301.

13. Zane/Segal, 146.

14. Harold C. Schonberg, "Lincoln Center Board to Begin the Search for President," *New York Times*, December 3, 1983, F-General Clippings, September–December 1983, B-270059, Archives of LCPA.

15. Zane/Segal, 146–147.

16. Samuel G. Freedman, "Lincoln Center Chief Is Resigning," *New York Times*, December 2, 1983, F-General Clippings, September–December 1983, B-270059, Archives of LCPA.

17. Transcript of interviews by Sharon Zane with Nathan Leventhal, October 28, 1991–January 15, 1992, August 17, 2000–September 15, 2000, New York City (hereafter Zane/Leventhal), LCPA Oral History Project (1991; 2000), Archives of LCPA, 66.

18. Ibid., 66.

19. Ibid.

20. Ibid., 66–67.

21. Zane/Segal, 148.

22. Zane/Leventhal, 69.

23. Ibid., 68.

24. Ibid.

25. Ibid., 71.

26. Ibid., 71–72.

27. Francis Blau, "Lincoln Center Shows Off Rebuilt State Theater," *New York Times*, August 25, 1982, F-Renovation NYST and Beaumont, B-270082, Archives of LCPA.

28. Ibid.

29. Donal Henahan, "City Opera: 'Merry Widow,'" *New York Times*, September 8, 1982, F-Renovation of NYST and Beaumont, B-270082, Archives of LCPA.

30. *New York Times*, August 25, 1982, F-Renovation of NYST and Beaumont, B-270082, Archives of LCPA.

31. *New York Times*, September 8, 1982.

32. Email from Robert Marx to the author, February 12, 2020.

33. Mel Gussow, "Can a Committee Revive the Beaumont?" *New York Times*, January 21, 1979, F-Beaumont Theater 1975–1985, B-270059, Archives of LCPA.

34. Craig Unger, "War at Lincoln Center," *New York Magazine*, February 6, 1984, F-February 1984 clippings, B-270059, Archives of LCPA.

35. *New York Times*, October 25, 1979.

36. Email from Robert Marx to the author, February 12, 2020.

37. Eleanor Blau, "Pei Resigns as Beaumont Architect," *New York Times*, February 25, 1982, F-Beaumont Theater 1979–1985, B-270059, Archives of LCPA.

38. Zane/Segal, 132.

39. Ibid., 132.

40. Unger, "War at Lincoln Center."

41. Ibid.

42. Ibid.

43. Ibid.

44. Ibid.

45. Harold C. Schonberg, "Troubles Stalk the Beaumont," *New York Times*, January 10, 1983, F-Beaumont 1975–1985, B-270059, Archives of LCPA.

46. Unger, "War at Lincoln Center."

47. Diana Maychick, "New Screws Put on the Beaumont," *New York Post*, August 23, 1983, F-Beaumont Theater-1975–1985, B-270059, Archives of LCPA.

48. Zane/Segal, 133.

49. Harold C. Schonberg, "Debate Stirring Anew over Beaumont Theater," *New York Times*, April 11, 1984, F-Beaumont Theater 1979–1985, B-270059, Archives of LCPA.

50. Harold C. Schonberg, "Beaumont Agreement Is Reached," *New York Times*, June 5, 1984, F-Beaumont Theater 1979–1985, B-270059, Archives of LCPA.

Chapter Nine. It Will Flourish as Long as a Civilized Society Survives

1. Transcript of interviews by Sharon Zane with Nathan Leventhal, October 28, 1991–January 15, 1992, August 17, 2000–September 15, 2000,

New York City (hereafter Zane/Leventhal), LCPA Oral History Project (1991; 2000), Archives of LCPA, 75.

2. Ibid., 89.

3. Email from Nathan Leventhal to the author, February 24, 2020.

4. Transcript of interview by Sharon Zane with Bernard Gersten, April 7, 1992, New York City (hereafter Zane/Gersten), LCPA Oral History Project (1993), Archives of LCPA, 24.

5. Zane/Leventhal, 90.

6. Zane/Gersten, 33.

7. Email from Nathan Leventhal to the author, February 24, 2020.

8. Zane/Leventhal, 93.

9. Martin E. Segal, "The Years June, 1981 to June, 1986," report presented at the annual meeting of the board of directors, June 2, 1986 cited in Transcript of interviews by Sharon Zane with Martin E. Segal, May 2, 1991–July 1, 1991, New York City, LCPA Oral History Project (1991), Archives of LCPA, app. 7.

10. Transcript of interviews by Sharon Zane with George Weissman, November 19, 1991–April 15, 1992, New York City (hereafter Zane/Weissman), LCPA Oral History Project (1992), Archives of LCPA, 1.

11. See Jennifer Dunning, *"But First a School": The First Fifty Years of the School of American Ballet* (New York: Viking Penguin, 1985).

12. See the author's article "An Unsettled Marriage: The Merger of the School of American Ballet and The Juilliard School," *Ballet Review*, Spring 2006.

13. Zane/Weissman, 59.

14. Zane/Leventhal, 133.

15. Author's recollection of Community Board #7 meeting, May 1986.

16. Charles V. Bagli, "Frederick P. Rose, 2nd-Generation Builder and a Major Philanthropist, Is Dead at 75," *New York Times*, September 16, 1999.

17. Zane/Leventhal, 140.

18. Ibid., 142.

19. Ibid., 144.

20. "Let Lincoln Center Grow," *New York Times*, August 13, 1986, F-Clippings New Building, Book II, B-200298, Archives of LCPA.

21. Jennifer Dunning, "New Ballet School Opens, but Kirstein Worries," *New York Times*, January 9, 1991, F-Clippings New Building, Book II, B-200298, Archives of LCPA.

22. Zane/Leventhal, 80–81.

23. Bernard Holland, "Hugh Southern Resigns as Met Opera Manager," *New York Times*, June 23, 1990.

24. Anna Kisselgoff, "George Balanchine, 79, Dies in New York," *New York Times*, May 1, 1983.

25. Michael Shnayerson, "One by One," *Vanity Fair*, August 21, 2013.

Chapter Ten. This Is a Dream Come True

1. Ralph Blumenthal, "Beverly Sills, at 66, Stars in Her Grandest Role," *New York Times*, February 13, 1996, Beverly Sills Book 1, B-200287, Archives of LCPA. (Spelling of "fazes" corrected.)

2. Anthony Tommasini, "Beverly Sills, All-American Diva, Is Dead at 78," *New York Times*, July 3, 2007.

3. Ibid.

4. Ibid.

5. Cheryl Hall, "Enterprising Encore," *Dallas Morning News*, October 6, 1996, Beverly Sills Book 1, B-200287, Archives of LCPA.

6. Mary Campbell, "Beverly Sills Takes on Yet Another Formidable Task," *Gannett Reporter Dispatch*, Beverly Sills Book 1, B-200287, Archives of LCPA.

7. Peter Goodman, "Lincoln Center Looks to Beverly Sills," *New York Newsday*, January 25, 1994, Beverly Sills Book 1, B-200287, Archives of LCPA.

8. Ibid.

9. Ibid.

10. Contemporaneous notes taken by Joseph W. Polisi in his daily diary, September 27, 1994. These diary notes are housed in the archives of the Lila Acheson Wallace Library of The Juilliard School and are currently closed to researchers.

11. Nathan Leventhal, phone interview by the author, February 26, 2020.

12. Blumenthal, "Beverly Sills."

13. Roy Furman, phone interview by the author, April 6, 2020.

14. Frank Bruni, "Diva among the Divas," *New York Times*, January 6, 2002, F-Beverly Sills 2000–6/2003, B-200333, Archives of LCPA.

15. Leventhal, interview.

16. "Lincoln Center Appoints John Rockwell to Head New Annual Performance Festival Beginning in 1996," Lincoln Center Productions News Release, September 21, 1994, F-Press Releases, September 1994. B-200405, Archives of LCPA.

17. Ibid.

18. Transcript of interviews by Sharon Zane with Nathan Leventhal, October 28, 1991–January 15, 1992, August 17, 2000–September 15, 2000, New York City (hereafter Zane/Leventhal), LCPA Oral History Project (1991; 2000), Archives of LCPA, 199, 221.

19. Lincoln Center News Release, September 21, 1994 (in the author's possession).

20. Zane/Leventhal, 223–24.

21. William Grimes, "Lincoln Center Feels Strain as It Prepares New Festival for 1996," *New York Times*, March 16, 1995, Beverly Sills Book 1, B-200287, Archives of LCPA.

22. Nathan Leventhal, phone interview by the author, date unknown.

23. Allan Kozinn, "Schwarz to Quit after 17 Years as Leader of Mostly Mozart," *New York Times*, October 26, 1999.
24. Grimes, "Lincoln Center Feels Strain."
25. Zane/Leventhal, 222.
26. Michael Cooper, "Lincoln Center to End Its Namesake Festival," *New York Times*, November 14, 2017.
27. Wynton Marsalis Official Website, accessed March 4, 2020, https://wyntonmarsalis.org/.
28. Peter Watrous, "Lincoln Center Elevates Status of Jazz," *New York Times*, December 19, 1995.
29. This space was initially named for its first donor, Herbert Allen, in 2004. In 2014, the chair of Jazz at Lincoln Center (JALC), Robert Appel, and his wife, Helen, gave a gift of $20 million to the JALC endowment fund. As a result, Allen generously gave back the naming rights to the room in honor of the Appel contribution.
30. "History," Jazz at Lincoln Center, accessed March 2, 2020, https://www.jazz.org/history/.
31. Watrous, "Lincoln Center Elevates Status."
32. Ibid.

Chapter Eleven. An Innovative, Risk-Taking, Adventurous, Artistic Entity

1. Frank Bruni, "Diva among the Divas," *New York Times*, January 6, 2002.
2. Heidi Waleson, *Mad Scenes and Exit Arias* (New York: Metropolitan Books / Henry Holt, 2018), 118.
3. Ibid., 120.
4. "Committee for the 21st Century: Report to the Lincoln Center Board of Directors," November 30, 1999, 28 (in the author's possession).
5. Ibid., 7.
6. Contemporaneous notes taken by Joseph W. Polisi in his daily diary, December 20, 1999. These diary notes are housed in the archives of the Lila Acheson Wallace Library of The Juilliard School and are currently closed to researchers.
7. Transcript of interviews by Sharon Zane with Nathan Leventhal, October 28, 1991–January 15, 1992, August 17, 2000–September 15, 2000, New York City (hereafter Zane/Leventhal), LCPA Oral History Project (1991; 2000), Archives of LCPA, 307.
8. "Committee for the 21st Century," 17.
9. Ibid., 19–20.
10. Zane/Leventhal, 257–58, 263.
11. Carol Vogel, "Lincoln Center Drops Plan to Sell Its Jasper Johns Painting," *New York Times*, January 26, 1999.
12. Ibid.

13. "'Numbers' at Lincoln Center," *New York Times*, January 13, 1999.

14. Zane/Leventhal, 261.

15. Edward Rothstein, "At Tully Hall, Celebration and Self-Searching," *New York Times*, September 14, 1994.

16. Zane/Leventhal, 324–25.

17. Ibid., 326.

18. Ibid., 369–70.

Chapter Twelve. We're Going to Have to Put Our Dreams on Hold

1. Ralph Blumenthal and Robin Pogrebin, "Conflicts Split Lincoln Center, with Redevelopment Project at Core; Proposals for Dome and New Opera House Are Proving Especially Volatile," *New York Times*, October 11, 2001.

2. Contemporaneous notes taken by Joseph W. Polisi in his daily diary (hereafter Polisi notes), November 9, 2000. These diary notes are housed in the archives of the Lila Acheson Wallace Library of The Juilliard School and are currently closed to researchers.

3. Ibid., November 29, 2000.

4. Katherine G. Farley, phone interview by the author, June 26, 2020.

5. Polisi notes, December 19, 2000.

6. Nathan Leventhal, phone interview by the author, April 6, 2020.

7. Ralph Blumenthal, "Insider Is Chosen to Lead Lincoln Center in Rebirth," *New York Times*, October 27, 2000.

8. Polisi notes, January 16, 2001.

9. Ralph Blumenthal, "Met Opera Rejects Plan for Renovation of Lincoln Center," *New York Times*, January 24, 2001.

10. Ibid.

11. Ralph Blumenthal, "Met Is Ready to Rejoin Lincoln Center Redevelopment under New Rules," *New York Times*, March 19, 2001.

12. Polisi notes, March 20, 2001.

13. Ibid.

14. Ibid.

15. Robin Pogrebin, "Met Is Rejoining the Project to Renovate Lincoln Center," *New York Times*, May 4, 2001.

16. Ibid.

17. Rebecca Robertson, phone interview by the author, April 15, 2020.

18. Polisi notes, May 15, 2001.

19. Ibid., May 17, 2001

20. Anthony Tommasini, "Arts Critic's Notebook: City Opera Trying to Recapture Its Concentration," *New York Times*, September 17, 2001.

21. Polisi notes, September 19, 2001.

22. Ralph Blumenthal, "Lincoln Center Sees Chief Quit in Abrupt Exit," *New York Times*, September 29, 2001.

23. Ibid.
24. Ibid.
25. Ibid.
26. Blumenthal and Pogrebin, "Conflicts Split Lincoln Center."
27. Andrew Rice, "Why Gordon Davis Left the Big Task at Lincoln Center," *Observer*, October 8, 2001.
28. Ibid.
29. Polisi notes, October 1, 2001.
30. Blumenthal and Pogrebin, "Conflicts Split Lincoln Center."
31. Ibid.
32. Working Notes of Marshall Rose for Lincoln Center Executive Committee Meeting, October 12, 2001 (in the author's possession).
33. Ibid.
34. Ibid. (emphasis mine).
35. Robin Pogrebin, "Chairman of Lincoln Center Redevelopment Resigns," *New York Times*, October 23, 2001.
36. Leslie Bennetts, "The Metropolitan Soap Opera," *New York*, February 4, 2002.
37. Blumenthal and Pogrebin, "Conflicts Split Lincoln Center."

Chapter Thirteen. I Would Have Preferred a More Collegial Approach

1. Contemporaneous notes taken by Joseph W. Polisi in his daily diary, January 17, 2002. These diary notes are housed in the archives of the Lila Acheson Wallace Library of The Juilliard School and are currently closed to researchers.
2. Ibid.
3. Ibid.
4. Ibid.
5. Leslie Bennetts, "The Metropolitan Soap Opera," *New York*, February 4, 2002.
6. Ibid.
7. Ibid.
8. Ibid.
9. Robin Pogrebin, "Head of Refugee Group Picked as President of Lincoln Center," *New York Times*, February 26, 2002.
10. Nekesa Mumbi Moody, "Chair of Lincoln Center Resigns," Associated Press, April 1, 2002, F-Beverly Sills 2000–6/2003, B-200333, Archives of LCPA.
11. Ralph Blumenthal, "Beverly Sills Names Date of Resignation," *New York Times*, April 2, 2002, F-Beverly Sills 2000–6/2003, B-200333, Archives of LCPA.
12. Ibid.

13. Ibid.

14. Ibid.

15. Robin Pogrebin, "Met Opera's Former Head Will Lead Lincoln Center," *New York Times*, June 18, 2002.

16. Ralph Blumenthal, "Enough Retirement Already: Beverly Sills to Be Met's Chairman," *New York Times*, October 12, 2002, F-Beverly Sills 2000–6/2003, B-200333, Archives of LCPA.

17. Ibid.

18. Verena Dobnik, "Beverly Sills Coming Out of Six-Month Retirement to Become New Metropolitan Opera Chair," Associated Press, October 12, 2002, F-Beverly Sills 2000–6/2003, B-200333, Archives of LCPA.

19. Richard Donadio, "Sills Faces Tough Financial Challenge at Opera," *The Sun*, October 18–20, 2002, F-Beverly Sills 2000–6/2003, B-200333, Archives of LCPA.

20. Blumenthal, "Enough Retirement Already."

21. Ibid.

22. Ralph Blumenthal and Robin Pogrebin, "The Philharmonic Agrees to Move to Carnegie Hall," *New York Times*, June 2, 2003.

23. Ibid.

24. Ibid.

25. Ibid.

26. Paul Lieberman, "Performing Arts: Big-City Hall Marks," *Los Angeles Times*, July 6, 2003.

27. Robin Pogrebin, "Orchestra Maneuver," *New York Times*, June 2, 2003.

28. Ibid.

Chapter Fourteen. Welcome to the Urbanism of Lilt and Swoon

1. Robin Pogrebin, "Lincoln Center Loses Official Who Oversaw Redevelopment," *New York Times*, June 13, 2003.

2. Ibid.

3. Rebecca Robertson, phone interview by the author, April 15, 2020.

4. Pogrebin, "Lincoln Center Loses Official."

5. Ibid.

6. Contemporaneous notes taken by Joseph W. Polisi in his daily diary, June 6, 2003. These diary notes are housed in the archives of the Lila Acheson Wallace Library of The Juilliard School and are currently closed to researchers.

7. "The Possibilities of Lincoln Center," *New York Times*, January 13, 2002.

8. Robin Pogrebin, "City Opera Considers Move to Ground Zero," *New York Times*, February 28, 2002.

9. Robin Pogrebin, "City Opera Focusing on Ground Zero Site," *New York Times*, August 24, 2002.

10. Alex Ross, "Coming Apart: City Opera vs. Lincoln Center," *New Yorker,* April 1, 2002.

11. Waleson, *Mad Scenes and Exit Arias,* 141.

12. Robin Pogrebin, "The Philharmonic and Carnegie Hall Call Off Merger," *New York Times,* October 7, 2003.

13. Ibid.

14. Ibid.

15. Ibid.

16. "Lincoln Center Selects Architectural Team for Redesign," Associated Press, February 24, 2003.

17. Clay Risen, "Can Crisis Save Lincoln Center from Disaster?" *Observer,* October 27, 2003.

18. Benjamin Forgey, "The Heirs Aberrant of Architecture," *Washington Post,* March 30, 2003.

19. Ibid.

20. Ibid.

21. Rebecca Robertson, phone interview by the author, April 15, 2020.

22. Justin Davidson, "Creating a Cultural Commons," *Newsday,* January 23, 2003.

23. Ibid.

24. Robin Pogrebin, "A Major Step forward for the Lincoln Center Plan," *New York Times,* April 1, 2004.

25. Ada Louise Huxtable, "Lincoln Center Rejoins the City," *Wall Street Journal,* July 1, 2009.

26. Robin Pogrebin, "A New Face For Lincoln Center; Plan Turns a Neglected Alley into a More Welcoming Space," *New York Times,* April 13, 2004.

27. Ibid.

28. Herbert Muschamp, "An Appraisal; A New Face for Lincoln Center," *New York Times,* April 13, 2004.

Chapter Fifteen. She Had Bet the Ranch

1. "Beverly Sills in a Great New Role: Chairman of the Met," *In the House,* Spring 2003, F-Beverly Sills Book I, B-200287, Archives of LCPA.

2. Bruce Crawford, phone interview by the author, May 4, 2020.

3. Ibid.

4. Ibid.

5. Daniel J. Wakin, "The Multiplex as Opera House: Will They Serve Popcorn," *New York Times,* September 7, 2006.

6. Memo from Danielle Collura to Beverly Sills, November 11, 2003, MOA.

7. Daniel J. Wakin, "Beverly Sills Quits Post at the Met," *New York Times,* January 26, 2005.

8. Verlyn Klinkenborg, "Beverly Sills: Appreciation," *New York Times,* July 4, 2007.

9. Robin Pogrebin, "Beverly Sills and the Future of City Opera," *New York Times*, March 30, 2002, F-Beverly Sills, MOA.

10. Ibid.

11. Ibid.

12. Robin Pogrebin and Daniel J. Wakin, "How People's Opera Orchestrated Its Peril," *New York Times*, June 15, 2011.

13. Ibid.

14. Waleson, *Mad Scenes and Exit Arias*, 154.

15. Ibid., 155.

16. Daniel J. Wakin, "City Opera Lures Director from Paris," *New York Times*, February 28, 2007.

17. Ibid.

18. Daniel J. Wakin, "Bold Impresario and City Opera Part Ways," *New York Times*, November 7, 2008.

19. Ibid.

20. Email from Robert Marx to the author, June 10, 2020.

21. Wakin, "Bold Impresario."

22. Waleson, *Mad Scenes and Exit Arias*, 165, 181, 166.

23. Robin Pogrebin, "Lincoln Center Chairman Is to Resign," *New York Times*, January 13, 2005.

24. Ibid.

25. Ibid.

26. Daniel J. Wakin, "North Koreans Welcome Symphonic Diplomacy," *New York Times*, February 27, 2008.

27. Ibid.

28. Ada Louise Huxtable, "Lincoln Center Rejoins the City," *Wall Street Journal*, July 1, 2009.

29. Ibid.

Chapter Sixteen. We Don't Have a Playbook for This

1. Waleson, *Mad Scenes and Exit Arias*, 183.

2. Ibid., 187.

3. Daniel J. Wakin, "City Opera Names Steel as General Manager," *New York Times*, January 14, 2009.

4. Ibid.

5. Waleson, *Mad Scenes and Exit Arias*, 198.

6. Ibid., 203.

7. Reynold Levy, *They Told Me Not to Take That Job: Tumult, Betrayal, Heroics, and the Transformation of Lincoln Center* (New York: Public Affairs, 2015), 149.

8. Robin Pogrebin and Daniel J. Wakin, "How Peoples' Opera Orchestrated Its Peril," *New York Times*, June 15, 2011.

9. Alex Ross, *Wagnerism* (New York: Farrar, Straus and Giroux, 2020), 440.

10. Alex Ross, "Diminuendo: A Downturn for Opera in New York City," *New Yorker,* March 5, 2012.

11. Robin Pogrebin, "Lincoln Center Turns to Broadway for Its Next Chief," *New York Times,* May 15, 2013.

12. Robin Pogrebin and Michael Cooper, "Lincoln Center's President Quits after a Single, Rocky Year," *New York Times,* April 6, 2018.

13. Caroline Polisi, "Weinstein Conviction Shows #MeToo Made Its Mark on Justice System," *CNN,* February 25, 2020.

14. Michael Cooper. "The 10 Biggest Upheavals of Lincoln Center's Tumultuous Year," *New York Times,* December 28, 2018.

15. Ibid.

16. Ibid.

17. Zachary Woolfe, "Philharmonic Players, Fired on Misconduct Grounds, Are Reinstated," *New York Times,* April 7, 2020.

18. Michael Cooper, "Lincoln Center Finds Its New President at the 92nd Street Y," *New York Times,* February 6, 2019.

19. Ibid.

20. "Working in Concert," Lincoln Center and New York Philharmonic News Release, December 2, 2019 (in the author's possession).

21. Zachary Woolfe, "Bored of the 'Ring,'" *New York Times,* May 14, 2019 .

22. Zachary Woolfe, "New York Philharmonic Cancels Rest of Season," *New York Times,* March 23, 2020.

23. Julia Jacobs, "No 'Nutcracker' This Year, New York City Ballet Says," *New York Times,* June 18, 2020.

24. Michael Cooper, "Metropolitan Opera Cancels Fall Season, Plunging into Crisis," *New York Times,* June 2, 2020.

25. "YSM Commitments to Racial Equity," Yale School of Music, June 14, 2020, accessed June 18, 2020, http://ysm.org/.

26. Lincoln Center for the Performing Arts, "Lincoln Center: A Week Ago We Promised a Renewed Focus . . . ," Facebook, June 9, 2020, accessed June 11, 2020, https://www.facebook.com/.

27. Anthony Tommasini, "To Make Orchestra More Diverse, End Blind Auditions," *New York Times,* July 19, 2020.

28. Zachary Woolfe and Joshua Barone, "Racial Equity and Auditions: Discuss," *New York Times,* September 13, 2020.

29. Ibid.

30. Christopher Lehmann-Haupt, "Eric Bentley, Critic Who Preferred Brecht to Broadway, Is Dead at 103," *New York Times,* August 7, 2020.

31. Holland Cotter, "Do Classic Paintings Get a Pass?" *New York Times,* August 13, 2021.

32. Bret Stephens, "Reading Orwell for the Fourth," *New York Times,* July 4, 2020.

Epilogue

1. Darren Walker, "Uncomfortable Questions," *New York Times*, July 5, 2020.

2. Colin Moynihan, "New York City's Arts and Recreation Employment Down 66%, Report Says," *New York Times*, February 24, 2021.

3. Jason Farago, "Can the Arts Bring Us Back? Yes, If We Bring Them Back First," *New York Times*, January 17, 2021.

4. Henry Timms, phone interview by the author, October 9, 2020.

5. Letter to LCPA Board of Directors from Henry Timms, June 2020 (in the author's possession).

6. Henry Timms, phone interview by the author, October 9, 2020.

7. Letter to LCPA Board of Directors from Henry Timms, June 2020.

8. Ibid.

9. "Lincoln Center in Search for Next Artistic Director," *Arts Journal*, December 2020.

10. Javier C. Hernández, "Lincoln Center Tries a New Approach," *New York Times*, August 4, 2021.

11. Michael Powell, "Blind to Hate, or Sounding Right Notes?" *New York Times*, February 15, 2021.

Bibliography

Oral Histories, Diary Notes, and Personal Interviews

Lincoln Center for the Performing Arts Oral History Project:

Abramovitz, Max. June 20, 1990–September 11, 1990.
Ames, Amyas. October 17, 1990.
Beranek, Leo L. October 4, 2001.
Chapin, Schuyler. January 7, 1991–January 22, 1992.
Gersten, Bernard. April 7, 1992.
Hoguet, Robert. October 25, 1990.
Johnson, Philip. August 14, 1990–October 4, 1990.
Leventhal, Nathan. October 28, 1991–January 15, 1992; August 17–
    September 15, 2000.
Mazzola, John W. December 15, 1991–January 29, 1992.
Segal, Martin E. May 2, 1991–July 1, 1991.
Weissman, George. November 19, 1991–April 15, 1992.
Whitehead, Robert. March 21, 1991.
Young, Edgar B. June 11, 1990–November 13, 1990.

Content from the oral history interview of the above subjects courtesy of Lincoln Center for the Performing Arts, Inc.
Perlis, Vivian. Interviews with William Schuman. February 2, 1997–November 16, 1997. Yale University American Music Series.
Polisi, Joseph W. Contemporaneous diary notes. September 4, 1984–June 30, 2018. Archives of the Lila Acheson Wallace Library of The Juilliard School.

Interviews with the Author

Borda, Deborah, President, the New York Philharmonic, June 23, 2020.
Crawford, Bruce, Chair Emeritus, Lincoln Center for the Performing Arts, May 4, 2020.

Farley, Katherine, Chair, Lincoln Center for the Performing Arts, June 26, July 31, August 13, 2020.

Furman, Roy, Member of the Board of Lincoln Center for the Performing Arts, April 6, 2020.

Leventhal, Nathan, President Emeritus, Lincoln Center for the Performing Arts, February 26, March 30, 2020.

Marx, Robert, President, Fan Fox and Leslie R. Samuels Foundation, February 17, May 11, July 2, July 25, 2020.

Robertson, Rebecca, President, Park Avenue Armory, April 15, 2020.

Solomon, Sarah Billinghurst, former Assistant General Manager for Artistic Affairs, Metropolitan Opera, April 27, 2020.

Timms, Henry, President, Lincoln Center for the Performing Arts, October 9, 2020.

Articles, Books, and Dissertations

Atkinson, Rick. *The British Are Coming.* New York: Henry Holt, 2019.

Bennetts, Leslie. "The Metropolitan Soap Opera." *New York,* February 4, 2002.

Bliven, Bruce, Jr. "Annals of Architecture: A Better Sound." *New Yorker,* November 8, 1976.

Brustein, Robert. *Seasons of Discontent.* New York: Simon and Schuster, 1965.

———. "Subsidized Rubbish." *New Republic,* April 11, 1964.

Carney, Saraleigh. "The Repertory Theater of Lincoln Center: Aesthetics and Economics, 1960–1973." PhD diss., City University of New York, 1976. University Microfilms, Ann Arbor, Michigan.

Caro, Robert A. *Working.* New York: Alfred A. Knopf, 2019.

Dunning, Jennifer. *"But First a School": The First Fifty Years of the School of American Ballet.* New York: Viking Press, 1985.

Goldner, Nancy. *The Stravinsky Festival of the New York City Ballet.* New York: Eakins Press, 1973.

Hannah-Jones, Nikole. "What Is Owed." *New York Times Magazine,* June 28, 2020.

Heimans, Jeremy, and Henry Timms. *New Power: How Power Works in Our Hyperconnected World—and How to Make It Work for You.* New York: Doubleday, 2018.

Jackson, Kenneth T., ed. *The Encyclopedia of New York City.* New Haven: Yale University Press, 1995.

Kazan, Elia. *Elia Kazan: A Life.* New York: Alfred A. Knopf, 1988.

Kerr, Walter. *Thirty Plays Hath November: Pain and Pleasure in the Contemporary Theater.* New York: Simon & Schuster, 1969.

Kirstein, Lincoln. *Thirty Years: Lincoln Kirstein's New York City Ballet.* New York: Alfred A. Knopf, 1978.

Levy, Reynold. *They Told Me Not to Take That Job: Tumult, Betrayal, Heroics, and the Transformation of Lincoln Center.* New York: Public Affairs, 2015.

Martin, Ralph G. *Lincoln Center for the Performing Arts.* Englewood Cliffs, NJ: Prentice-Hall, 1971.

Polisi, Joseph W. *American Muse: The Life and Times of William Schuman.* New York: Amadeus Press, 2008.

———. "An Unsettled Marriage: The Merger of the School of American Ballet and The Juilliard School." *Ballet Review*, Spring 2006.

Rich, Alan. *The Lincoln Center Story.* New York: American Heritage Publishing, 1984.

Roberts, Kenneth H. "The Lincoln Center Repertory Theatre, 1958–1965." PhD diss., The Ohio State University, 1966. University Microfilms, Ann Arbor, Michigan.

Ross, Alex. *Wagnerism.* New York: Farrar, Straus and Giroux, 2020.

Sanderson, Eric W. *Mannahatta: A Natural History of New York City.* New York: Harry N. Abrams, 2009.

Schonberg, Harold C. "Six Architects in Search of a Center." *New York Times Magazine*, February 6, 1959.

Scott, William B., and Peter M. Rutkoff. *New York Modern.* Baltimore: Johns Hopkins University Press, 1999.

Shnayerson, Michael. "One By One." *Vanity Fair*, August 21, 2013.

Taper, Bernard. *Balanchine: A Biography.* Berkeley: University of California Press, 1987.

Unger, Craig. "The War at Lincoln Center." *New York*, February 6, 1984.

Waleson, Heidi. *Mad Scenes and Exit Arias.* New York: Metropolitan Books / Henry Holt, 2018.

Young, Edgar B. *Lincoln Center: The Building of an Institution.* New York: New York University Press, 1980.

Zipp, Samuel. *Manhattan Projects: The Rise and Fall of Urban Renewal in Cold War New York.* New York: Oxford University Press, 2010.

Acknowledgments

THE PROCESS OF RESEARCHING and writing this book has been a solitary one. In turn, the people and organizations I encountered while telling the story of Lincoln Center brought me to a fresh sense of community during the evolution of this history, which provided a type of companionship, if only vicariously. However, individuals who directly interacted with me during my development of this book have provided a personal solace and professional focus which have enhanced my mental well-being and made the entire process considerably less cloistered.

About one-third of this book was written during the COVID-19 pandemic of 2020. Fortunately, most of my research requiring physical visits to archives and libraries had been completed before the national lockdown occurred in mid-March 2020. I was able to complete the balance of my research online and through telephone interviews with individuals without any negative impact on my work.

Since Lincoln Center's creation evolved through the vision and leadership of John D. Rockefeller 3rd, the Rockefeller Archive Center in Sleepy Hollow, New York, provided invaluable primary materials that illuminated JDR 3rd's thinking in bringing the Center to life. The Archive, located in a gracious home built for Martha Baird Rockefeller, the second wife of John D. Rockefeller, Jr., is a perfect setting for research, with a professional and helpful staff, ample space for work, and even a complimentary lunch for researchers every Tuesday. I am grateful to James Allen Smith, former vice president and director of research and education at the Archive Center, for his hospitality and professional support, as well as to Monica Blank, archivist at the Center, who was always able to find the "correct" archival box or photo for my review.

In addition, my gratitude goes to Jane Gottlieb, vice president for library and information resources of The Juilliard School; Gabryal Smith, director, Archives and Exhibitions, New York Philharmonic Leon Levy Digital Archives; Peter Clark, director of the Metropolitan Opera Archives; Bonnie Marie Sauer, former director, Lincoln Center Archives and Records Management; and Thomas G. Lannon, assistant director of manuscripts, archives, and rare books at the New York Public Library.

Many individuals with firsthand knowledge of the history of Lincoln Center have graciously spent hours with me on the phone or through email and read and commented on my draft chapters. Nathan Leventhal, president emeritus of Lincoln Center, was enormously generous, reading the entire book and providing insights and corrections that greatly strengthened the text. In addition, Robert Marx, president of the Fan Fox and Leslie R. Samuels Foundation, reviewed all the chapters. His encyclopedic knowledge of not only many elements of the Center's history but also the history of the performing arts in America opened new vistas for my writing and allowed me to tell the Center's story more accurately and with greater texture.

My dear colleague and friend Jane Gottlieb was kind enough not only to read my draft chapters but also to point me toward the most helpful archival and bibliographical sources. Her encouragement and intellectual focus motivated me to seek out new research that enhanced the history.

I am indebted to my many Juilliard, Lincoln Center, and professional colleagues and friends who read selected chapters, provided insightful edits, and took time for phone interviews. Much thanks goes to Juilliard's president Damian Woetzel and his wife, Heather Watts, both of whom were especially helpful in describing the Balanchine years at the New York City Ballet and the extraordinary Stravinsky Festival of 1972; Bruce Kovner, Juilliard's board chair, who reviewed several chapters dealing with the story of the Center's Sixty-Fifth Street renovation; my colleague and friend Ara Guzelimian, former provost and dean of The Juilliard School, who read several chapters; Benjamin Sosland, the provost of the New England Conservatory, whose great talent as a writer and editor improved many elements of my narrative; the current chair of Lincoln Center, Katherine Farley, and the Center's president, Henry Timms, who very kindly reviewed many chapters, participated in phone interviews, and brought to light future plans for the Center; Mary Lou Falcone, a great friend and colleague; and Maurice Edelson, Juilliard's general counsel, who provided helpful edits and much support.

Much gratitude also goes to Deborah Borda, president of the New York Philharmonic; Bruce Crawford, chair emeritus of Lincoln Center; Sarah Billinghurst Solomon, former assistant general manager for artistic affairs of the Metropolitan Opera; Rebecca Robertson, president and executive producer of the Park Avenue Armory; and Lincoln Center board members Bart Friedman and Roy Furman, all of whom participated in phone interviews and provided helpful edits. Finally, I wish to acknowledge my friend of many years Robert Blocker, dean of the Yale School of Music, and thank him for his generosity in introducing me to Yale University Press and assisting me in the publication of this book.

The initial editing of the book's draft was done, in part, with great precision and care by Mary Belanger, my assistant for many years during my tenure as president of The Juilliard School. Much gratitude goes, as well, to Heather Foye, my former assistant in support of my work as Juilliard's chief China officer, who was meticulous in providing numerous readable reproductions of photos taken by me of archival materials, as well as finding a myriad of facts concerning both individuals and organizations. In addition, two exceptional members of the Juilliard Library staff, Stephanie Bazirjian and Katrina Art, supplied invaluable help in identifying photos for my book and assembling the final manuscript. Jeni Dahmus, the Juilliard Library archivist, also provided important information in tracking down permission for photos and identifying several images used in the book.

I extend my sincere gratitude to Yale University Press editor Adina Berk for her work regarding the early evolution of my manuscript, and special thanks to Susan Laity, a senior manuscript editor at Yale, for her meticulous reading of the book and her uplifting support regarding the overall publication of my work. My great thanks go, as well, to copy editor Nicholas Taylor, who edited the entire text with great professionalism and accuracy, and to Alexa Selph, who showed that creating a book index is an artful process when placed in her hands.

I also wish to acknowledge the recommendations made by three anonymous reviewers working with Yale University Press who read my manuscript. Their suggestions allowed me to address certain topics which enhanced the book's narrative significantly.

Much of my writing during the warmer months took place at the Shenorock Shore Club in Rye, New York, overlooking Long Island Sound. This idyllic venue provided me with the perfect place to think clearly and write while enjoying fresh air and sun. I wish to thank my Shenorock neighbors Jane and Joe Burke, Meighan and Michael Corbett, Gaye and Scott Geiger, Susan Holden, Marcy and Paul Kalkut, Suzanne and Bob Luckey, Kristy and Bob McKeon, Kathy Miller, Jane and Mark Mittler, Dorie and Paul Reisner, and Lanier Saperstein for their goodwill and encouragement as they frequently checked in on my progress.

A project of this all-consuming nature is enhanced enormously by the support and encouragement of one's family. To my beloved wife, Elizabeth, I express my deepest gratitude for her patience and indulgence during times when my focus was far away from family matters. Also, to my daughter Catherine, my son Ryan, my daughter-in-law Caroline, and my son Christopher—who in particular was enormously helpful with various computer issues involving the writing of the book—thank you all for your support and efforts to keep the grandchildren's shells and rocks off of Pop's writing table.

This book is dedicated to those grandchildren: Creighton (twelve), Adeline (eleven), Teague, (ten), and Will (eight). All four watched with varying degrees of interest while this book was written, occasionally helping with a research assignment or two. In this difficult time, they give me hope for the future.

Index

Aalto, Alvar, 16
Abramovitz, Max, 28, 29, 30, 46, 47, 79, 101
Actors Studio, 54
AIDS epidemic, impact of, on the Lincoln Center community, 158–59
Ailey, Alvin, 71
Albee, Edward, 133; *A Delicate Balance*, 182
Albert A. List Foundation, 76
Alice Tully Hall, 1, 19, 77, 83, 84–85, 87, 259; and the Lincoln Center redevelopment project, 217, 218; and the opening of the Juilliard School building, 89–90; reopening of, 231–32
Allen, Reginald, 24–25, 42, 48
Allen, Vivian Beaumont, 26, 65; as donor for the Repertory Company, 56. *See also* Beaumont Theater
Allen, Woody, 133; *The Floating Light Bulb*, 134
Amara, Lucine, 42
American Ballet Theatre, 50
American Federation of Musicians, 72
American National Theater and Academy (ANTA), 56–57, 133
American Red Cross, 16
American Songbook series, 184, 201

Amerindo Investment Advisors, 181
Ames, Amyas, 86, 87; and the Beaumont Theater, 104–5, 107–8, 109–10; as chair of Lincoln Center, 92–96, 98, 100, 103, 108, 109, 110, 120, 126; as chair of the New York Philharmonic, 92, 124; and constituents of Lincoln Center, 92–93; and fundraising for Lincoln Center, 95–98; leadership style of, 94; and Joseph Papp, 109–10; and Philharmonic Hall, 96–98, 100–102
Ames, Evvie, 114
Ammidon, Hoyt, 64
Ansermet, Ernest, 44
Appel, Helen, 171
Appel, Robert, 171
Appel Room, 171
Arrau, Claudio, 139
art, as displayed at Lincoln Center, 73–77
Art Commission (New York City), 75, 76
arts, the: and "culture war," 263–64; experimentalism in, 256; government funding for, 96; as healing force, 259; impact of the pandemic on, 251–52, 259, 260, 261; role of, in a world of social change, 253–56, 258–59

Ash, Aesha, 255
Atkinson, Brooks, 54
Audition Bootcamp, 254
Avery Fisher Fellowship Program, 97
Avery Fisher Hall, 97; opening of, 101–2; renaming of, 212; renovations of, 100–101, 173, 212
Ax, Emanuel, 139

Bach, Johann Sebastian, *St. Matthew Passion*, 237–39
Baker, Susan, 225, 226–27, 233, 234, 235
Balanchine, George, 21, 22, 49, 61, 62, 147, 182, 260; *Allegro Brillante*, 61; *Apollo*, 140; death of, 158; *Stars and Stripes*, 61; and the Stravinsky Festival, 120–21
Ballard, William F. R., 75, 78
Ballet Russe de Monte Carlo, 49
Barber, Samuel, 45, 84; *Antony and Cleopatra*, 71–72, 115; *Vanessa*, 71
Barenboim, Daniel, 159
Barnes, Clive, 106
Barr, Alfred H., Jr., 75–76
Barry, Philip, *The Philadelphia Story*, 134
Baryshnikov, Mikhail, 168
Baum, Morton, 51, 52–53
Bay of Pigs invasion, 39–40
Beaumont Theater: directorate for, 133–34; leadership of, 132–33; John Lindsay as chair of, 143; ongoing problems associated with, 103–8, 132–39; Joseph Papp as head of, 109–11, 112–13; as part of Lincoln Center, 56, 57, 65–66, 91; renovation proposed for, 134–36
Beckett, Samuel, 167; *Not I*, 107
Beeson, Jack, *Lizzie Borden*, 182
Beethoven, Ludwig van, 36, 44
Behrman, S. N., *But for Whom Charlie*, 58, 59

Belluschi, Pietro, 16, 21, 28; as architect for the Juilliard School building, 28, 29, 30–31, 67
Belmont, Mrs. August, 73
Benedict, Steven, 86
Bennack, Frank A., Jr., 171, 193, 200; as chair of Lincoln Center, 228, 235, 239
Bennett, Michael, 109
Bennetts, Leslie, 198–99
Bentley, Eric, 256
Beranek, Leo L., 44, 46–47
Bergen, Candice, 177
Bergsma, William, 45
Berlin Philharmonic, 237–38
Bernstein, Jed, as president of Lincoln Center, 240–41
Bernstein, Leonard, 8, 35, 41, 42, 46, 158; as conductor of the New York Philharmonic, 43–44, 89–90, 92, 99, 157, 158; *A Quiet Place*, 234, 235
Beyer Blinder Belle, 176, 213
Biden, Joseph R., Jr., 258
Biggs, E. Power, 45
Bing, Rudolf, 42, 59, 60, 71, 72–73, 119, 161
Bishop, André, 165
Bizet, Georges, 36
Black Lives Matter movement, 252–53, 258
Blair, Floyd, 13
Blakey, Art, 169
Blanchard, Terrence, *Fire Shut Up in My Bones*, 260
Blau, Herbert, 64–65, 66, 81, 103, 104, 132
Bliss, Anthony, 59, 68, 77, 119, 142, 156–57
Bloch, Richard, 245
Bloomberg, Michael, 184, 205, 217, 240
Bloomgarden, Alina, 170
Blum, Robert, 13
Blumenthal, Ralph, 188, 194

Board of Directors of Lincoln Center for the Performing Arts: creation of, 14–15; Kirstein's resignation from, 33–34

Boccadoro, Patricia, 73

Bolt, Richard, 16

Bolt Beranek & Newman, 46

Bondy, Luc, 236

Borda, Deborah, 222; as president of the New York Philharmonic 246–47, 248–49, 251–52, 260

Boston Symphony Orchestra, 44

Boulez, Pierre, 84, 92, 98, 99, 100, 101, 102, 157

Brain Opera, 168

Braislin, Porter & Wheelock, 9

Brandeis Annex, 68

Brandenburg Ensemble, 139

Brannigan, Robert, 105

Brecht, Bertolt, *The Caucasian Chalk Circle*, 65

Breuer, Marcel, 16

Brey, Carter, 205

Broadway, 6

Brook, Peter, 62–63; *La Tragédie de Carmen*, 136–37, 138

Brown, Michael, 252

Browne, Mahogany L., as poet in residence at Lincoln Center, 263

Browning, John, 45

Browning, Kirk, 44

Bruno Walter Auditorium, 67, 158

Brustein, Robert, 58–59, 112, 114, 135

Brutalist style (of architecture), 30–31

Büchner, Georg, *Danton's Death*, 65, 104

Bunshaft, Gordon, 28–29, 30, 65, 69

Burgee, John, 131

Burke, Tarana, 243

Butcher, Willard, 150

Cage, John, 168

Calder, Alexander, *Le Guichet*, 75–76

Caldwell, Sarah, 133, 134

CAMI Video, 223

Capobianco, Tito, 115

Carnegie Hall, 10, 237; concerns regarding its impact on Lincoln Center, 48; and possible merger with the New York Philharmonic, 203–5, 206–7, 210–11

Carney, Saraleigh, 106

Carter, Jimmy, 124

Casals, Pablo, 45–46

Castro, Fidel, 2, 39

Catalano, Eduardo, 28

Catazaro, Zachary, 245

Central Park, 6

Chagall, Marc, 73, 74

Chamber Music Society, 231; JDR 3rd's concerns regarding, 82–83, 85–86; as part of Lincoln Center, 87, 147, 183, 216; as priority for Schuman, 82–85, 86; Young's concerns regarding, 85–86

Channing, Stockard, 182

Chapin, Schuyler, 41, 51, 59, 60, 77, 90, 119, 193

Chaplin, Charlie, 78

Chapman, Gilbert W., 67

Chauvin, Derek, 252

Chavez, Carlos, 84

Chorus Line, A, 109

Churchill, Winston, 2

Citizens Committee for Carnegie Hall, 48

Ciulei, Liviu, 133

Civil Rights Acts, 2

Cleveland Orchestra, 44, 46

Cliburn, Van, 45, 89, 118

Clurman, Richard, and the Beaumont Theater, 105, 106, 107

Coffin, William Sloane, 122

Coggeshall, Clarke, 107

Cohen, Alexander, 136

Cold War, 2

Collura, Danielle, 223

Columbia University School of the Arts, 23

Columbus Boychoir, 44
Committee for the 21st Century
    (Lincoln Center), 173, 176; and the
    Project Leadership Committee,
    176–77, 186–87; Redevelopment
    Committee, 177
Committee on Slum Clearance, 8,
    14, 25
Conlon, James, 229
Conroy, Frances, 182
Cooke, Alistair, 44
Cooper Robertson, 176, 190, 213
Copland, Aaron, 19, 21, 35, 44, 45
Corey, Emilie, 225, 235
Corigliano, John, 84, 159
Cotter, Holland, 256
COVID-19 pandemic: economic im-
    pact of, 251–52, 260, 261; impact of,
    on Lincoln Center, 251–52, 258–59
Cowell, Henry, 44
Crawford, Bruce E., 221; as chair of
    Lincoln Center, 202, 204, 205, 207–
    8, 211, 216, 217; as general manager
    of the Metropolitan Opera, 156,
    157; legacy of, 228; resignation
    of, 228; and the Philharmonic-
    Carnegie merger, 206
Crimmins, Craig S., 132
Crinkley, Richmond, 133–34, 136–37,
    138, 143
Cronin, Hume, 107
Cronson, Mary, 233–34
Crozier, Catharine, 45
Cunningham, Merce, 168
Cuomo, Andrew M., 251
Curtin, Phyllis, 115

Dachs, Joshua, 249
Dallas Opera, 234
Dalrymple, Jean, 49
d'Amboise, Jacques, 61
Damrosch Park, 31, 212–13, 216, 260
David Geffen Hall, 1, 212; renovation
    of, 241, 242, 246, 247–50, 259

David H. Koch Theater, 235
David Rubinstein Atrium, 176, 242
Davies, Dennis Russell, 168
Davis, Brody & Associates, 150
Davis, Gordon, 150, 151, 170, 177–78;
    background of, 187; as president of
    Lincoln Center, 187–88, 189, 191,
    198, 199; resignation as president of
    Lincoln Center, 192–93, 194
Davis, Lew, 150–51
Davis, Miles, 169
Davis, Shelby Cullom, 67, 157
Day & Zimmermann, 11, 14, 18, 22,
    23, 38
Debussy, Claude, *Pelléas et Mélisande*, 226
DeIntinis, Ranier C., 102
de Larrocha, Alicia, 156
de Mille, Agnes, 147
de Paur, Leonard, 118
Diamond, Irene, 166, 172, 182, 231,
    232
Diamond Schmitt Architects, 249, 250
Diaz, Justino, 71
Diller, Elizabeth, 213–14, 217
Diller Scofidio + Renfro (DS + R), as
    architects for Lincoln Center re-
    development project, 213–16, 232
Dilworth, J. Richardson, 122
Dinkeloo, John, 57
Dinkins, David, 128, 187
Dollard, Charles, 23
Domingo, Plácido, 175, 222, 245
Drye, John, 14
Dubinsky, David, 32
Dudamel, Gustavo, 246–47
Dufy, Raoul, 73
Dunaway, Faye, 57
Durning, Charles, 112
Dutoit, Charles, 246

Eisenhower, David, 89
Eisenhower, Dwight D., 13; at the
    Lincoln Center groundbreaking
    ceremony, 34–35, 36–37

Eisenhower, Julie Nixon, 89
Elinor Bunin Munroe Film Center, 218
Elliott, Donald H., 78
Ellis, Adrian, 235
Emerson Quartet, 139
Exploratory Committee for a Musical Arts Center, 10–11, 13–14; JDR 3rd as chair of, 3, 14–15, 20, 21, 24, 27–28, 32; members of, 13–14. *See also* Lincoln Center for the Performing Arts

Falla, Manuel de, 45
Fan Fox and Leslie R. Samuels Foundation, 111, 130, 134
Farley, Katherine G., 186; as chair of Lincoln Center, 239–40, 241, 242–43, 248, 249, 254, 261
Farrell, Eileen, 44
Fashion Week, at Lincoln Center, 212–13
Faubus, Orval, 2
Federal Housing Act (1949), 8, 17, 25
Fein, Fiona Morgan, 155
Feld, Eliot, *Sir Isaac's Apples*, 220–21
Feldman, Morton, 167
Fellrath, Basil, 15
Ferguson, Glenn W., as president of Lincoln Center, 127–28, 129
Film Society of Lincoln Center, 77–78, 125, 146, 147, 216; new venue for, 218
Finkel, David, 183
Finlay, Chase, 245
Fiorello H. La Guardia High School of Music & Art and Performing Arts, 16
Fisher, Avery, 97–98, 99, 100, 101, 102
Fisher, Janet, 212
Fisher Dachs Associates, 249
Fitch, Doug, 230
Fleisher, Leon, 231
Floyd, George, 252

Ford, Gerald, 67, 124
Ford Foundation, 25
Fordham University, and the slum clearance project, 16, 26–28
Forum Theater, 112
Foster, Norman, 207, 212
Fowler, A. L., 14, 18
Fox, Virgil, 45
Fox & Fowle Architects, 213
Francis, Clarence, 26
Franco, Francisco, 46
Furman, Roy, 163, 176

Gardiner, John Eliot, 167
Gatti, Daniele, 246
Geffen, David, 212, 242, 248. *See also* David Geffen Hall
Gehry, Frank O., and design proposal for Lincoln Center, 190–91, 207
Gelb, Arthur, 43
Gelb, Peter, 213, 244, 248; as general manager of the Metropolitan Opera, 222–23, 225, 229; on the impact of the pandemic, 252; and Reynold Levy, 240
Gentele, Göran, 119
Gergiev, Valery, 229
Gersten, Bernard, 111, 143–44, 165
Gibson, Rob, 170, 174, 186
Gilbert, Alan, named music director of the New York Philharmonic, 230
Gilbert and Sullivan, *The Mikado*, 192
Gilman, Richard, 104
Ginastera, Alberto, 84
Giuliani, Rudolph, 229; and funding for Lincoln Center redevelopment project, 178, 187, 195; as mayor of New York City, 192
Giuliani Partners, 229
#GivingTuesday, 248
Glass, Philip, 227; *Einstein on the Beach*, 226
Glorya Kaufman Dance Studio, 232
Goberman, John, 118, 139

Goetz, Ruth and Augustus, *The Heiress*, 182
Gold and Fizdale, 44
Gorky, Maxim, *Enemies*, 107
Graham, Martha, 42, 50
Granet, Russell, 242
Great Performers series, 139
Greenberg, Noah, 44
Greene, Jerome L., 134–35, 137, 166
Greenough, Meredith (Muffy), 161
Greenough, Peter B., 160–61, 223
Greenough, Peter, Jr. (Bucky), 161
Greenway, G. Lauder, 71
Gregorian, Vartan, 142, 157
Guenther, Paul, 197, 198, 203, 204, 207, 210, 211
Guggenheim Museum, 209
Gussow, Mel, 111

Hall, Peter, 137
Hamburg Opera, 81
Hamlisch, Marvin, 109
Hammerstein, Oscar, 19
Handel, George Frideric, 36; *Giulio Cesare*, 115, 116, 161
Hardy, Hugh, 219
Harnoncourt, René d', 29
Harrell, Lynn, 139
Harris, Cyril, 100, 101, 135
Harris, Rosemary, 182
Harrison, Wallace K., 10, 11, 13, 14; as architect for the Metropolitan Opera House, 68–69, 72; as coordinating architect for Lincoln Center, 15, 28, 29, 31, 79
Harrison & Abramowitz, 99
Harth, Robert J., 204, 210, 211
Healy, Timothy, 157
Heimans, Jeremy, 248
Helen Huntington Hull Fund, 130–31
Hellman, Lillian, *The Little Foxes*, 182
Henahan, Donal, 103, 131
Henry L. and Grace Doherty Charitable Foundation, 71

Hess, Leon, 125
Hess, Norma, 125
Hill, Martha, 147–48
Hindemith, Paul, *Mathis der Maler*, 159, 182
Hitchcock, Henry-Russell, Jr., 30
Hoguet, Robert L., Jr., 58, 59, 64, 65–66, 103–4
Holden, Mark, 232
Holm, Hanya, 50
Horne, Marilyn, 139
Horowitz, Vladimir, 120, 223
Houghton, Arthur A., Jr., 10, 13, 74, 83
Hoving, Thomas P. F., 78–79
Hudson, Henry, 6
Hurok, Sol, 20, 223
Huxtable, Ada Louise, 72, 79, 232

International Alliance of Theatrical Stage Employees, 260
International Film Festival, 77
International Rescue Committee, 200
International Style (of architecture), 30
International University Choral Festival, 91
Irene Diamond Education Center, 172
Irving, Jules, 81; as artistic director of the Beaumont Theater, 64–65, 66, 103, 106–7, 132, 133
Irving, Washington, 6

Jack, Hulan, 36
Jackson, C. D., 10–11, 13
Jacobs, Jane, 216
Jacobs, Paul, 158
Jaffe Holden, 218
Janáček, Leoš, *The Makropulos Affair*, 226
Janklow, Linda, 138, 178–79, 193
Jazz at Lincoln Center, 169–72, 182, 231, 259; new theater for, 174
Jazz Messengers, 169
Johns, Jasper, and possible sale of *Numbers 1964*, 179–80

Johnson, "Lady Bird," 70, 71
Johnson, James P., 7–8
Johnson, Lyndon B., 96
Johnson, Philip, 16, 28, 29, 30, 31,
    49, 61, 79, 179; as architect for the
    renovation of Avery Fisher Hall,
    100–101, 102; and renovation of the
    New York State Theater, 130–31
Johnson, Russell, 46
Jones, Cherry, 182
Josephs, Devereaux, 13, 68, 87, 88
Josie Robertson Plaza, 177, 216, 248
Joyce Theater, 208, 209–10
Judd, George E., Jr., 42
Juilliard, Augustus, 190
Juilliard Chorus, 35, 44
Juilliard Graduate Institute, 190
Juilliard Orchestra, 44, 231, at the
    opening of the Juilliard School
    building, 89
Juilliard School building: opening
    ceremony for, 88–89; Peter J. Sharp
    Theater in, 174; renovation of, 232
Juilliard School of Music, The, 1, 18,
    92, 97, 119, 231; architect for, 28,
    30–31, 67; centennial celebration
    of, 220–21; changes at, 24; concerns
    regarding, 22–23; dance studio
    at, 232; equity and diversity as
    addressed by, 253–54; jazz studies
    at, 172; operating deficit of, 117;
    leadership changes at, 157; Lincoln
    Center constituents as faculty at,
    154; and the Lincoln Center re-
    development project, 217; Wynton
    Marsalis as student at, 169; as part
    of Lincoln Center, 23–24, 67–68,
    91, 139, 216
Juilliard String Quartet, 44

Kahn, Madeline, 112
Kazan, Elia, 21, 22, 132; and the Lin-
    coln Center Repertory Company,
    54, 55, 57, 59, 60

Keene, Christopher, 158–59, 182
Keilholz, Heinrich, 47, 98, 99
Keiser, David, 14, 36, 92
Keller, Johanna, 155
Kellogg, Paul: as general manager of
    the New York City Opera, 174–75,
    182, 187–88, 191, 192, 198, 199,
    203, 208, 209, 225; retirement of,
    210
Kennedy, Jacqueline, 43
Kennedy, John F., 2, 40
Kennedy, Joseph P., 17
Kennedy Building, 17
Keppel, Francis, 120
Kerr, Walter, 22, 54, 104
Kiley, Dan, 218
Kinnear, James W., 203
Kirstein, Lincoln, 13, 16, 21, 62, 154;
    and dance at Lincoln Center, 49,
    61, 62, 120, 121, 142, 147, 148,
    149, 231; death of, 182; and music
    education at Lincoln Center, 22, 23;
    and the New York State Theater,
    61; resignation of, 33–34; tempera-
    ment of, 51–52
Kisselgoff, Anna, 158
Klinkenborg, Verlyn, 223–24
Knudsen, Vern O., 47
Koch, Charles, 247
Koch, David, 247–48
Koch, Edward, 128, 129, 131, 187
Koch, Fred, 134
Köchel, Ludwig von, 155
Koch Hall, 1
Kolodin, Irving, 21
Kostelanetz, Andre, 102
Kovner, Bruce, 190, 193; and the Lin-
    coln Center redevelopment project,
    196, 197, 198
Krawitz, Herman, 59–60, 69
Kushner, Tony, *Angels in America*, 159

labor unions, and construction of Lin-
    coln Center, 32

LaChiusa, Michael John, 182
La Guardia, Fiorello H., 49
Lamos, Mark, *Paul Bunyan*, 182
Lang, Paul Henry, 21
Larkin, June Noble, 218
LCT 3, 219
Lee, Ming Cho, 115
Lee, Sherman E., 122
Lehár, Franz, *The Merry Widow*, 64, 131
Lehmbruch, Wilhelm, 73
Lehrer, Peter M., 202, 206–7, 208, 239
Leigh, Mitch, *Man of La Mancha*, 58
Leinsdorf, Erich, 44, 156
Lenni-Lenape, 6
Leoncavallo, Ruggero, 35–36
Lepage, Robert, 237, 238
Leppard, Raymond, 155
Leventhal, Nathan: departure of, from Lincoln Center, 183–84, 186; and Jazz at Lincoln Center, 170; legacy of, 184; and the Lincoln Center Festival, 165–66, 167; and Lincoln Center redevelopment project, 173–74, 177–78; as president of Lincoln Center, 128–30, 138, 141–44, 146, 150, 152–53, 154; and sale of Jasper Johns painting, 179–80; and Martin Segal, 142–43; and tensions with Beverly Sills, 163–64
Levin, Kate D., 205
Levine, James, 139, 155; and accusations of sexual abuse, 243–44; as music director of the Metropolitan Opera Orchestra, 157, 181
Levy, Reynold, 171, 201, 231, 238; and the possible Philharmonic-Carnegie merger, 206; as president of Lincoln Center, 200, 202, 204, 205, 211, 212–13, 217, 219, 228; resignation of, 240; and George Steel, 235; *They Told Me Not to Take That Job*, 240
Library-Museum, 25, 29, 31, 65, 66–67
Lieberson, Goddard, 21
Liebling, Estelle, 160

Ligeti, György, *Le Grand Macabre*, 230
Limón, José, 24, 50, 147
Lincoln, Abraham, 7
Lincoln Center Constituent Development Project, 177, 188, 202, 216
Lincoln Center Corporate Fund, 96, 117, 126–27, 137, 148
Lincoln Center Council, 142, 166, 185–86, 202, 229; and Mozart Bicentennial Festival, 154; tensions among members of, 187–88, 189, 195
Lincoln Center Endowment Fund, 122–23, 125
Lincoln Center Festival, 164–65, 174, 201; content of, 167–68; public response to, 167; and tensions with constituents, 165–67
Lincoln Center Film Society, 1, 77–78, 125, 146, 147, 156
Lincoln Center for the Performing Arts: Amyas Ames as chair of, 92–96, 98, 100, 103, 108, 109, 110, 120, 126; architects for, 28–31; architects for redevelopment of, 213–16; architecture of, 15–16, 30–31, 68–69, 72; Art Committee of, 74–75; aspirations for, 1–3, 4, 9–11; autonomy of constituents of, 24–25, 122, 141–42; Frank Bennack as chair of, 228, 235, 239; Jed Bernstein as president of, 240–41, 242; Black workers at, 32–33; chamber music constituent proposed for, 81, 82–85; cooperation among constituents of, 154–56; complex early history of, 4–5, 8; concept and mission of, 13, 21–22, 25, 41–42, 215, 264; constituents of, 1, 16, 19–20, 54–55, 91, 92–93, 139; construction workers for, 31–33; dance at, 33, 49–50, 51, 52, 61; Gordon Davis as president of, 192–93, 194, 242; and displacement of families in the Lincoln Square neighborhood, 3–4, 8–9, 13,

14–15; drama constituent at, 54–56; early budgeting for, 25; economic impact of, 178; educational programs at, 22–24, 119–20, 170, 172; equity and diversity as addressed by, 253–55, 262–63; expansion of, 149–54; Katherine Farley as chair of, 239–40, 241, 242–43, 248, 249, 254, 261; Fashion Week at, 212–13; Glenn Ferguson as president of, 127–28, 242; film presented at, 77–78; financial challenges affecting, 81–82, 87–88, 94–95, 116–18, 130; and Fordham University, 26–28; friction among constituents of, 81, 92–93, 141–44, 193–94; funding and fundraising for, 25–26, 50–51, 66, 91, 94, 95–96, 105, 117, 125, 130–31, 144–45, 152–53, 176, 177–78, 181, 187, 195, 212, 259; Frank Gehry's design proposal for, 190–91; groundbreaking ceremony for, 33, 34–37; high-quality performances presented by, 139–40, 180–83; impact of, on surrounding community, 216; impact of the pandemic on, 251–52, 258–59; JDR 3rd as board chair of, 89; JDR 3rd as founding president of, 3, 14–15, 20, 21, 24, 27–28, 32, 40, 52, 215; Jewish leadership at, 129–30; land acquisition for, 17–18, 25, 26; Nathan Leventhal as president of, 128–30, 138, 141–44, 146, 150, 152–53, 154; Reynold Levy as president of, 200, 202, 204, 205, 211, 212–13; location of, 16; major redevelopment project for, 173–74, 176–79, 185–86, 187, 189–91, 194–95, 196–200, 206, 208, 211–12, 216–19, 230–32, 242; mall concept proposed for, 78–79; John Mazzola in leadership positions at, 85, 87–88, 93–94, 96, 97, 101, 105, 109, 113, 114, 124–25, 126, 127; and the #MeToo movement, 243–46; new theater proposed for, 173–74; opening week of, 44–45; opposition to, 26–28; planning stages of, 14; priorities for, 262; William Schuman as president of, 40–42, 49, 52, 77, 80, 90, 129, 142; seating capacity for venues at, 19, 69, 171, 174; search for first CEO of, 38–39; Martin Segal as chair of, 124–30, 144–45; and September 11, 2001 attacks, 191–92; Deborah Spar as president of, 241–42; Maxwell Taylor as president of, 39–40, 242; tensions among leaders of, 52–53, 186–89, 193–94, 196–200, 207–8; Shanta Thake as chief artistic officer of, 262–63; Henry Timms as president of, 248–49, 254, 261–62; twenty-fifth anniversary of, 140; violence at, 131–32; visual arts as part of, 73–77; website for, 188; George Weissman as chair of, 145–47; work environment at, 41. *See also* Committee for the 21st Century; Exploratory Committee for a Musical Arts Center; *and names of constituent organizations*

Lincoln Center Institute, 120
Lincoln Center Labor Advisory Committee, 32
Lincoln Center Legends, 241
Lincoln Center Out of Doors, 118, 139
Lincoln Center Productions, 162
Lincoln Center Repertory Company, 55–60, 105, 112; negative reviews of, 58–59; new leadership at, 64–65; tensions within, 56–57
Lincoln Center Theater Company, 1, 55–56, 114, 138, 143, 181–82, 193, 216
Lincoln Square, 3–4, 7–8
Lincoln Square Urban Renewal Project, 9–10, 11; opposition to, 26–28; support for, 28

Lindsay, John V., 78, 79, 128; as chair of the Beaumont Theater, 143
Lipman, Howard, 75
Lipman, Jean, 75
Liszt, Franz, 89
Live from Lincoln Center, 118, 139, 140, 220
Live from the Met, 140
L'Observatoire International, 213
Lockwood, William, 155, 165
Loden, Barbara, 57
Loesser, Frank, 41
London, George, 44
Long, Catherine, 22
Louis Philippe, King, 6
Lupone, Patti, 152

Maazel, Lorin, 180–81, 229
Machover, Tod, 168
Mahler, Gustav, 44, 101; Second (Resurrection) Symphony, 260
Maillol, Aristide, 73
Malkin, Isabel, 148
Mamet, David, 143
Manhattan, early history of, 6–7
Manuti, Al, 32
Marcos, Ferdinand, 70, 71
Marcos, Imelda, 70, 71
Markova, Alicia, 42
Marsalis, Dolores, 169
Marsalis, Ellis, 169
Marsalis, Wynton, 171, 174, 182; *Blood on the Fields,* 169; as classical trumpeter, 169; criticism of, 172; educational programming of, 170, 172; and Jazz at Lincoln Center, 169–72
Martin, John, 49
Martins, Peter, 140, 182, 191, 231, 245
Marx, Robert, 111, 113, 157–58, 227
Maslow, Sophie, 50
Masur, Kurt, 157, 167, 180, 246
May, William F., 77
Mayfair Associates, 150

Mazzola, John, 84; as head of Lincoln Center, 85, 87–88, 93–94, 96, 97, 101, 105, 109, 113, 114, 124, 126, 127; resignation of, 127
McBride, Patricia, 61
McCarthy, Joseph, 78
McClellan, George B., 7
McCluskie, Gary, 249
McDonald, Audra, 182
McGinley, Father Laurence J., 28
McHenry, W. Barnabas, 137
McNulty, John W., 81
Mehta, Zarin, 204, 205, 207, 210, 211, 246
Mehta, Zubin, 103, 155, 157
Meisner, Sanford, 22
Mendelson, Ralph, 100
Mennin, Peter: as president of The Juilliard School, 88, 157; and the School of American Ballet, 147–48; and William Schuman, 89
Merce Cunningham Dance Company, 168
Mertz, LuEsther, 111
Messiaen, Olivier, 84; *St. Francis of Assisi,* 166, 226
#MeToo movement, impact of, on Lincoln Center, 243–46
Met Opera Presents, The, 223
Metropolitan Opera: financial challenges experienced by, 117; and labor negotiations with stagehands, 260; leadership changes at, 156–57; and the Lincoln Center redevelopment project, 188, 189; as part of Lincoln Center, 10, 17, 19, 20, 45, 51, 68–69, 91, 181, 185–86, 188–89; Beverly Sills as chair of, 203, 221–23; Joseph Volpe as general manager of, 157, 166, 181, 186, 198, 201, 202, 222, 229
Metropolitan Opera House, 1, 63, 76–77; architecture of, 28, 68–69, 72; art displayed in, 73; Peter Gelb as general manager of, 222–23, 225, 229,

236, 237; murder at, 131–32; opening night of, as part of Lincoln Center, 70–73; Beverly Sills as chair of, 203

Metropolitan Opera Orchestra, 44; labor negotiations with, 72–73; members of, as faculty at The Juilliard School, 154

Met Titles, 181

Middleton, Thomas, *The Changeling*, 58–59

Midsummer Night Swing, 184

Mielziner, Jo, 57, 65, 105–6

Milano, Alyssa, 243

Milhaud, Darius, 84

Miller, Arthur, 60; *After the Fall*, 57, 58; *Incident at Vichy*, 59

Minghella, Anthony, 236

Mintiks, Helen Hagnes, 131–32

Mitzi Newhouse Theater, 65

modern dance, at Lincoln Center, 24, 49, 50

Monk, Thelonious, 7

Monroe, Marilyn, 57

Montrone, Paul M., 185, 186, 188, 197–98, 203

Moore, Douglas, *The Ballad of Baby Doe*, 118

Moore, Henry, 218; *Reclining Figure*, 76

Morel, Jean, 44, 89

Morris, Mark, 225

Morris, Newbold, 16–17; and controversy over Calder sculpture, 75–76

Morse, Enid (Dinny), 148

Mortier, Gerard: as general manager of the New York City Opera, 225–27; new works presented by, 226; resignation of, 227, 233

Moseley, Carlos, 92, 97, 98, 100

Moses, Robert, 8–9, 18, 36, 60, 69; and Lincoln Center, 9–10, 13, 14, 16, 31, 35, 50, 79, 216; on the Metropolitan Opera House, 72; and slum clearance, 8–9, 14, 26, 27

Mosher, Gregory, 143–44, 165

Moss, Jane, 163, 165, 166, 167, 168, 237, 238

Mostly Mozart Festival, 82, 139, 168; criticism of, 166

Mozart, Wolfgang Amadeus: *The Magic Flute*, 73; and bicentennial honoring of death of, 154–56

Mozart Bicentennial Festival, 154–56, 184

Muckey, Matthew, 245

Murray, Albert, 170

Muschamp, Herbert, 219

Museum of Modern Art, 29

Music, Inc., 11

Music Theater of Lincoln Center, 61, 63–64, 91

Nadelman, Elie, 51–52; *Two Circus Women*, 76

National Endowment for the Arts, 96

National Endowment for the Humanities, 96

National September 11 Memorial and Museum, 210

National Student Film Awards Competition, 77

Nelson, Otto L., Jr., 15, 38

Neuhaus, Mark, 233

Newhouse, Mitzi E., 110, 112

New York City: early history of, 6–8; and funding for Lincoln Center redevelopment project, 178; new space proposed for, 191; "slum clearance" in, 8–9, 16, 26–28

New York City Ballet, 1, 11, 16, 63, 231, 260; and allegations of sexual misconduct, 245; as part of Lincoln Center, 33, 49, 51, 52, 61, 63, 91, 139, 182, 205

New York City Center of Music and Drama: and the Beaumont Theater, 105; drama component of, 54–56; as part of Lincoln Center, 16–17, 33, 48–51, 52, 93, 114

New York City Opera, 11, 205, 231; bankruptcy of, 236; challenges faced by, 224, 227–28, 235–36; Christopher Keene as director of, 158–59, 182; Paul Kellogg as director of, 174–75, 182, 187–88, 191, 192, 198, 199, 203, 208, 209, 225; Gerard Mortier as director of, 225–27; new performance space sought for, 174–76; new works presented by, 226; as part of Lincoln Center, 49, 51, 52, 61, 91, 139, 173, 182, 201; and possible move to Ground Zero complex, 208–9; Beverly Sills at, 114–16, 160–63; George Steel as director of, 233–36

New York City Opera House, 176, 187

New York Community Trust, 11

New York Film Festival, 77

New York Foundation, 11

New York Philharmonic: Amyas Ames as chair of, 92, 124; Deborah Borda as president of, 246–47, 248–49, 251–52; changes in leadership at, 157, 246–47; and decision to remain at Lincoln Center, 211; members of, as faculty at The Juilliard School, 154; moving forward after 2020, 259–60; and musicians' strike, 99–100; and opening week at Lincoln Center, 44; as part of Lincoln Center, 1, 10, 11, 17, 19, 35, 81, 91, 139; performances in North Korea, 229–30; possible merger with Carnegie Hall, 203–5, 206–7, 210–11. *See also* Avery Fisher Hall; Philharmonic Hall; and individual music directors

New York Pro Musica, 44

New York Public Library for the Performing Arts, 66, 67, 142, 178; leadership changes at, 157–58. *See also* Library-Museum

New York Shakespeare Festival, 109; as part of Lincoln Center, 111–12, 113

New York State Theater, 19, 32, 42, 59, 50–51, 52, 60–63, 64; acoustical problems at, 62–63, 131, 175, 208; renaming of, 247–48; renovations of, 130–31, 145, 161, 226, 227

New York University, 56–57

New York World's Fair (1964), 42, 50, 60, 63

Nézet-Séguin, Yannick, 244–45, 260

Nixon, Pat, 89

Nixon, Richard M., 67, 88, 124

North Atlantic Treaty Organization, 2

North Korea, New York Philharmonic's performances in, 229–30

Obama, Barack, 248; election of, 233

O'Brien, Donal C., Jr., 122

Ogilvie, David, 145–46

Ohnesorg, Franz Xaver, 186

O'Keefe, John, 94, 96

Olds, Irving S., 13

Olin Partnership, 213

Omega Seven, 131

O'Neill, Eugene, *Marco Millions*, 57–58

Opera Ballet School, 22

Oppenheimer, Martin, 196, 197, 202

Ormandy, Eugene, 19, 44

Ozawa, Seiji, 223

Paganini, Niccolò, 89

Paine, Peter, 127

pandemic. *See* COVID-19 pandemic

Papp, Joseph, 54–55, 108, 143; background of, 109; at the Beaumont Theater, 109–14 132

Park Avenue Armory, 230, 237–38, 239

Parks, Rosa, 2

Pavarotti, Luciano, 118, 120, 139

Pei, I. M., 134, 135

Pence, Mike, 258

Perelman Performing Arts Center, 210

Perlman, Itzhak, 89, 140

Persichetti, Vincent, 44–45

Peter J. Sharp Foundation, 234

Philadelphia Orchestra, 44

Philharmonic Hall, 48, 63; acoustical problems at, 42, 46–47, 98–99, 100; architect for, 28; and donation from Avery Fisher, 97–98; financial challenges facing, 96–97; opening week of, 42–45; pipe organ in, 45; renovation of, 100–102. *See also* Avery Fisher Hall

Phillips, Robin, 133

Picker, Tobias, *Emmeline*, 182

Pinero, Miguel, *Short Eyes*, 112

Piston, Walter, 45

Pixley, Dorothy, 42

Pogrebin, Robin, 194, 228

Polisi, Joseph W., 178; and the Mostly Mozart Festival, 155; as president of The Juilliard School, 157, 248

Pomerance, Bernard, *The Elephant Man*, 133

Pomerance & Breines, 48

Pope, Josephine, 65

Porter, Cole, *Anything Goes*, 152

Powers, William, 38

Present, Harris L., 27

Previn, André, 118

Price, Janice, 193

Price, Leontyne, 71, 72, 122, 241

Prince, Hal, 241

Project Leadership Committee, 176–77, 186; Gordon Davis as member of, 186; Joseph Volpe as member of, 186–87

Prokovsky, André, 61

Public Theater, 54–55, 109, 111, 112, 113

Puccini, Giacomo: *Madama Butterfly*, 236; *Tosca*, 140, 236; *Turandot*, 118

Quintero, José, 58

Raab, Ellis, 107, 133, 134

Rabe, David, *In the Boom Boom Room*, 112

racial justice. *See* Black Lives Matter movement; social change

Raitt, John, 61

Ramasar, Amar, 245

Rattle, Simon, 237–38

Redden, Nigel, 165, 168

Reich, Steve, *Drumming*, 221

Renfro, Charles, 213, 214

Robards, Jason, Jr., 57

Robbins, Jerome, 121; death of, 182

Robertson, David, 231

Robertson, Jaquelin, 190

Robertson, Julian, 177

Robertson, Rebecca, and the Lincoln Center redevelopment project, 177, 183, 190, 191, 207, 208, 211, 215, 217, 219, 230

Rockefeller, David, Jr., 78

Rockefeller, John D., Sr., 117

Rockefeller, John D., Jr., 11, 25–26, 37

Rockefeller, John D. 3rd (JDR 3rd), 11, 13, 18, 43; background of, 11–12; and Morton Baum, 53; as board chair of Lincoln Center, 39; and Pablo Casals, 45–46; and concerns regarding chamber music constituent for Lincoln Center, 82–83, 85–87; and City Center, 52; death of, 122–23; as founding president of Lincoln Center, 3, 14–15, 20, 21, 24, 27–28, 32, 40, 52; and groundbreaking for Lincoln Center, 34–37; and Wallace Harrison, 68–69; and the Juilliard School building, 88; and Lincoln Kirstein, 33, 34; and the Metropolitan Opera House, 68–69, 70, 71; and rift with William Schuman, 79–83, 90; stepping down from leadership of Lincoln Center, 91–92; as supporter of the arts, 12–13

Rockefeller, John D., IV, 122

Rockefeller, Martha Baird, 94

Rockefeller, Nelson, 35, 48, 50, 52, 60

Rockefeller, Steven C., 122
Rockefeller, William, 117, 126–27
Rockefeller Foundation, 9, 11–12, 25
Rockwell, David, 218
Rockwell, John, 164–65, 166
Rodgers, Richard, 19, 52; as president
  of the Music Theater of Lincoln
  Center, 64; and William Schuman,
  63
Rodgers and Hammerstein, *Carousel*,
  61, 182; *The King and I*, 64
Rogers, Slade & Hill, 38
Rolling Stones, 220
Rome Opera, 81
Rose, David, 153
Rose, Frederick Phineas, 31, 150, 152,
  153, 171
Rose, Leonard, 45
Rose, Marshall, 177, 183–84, 188, 190,
  198, 199; and resignation from the
  redevelopment committee, 194–95;
  and Joseph Volpe, 189
Rose, Samuel, 153
Rose, Sandra Priest, 152
Rose Building, 68, 145, 148, 149–54,
  184
Rose Hall, 228, 259
Rosenberg, Anna M., 32
Rose Theater, 171
Ross, Alex, 209, 237
Rowley, William, *The Changeling*,
  58–59
Royal Shakespeare Company, 62
Rudel, Julius, 115, 161
Rudolf, Max, 23
Rug Concerts, 102–3
Rusk, Dean, 9, 11
Rutkoff, Peter M., 13

Saariaho, Kaija, 225
Saarinen, Eero, 29, 65, 69, 105
Salonen, Esa-Pekka, 246–47
Samuel B. and David Rose Building.
  See Rose Building

Samuels, John S. 3rd, 132–33, 134–35,
  137
Samuels, Leslie R., 135
San Juan Hill, 7–8
Sartre, Jean-Paul, *The Condemned of
  Altona*, 65
Savall, Jordi, 231
Scarbrough, Paul, 249
Scherzer, Irwin, 86
Schippers, Thomas, 71
Schneiderman, Irwin, 197
Schoenberg, Arnold, *Erwartung*, 234;
  Moses und Aron, 182
Schola Cantorum of New York 44
Schonberg, Harold C., 29–30, 46,
  72; on the acoustics in Philhar-
  monic Hall, 99; as critic of Schu-
  man, 81
School of American Ballet (SAB), 22,
  158; and dancers of color, 254–55;
  and The Juilliard School of Music,
  147–48; Lincoln Kirstein Wing
  of, 231; as part of Lincoln Center,
  148–49, 216, 231
Schroeder, Manfred, 47
Schubart, Mark, 119, 120
Schuman, William, 22, 23, 24, 35, 76;
  artistic initiatives proposed by,
  80–82; and chamber music as constituent at Lincoln Center, 82–85,
  86; and crisis involving the Repertory Company, 59–60; heart attack
  suffered by, 85; and Peter Mennin,
  89; as president of The Juilliard
  School of Music, 40; as president of
  Lincoln Center, 40–42, 49, 52, 77,
  80, 90, 93, 129, 160; resignation of,
  88; and rift with JDR 3rd, 79–83,
  90; and Richard Rodgers, 63
Schwartz, Stephen, 234; *Séance on a Wet
  Afternoon*, 235
Schwarz, Gerard, 139, 155, 166–67
Scofidio, Ric, 213–14
Scofield, Paul, 62

Scott, William B., 13

Segal, Martin E., 77, 78, 117, 146, 150, 160, 166–67, 176, 205; background of, 125–26; as chair of Lincoln Center, 124–30, 144–45; leadership style of, 126–27, 162; and Nathan Leventhal, 142–43; resignation of, 144; and tensions involving the Beaumont Theater, 135–39

Sellars, Peter, 133, 166, 225, 237–38

Semkow, Georg, 100

Serkin, Peter, 139

Serkin, Rudolf, 45, 99

Shakespeare, William: *King Lear*, 62–63; *Macbeth*, 112, 134; *The Tempest*, 112; *Troilus and Cressida*, 112

Sharp, Peter Jay, 156, 234

Sherry, Fred, 183

Shifrin, David, 183

Shinn, Richard, 138, 150

Signature Theater, 209–10

Sills, Beverly, 182; background of, 160–61; as chair of Lincoln Center, 160, 161–64, 184, 186, 188, 191, 192, 193; as chair of the Metropolitan Opera board, 203, 221–23; death of, 223–24; as director of the New York City Opera, 114–16, 131, 142; legacy of, 200–201; and the Lincoln Center redevelopment project, 173, 176, 177–78, 185, 193, 197, 198, 199, 200, 201; and the Mostly Mozart Festival, 166; as performer with the New York City Opera, 160–61; and resignation as chair of Lincoln Center, 200; and sale of Jasper Johns painting, 179–80; and sound enhancement system at the New York State Theater, 175, 176; and tensions with Leventhal, 163–64; and Joseph Volpe, 189, 221–22

Silverstein, Joseph, 121

Simon, Robert E., 48

Singer, Norman, 105

Sixty-Fifth Street, as site for Lincoln Center redevelopment project, 216–19, 230–31, 232

Skidmore, Owings & Merrill, 28–29, 65

social change, and the role of the arts, 253–56, 258–59. *See also* Black Lives Matter movement; #MeToo movement

Sokolow, Anna, 50, 147

Solomon, Howard, 197

Sony Classical Records, 223

Sousa, John Philip, 36, 61

Southern, Hugh, 157, 202

Spar, Debora L., 168; as president of Lincoln Center, 241–42

Spofford, Charles M., 10, 13, 49, 59

Stafford, Jonathan, 245

Stanton, Frank, 73

Stapleton, Maureen, 60

Steel, George: as director of the New York City Opera, 233–36; programming of, 234–35

Stein, Gertrude, 168

Steinberg, William, 99

Stern, Isaac, 45, 48

Stevens, Risë, 36

Stevens, Roger, 21, 133

Stevenson, Adlai, 45

Stillman, Abbott, 150

Stillman, Alan, 150

Stoddard, George D., 49, 54

Stokowski, Leopold, 46, 89

Stoppard, Tom, *Arcadia*, 182

Strasberg, Lee, 54

Strauss, Johann, *Die Fledermaus*, 160, 225

Strauss, Richard, *Intermezzo*, 234, 235

Stravinsky, Igor, 101; *Apollo*, 140; *Pulcinella*, 121; Symphony in Three Movements, 121; Symphony of Psalms, 121; Violin Concerto, 121

Stravinsky Festival, 120–21

Strindberg, August, *Dance of Death*, 112

Stritch, Elaine, 182
Sulzberger, Arthur Ochs, Sr., 86
Sutherland, Dame Joan, 120, 139
Szell, George, 44, 46, 119

Tallchief, Maria, 61
Talleyrand-Périgord, Charles-Maurice
    de, 6
Tandy, Jessica, 107
Tan Dun, *The Voyage of Marco Polo*,
    182
Taplin, Frank, 84, 85, 87
Taubman, Howard, 21, 22, 23, 55–56
Taylor, Breonna, 253
Taylor, Maxwell Davenport: back-
    ground of, 39; as chair of the Joint
    Chiefs of Staff, 40; as president of
    Lincoln Center, 39–40
Taymor, Julie, 223
Tchaikovsky, Pyotr Ilich: *Swan Lake*,
    118; Violin Concerto, 140
Ter-Arutunian, Rouben, 121
Terry, Walter, 21, 49
Thake, Shanta, as chief artistic officer
    of Lincoln Center, 262–63
Thang Long Water Puppets, 167
Theater for Dance and Operetta, 19,
    49, 50
Thomson, Virgil, 21, 44, 168
Timms, Henry, as president of Lincoln
    Center, 248–49, 254, 261–62
Titian, 256
Tod Williams Billie Tsien Architects,
    249, 250
Tommasini, Anthony, 255
Tourel, Jennie, 44
Tow, Leonard, 219
Treigle, Norman, 115
Trump, Donald, 153, 251; political
    climate created by, 256–57, 258
Tucker, Richard, 44
Tully, Alice, and the chamber music
    constituent of Lincoln Center,
    83–84, 87. *See also* Alice Tully Hall

Turnage, Mark-Anthony, *Anna Nicole*,
    236
Tynan, Kenneth, 56

Uchida, Mitsuko, 156
United States: racial divide in, 2; after
    World War II, 2
urban renewal, and the building of
    Lincoln Center, 4, 9–10, 13

Vacchiano, William, 169
Van Arsdale, Harry, Jr., 32
VanBesien, Matthew, 246
van Zweden, Jaap, 246, 247, 260
Vaughan Williams, Ralph, 44
Veneklasen, Paul, 47
Verdi, Giuseppe: *La Traviata*, 146;
    Requiem, 260–61
Verrett, Shirley, 44, 89
Vickers, Jon, 44
Vietnam War, 2, 40, 95
Vilar, Alberto, 181
Vincent, Edgar, 164
Viñoly, Rafael, 171
Vogel, Amos, 77
Volpe, Joseph, 175–76, 177–78; as gen-
    eral manager of the Metropolitan
    Opera, 157, 166, 181, 186, 198, 201,
    202, 222; and the Lincoln Center
    redevelopment project, 188–89, 193,
    195, 196–97, 199–200; resignation
    of, 229; and Marshall Rose, 189; and
    Beverly Sills, 189, 221–22

Wadsworth, Charles, 85, 86, 87, 183
Wagner, Richard: *Das Rheingold*, 237,
    238; *Der Ring des Nibelungen*, 237;
    Die Walküre, 237, 250; *The Flying
    Dutchman*, 192; *Götterdämmerung*,
    237; *Siegfried*, 237
Wagner, Robert, 9, 18, 35, 36, 75–76
Wakin, Daniel J., 229
Waleson, Heidi, 210, 227, 233
Walker, Darren, 258

Wall, Charles, 235
Wang, Liang, 245
Wardwell, Edward, 87
Warren, Leonard, 36
Warsaw Pact, 2
Washington, George, 6
Webster, Albert K. (Nick), 142, 154
Weidman, Charles, 50
Weill, Sanford I., 204, 211
Weinstein, Harvey, 243
Weissman, George: background of, 145–46; as chair of Lincoln Center, 145–47, 149, 150, 160, 170
Weldon, Joan, 61
Westermann, Helge, 28
West Side Armory, 7
West Side Story, 8
Wheeldon, Christopher, 260
Whelan, Wendy, 245
Whitehead, Robert, 42, 132; and the Lincoln Center Repertory Company, 54, 55, 56–57, 59, 60
White Light Festival, 168, 237
Whitney Museum of American Art, 214–15
Wien, Lawrence A., 95–96, 148

Wien, Mae L., 148, 149
Wilson, Malcolm, 35, 36
Wilson, Robert, 167–68, 186–87, 208, 224
Witte, Michael, 198, 199
WNET, 231
Woetzel, Damian, 248, 253–54
Woods, George D., 55, 56–57, 58
World's Fair Festival, 63
Wu Han, 183
Wuorinen, Charles, 227
Wycherley, William, *The Country Wife*, 65

Young, Edgar, 14, 23, 32, 33, 49, 60, 75, 87; as acting president of Lincoln Center, 40; and concerns regarding the chamber music constituent, 85–86; and the Metropolitan Opera House, 68; and plans for the Juilliard School building, 68

Zambello, Francesca, 233
Zaslaw, Neal, 155, 156
Zeffirelli, Franco, 71